Beiträge zur Finanzwissenschaft

herausgegeben von

Hans-Werner Sinn und Wolfgang Wiegard

14

Georg Hirte

Pension Policies for an Aging Society

Mohr Siebeck

Georg Hirte, born 1960; 1981–88 studied economics and theology at the University of Regensburg; 1989–2001 assistant lecturer at the University Hohenheim and the Catholic University of Eichstätt; 1995 Dissertation; 2000 Habilitation.

Die Deutsche Bibliothek – CIP-Einheitsaufnahme

Hirte, Georg:
Pension policies for an aging society / Georg Hirte. –
Tübingen : Mohr Siebeck, 2001
(Beiträge zur Finanzwissenschaft ; Bd. 14)
ISBN 3-16-147539-9

The book was printed by Gulde-Druck in Tübingen on non-aging paper and bound by Heinr. Koch in Tübingen.

ISSN 0940-4155

To Lydia

Preface

This book discusses the incidence, welfare, redistribution, economic effects, and the feasibility of pension policies in an aging society. These are some of the most prominent subjects in current economic research. My own experience and my knowledge of dynamic simulation techniques and studies on this topic convinced me that a simulation study of pension policies is the best approach to evaluating different aspects of social security. The results of this study also convinced me that a pure theoretically analysis might be misleading with respect to the effects of pension policies. Such an analysis provides no orientation about the significance of the different effects and cannot identify the various interdependencies between different institutions or the significance of specific institutional regulations. These are some reasons for my decision to carry out a large CGE study on pension reforms in an aging society.

It was mainly the feedback from a paper written together with Reinhard Weber that stimulated me to further examine this topic and some technical issues. This decision has been encouraged by my supervisor Joachim Genosko who always tried to give me enough independence. Many aspects of this study have been inspired by other colleagues. Especially, I would like to thank Hans Fehr, Joachim Genosko, Glenn W. Harrison, Wolfgang Peters, Reinhard Weber, and Wolfgang Wiegard.

A previous version of this study was accepted as habilitation thesis at the Catholic University of Eichstätt in summer 2000. I would like to thank Johannes Schneider who served as referee for the habilitation committee together with Joachim Genosko. I am deeply indebted to Robert Bell for correcting my English. Last but certainly not least, I owe an unrepayable debt to my wife, Lydia, for her continuous support and encouragement.

Ingolstadt, March 2001

Contents

List of Figures

List of Tables

Abbreviations

AK-Model	Auerbach-Kotlikoff Model
CES	constant elasticity of substitution
CGE	computable general equilibrium
HI	health insurance
OLG	overlapping generation
PAYGO	pay-as-you-go public pension system
UI	unemployment insurance
UI-benefits	unemployment benefits

List of Symbols

Indices

M	first year of retirement
J	last year of life
i, j, ν	index for age
t, s	index for years

Prices

r_s^g	gross interest rate in period s
r_s	interest rate net of factor tax (interest rate)
$r_s^{n,i}$	net interest rate of individual i
r_s^m	marginal net interest rate
w_s	wage after factor tax (wage)
w_s^i	wage of individual i
$w_s^{a,i}$	reservation wage of individual i
w_s^c	unit cost of labor in period s
$w_s^{e,i}$	effective wage of individual i
w_s^g	gross wage in period s
$w_s^{m,i}$	marginal net wage of individual i
$w_s^{n,i}$	net wage of individual i
$w_s^{w,i}$	true wage of individual i in period s
$w_s^{\mu,i}$	shadow wage of leisure

Production Sector and Unemployment

$F(\cdot)$	production function
F_{K_s}	marginal product of capital input in year s
F_{L_s}	marginal product of efficient labor input in year s
L_s	aggregated labor input in efficiency units in year s
Q_s	outside opportunity (wage expected outside of the firm)

$q(\cdot)$	quitting function or function of additional labor costs
w^q	replacing costs
x_s	rate of unemployment
β	mark-up on unit labor costs in period s
ε_L	elasticity of additional labor costs with respect to labor demand
ε_w	elasticity of additional labor costs with respect to the gross wage
λ	response parameter of the quitting function
Π_s	profit of the production unit
$\widetilde{\pi}_s^x$	replacement rate of UI with respect to unit labor costs
Φ	scale parameter of the Cobb-Douglas production technique
ψ	share parameter of the Cobb-Douglas production function

Taxes, tax and rates of contribution

P_s	net pension benefits
T_s	overall tax revenue
T_s^b	revenue of the tax on pension benefits
$T_s^{b,i}$	liability of individual i of the tax on pension benefits
T_s^c	revenue of the consumption tax
T_s^k	revenue of capital taxes
$T_s^{H,i}$	individual contributions to health insurance
$T_s^{P,i}$	individual contributions to the pension sector
T_s^r	revenue of the capital income tax
$T_s^{r,i}$	tax liability of individual i of the capital income tax
T_s^w	revenue of the wage tax
$T_s^{w,i}$	tax liability of individual i of the wage tax
$T_s^{X,i}$	individual contributions to unemployment insurance
$\phi_s^{P,i}$	marginal rate of pension benefits of an individual i
$\phi_s^{X,i}$	marginal rate of unemployment benefits of an individual i
θ_s^P	rate of contribution to public pension sector
θ_s^{SI}	rate of aggregate contribution to social insurance
θ_s^X	rate of contribution to unemployment insurance
$\overline{\tau}_s^{b,i}$	average tax rate of individual i on pension benefits
$\tau_s^{b,i}$	marginal tax rate of individual i on pension benefits
τ_s^c	rate of consumption tax
τ_s^H	rate of contribution to health insurance
τ_s^k	rate of capital tax
τ_s^P	marginal rate of implicit tax of the public pension sector

$\overline{\tau}^r_s$	average tax rate of capital income tax
τ^r_s	marginal rate of capital income tax
$\tau^{X,i}_s$	marginal rate of implicit tax of unemployment insurance
$\overline{\tau}^{w,i}_s$	average rate of wage tax
$\tau^{w,i}_s$	marginal rate of wage tax
$\tau^{\pi,i}_s$	marginal tax rate on pension benefits
ξ^b_k	tax allowance of the tax on pension benefits
ξ^r_s	tax allowance of the capital income tax
ξ^w_s	tax allowance of the wage tax

Private Sector

a^i_s	assets of individual i in period s
$b^{P,i}_s$	pension benefits of individual i in period s
$b^{X,i}_s$	unemployment benefits of individual i in period s
c^i_s	consumption demand of individual i in period s
h	time endowment
ℓ^i_s	leisure demand of individual i in period s
l^i_s	labor supply of individual i in period s
$l^{g,i}_s$	labor supply if the individual is not rationed
p^i_s	probability of being alive in the next year
R^m_s	discount factor with r^m_s
$R^{n,i}_s$	discount factor with $r^{n,i}_s$
$U^j_t(\cdot)$	lifetime utility function of in individual born in period t
u^i_s	temporal utility function
$\tilde{u}^i_s$	time variant part of the temporal utility function
W^i_t	wealth endowment of individual i born in t
α^i_s	strength of the preference for leisure
Γ^j_t	distribution part of the consumption function
γ	intertemporal elasticity of substitution
ζ^j_s	factor of the consumption function
η	Lagrange multiplier of the intertemporal budget constraint
μ^i_s	Lagrange multiplier of the time restriction
ϑ	pure rate of time preference
ρ	elasticity of substitution between consumption and leisure
Ω_s	average to marginal net interest rate correction factor

Public and Macroeconomic Variables

A_s	aggregate individual assets
a^F	weight of the type of pension
a_s^R	current pension value
BE_s	average wage income in period s
B_s^P	aggregate pension benefits
$b_s^{P,i}$	pension benefits to individual i
B_s^X	aggregate unemployment benefits
$b_s^{X,i}$	unemployment benefits to individual i
C_s	aggregate consumption
D_s	accumulated public debt
D_s^f	accumulated net foreign assets
$E_t^{P,i}$	earning points credited for exempt periods
$e_t^{P,M}$	earning points of an individual born in period t
G_s	public consumption
I_s	aggregate investment outlays
N_s^i	number of individuals ofπ generation i in period s
NQ_{s-1}	ratio of average wage to net wage income in period $s-1$
R_s	discount factor of government and current account
S_s	aggregate savings
T_s	overall tax revenue
X_s^P	contributions to the pension system paid by the UI insurance
x_s^i	rate of unemployment of cohort i
Z_s^X	grants to unemployment insurance
θ_s^z	supplement rate to pension benefits
π_s^X	replacement rate of unemployment benefits

Chapter 1

Introduction

Social policy has become a major subject of public discussion in almost all industrial nations. Some of these states such as Germany are under exceptionally great pressure to redesign their social insurance system. The adverse demographic prospects due to low fertility rates and a rise of life expectancy, a high rate of unemployment, and an already high tax burden endanger the sustainability of the social insurance systems. For example the Statistical Office of Germany forecast that the ratio of individuals older than 60 years to individuals aged between 20 and 59 will rise from 37% in 1996 to 68.5% in 2035 (Statistisches Bundesamt, 1994). A working group of some ministries estimate a raise to 76.6% in 2035 (Wissenschaftlicher Beirat, 1998, p. 6, see also Figure 1.1). This in turn means that there will be only 1.25 employees to finance a single retiree in 2040, while 2.7 employees 'fed' one pensioner in 1996.

Consequently, the rate of contribution to the German public pension system is expected to increase from 19.2% in 1996 to more than 30% in the 2040s if the effects of those regulations of the Pension Act of 1992 which will take effect in 2001 and the reform of 1999 are disregarded (Wissenschaftlicher Beirat, 1998). Moreover, as health expenditure rises with age, and the contributions of pensioners are less than the cost of their medical treatment, the aging process puts a strong financial strain on the health and long term care insurance system. For this reason the rate of contribution to German health insurance is forecast to increase from 13.5% in 1996 to about 25% in 2030 (Knappe and Rachold, 1999) and that of long term care insurance from 1.3% to 2.8% (Eckerle and Oczipka, 1998, p. 95). Adding these figures and the rate of contribution for unemployment

Figure 1.1: Old age dependency ratio (in the present study)

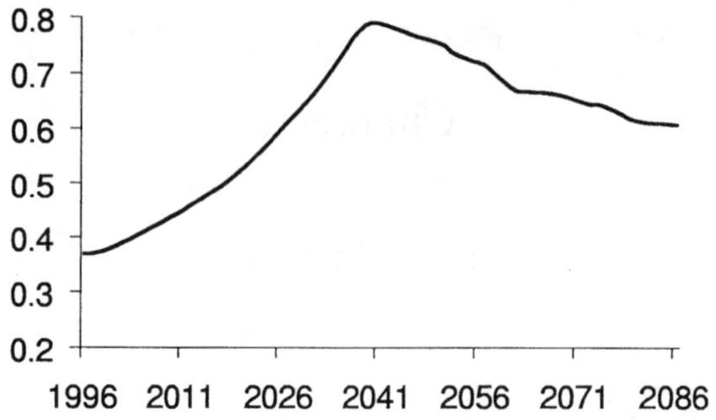

insurance to the rate of contribution for the pension system produces an aggregate rate of contribution of about 62% of wage income in the 2040s. Assuming for the time being that the rate of contribution is equivalent to the effective tax rate of the social insurance system, the average marginal rate of wage tax net of employers contributions will then exceed 60%[1]. Such a huge rate is beyond imagination and certainly not enforceable. This emphasizes that the social insurance system is not sustainable in its current form and the system must be vastly changed.

These are some of the reasons why the pension system and health insurance have been subject to many policy reforms in Germany and also in most industrialized nations. In the German case changes in pension policies in the 1990s have been enacted by the previous government in the Pension Act of 1992 (Rentenreformgesetz, RRG 1992), the Growth and Employment Act (Wachstums- und Beschäftigungsförderungsgesetz, WWG), and the Pension Act of 1999 (Rentenreformgesetz, RRG 1999). Among the regulations are the switch from the use of gross wages instead of net wages in calculating pension benefits, a rise of the mandatory retirement age accompanied by reduced benefits in the case of early retirement, and a demographic factor reducing the level of pension benefits if the average life expectancy increases. Since these measures certainly disadvantage current or future pensioners, pension policies were a major theme of the election campaign of the Social Democratic Party (SPD) in 1998. According to

[1]Note that contributions are shared equally between employees and employers.

some analysts the promise to suspend some of the regulations enacted by the former government was one of the major reasons for the change in government. In the Pension Correction Act (Rentenkorrekturgesetz) this promise was fulfilled and the introduction of the demographic factor suspended, at least until the end of 2000. Nonetheless, the new government had also to carry out some reforms. As a first step it suspended the net wage adjustment and announced that pensions will grow only in accordance with the inflation rate in 2000 and 2001. This is expected to reduce the gross replacement rate of a retiree who worked for 45 years and earned the average income in each year from 70.2% in 1996 to roughly 67%. Further reform schemes are under discussion and a huge reform is intended to pass through parliament in 2001. This reform includes an introduction of a non-mandatory private insurance component which compensates for the reduction in public pension benefits occurring in the next three decades.

There is also a tremendous number of publications[2] on pension policies suggesting a large number of specific reform schemes sometimes differing in only one detail. Among the reform schemes discussed are the transition to a fully funded system (e. g. Feldstein, 1996, Glisman and Horn, 1997, Holzmann, 1997, Neumann, 1997), the transition to a hybrid system where part of the pension benefits stem from a public pension system and the rest from a private pension plan (e. g. Wissenschaftlicher Beirat, 1998, Neumann, 1998, Sinn 1999, Raffelhüschen, 1997), and a switch to a public pension system purely financed by tax, which is usually a flat basic pension system (e. g. Miegel and Wahl, 1985 and 1999). In addition a lot of other, less fundamental reform schemes have been suggested (e. g. Schmähl, 1993). Instead of reviewing all these proposals we prefer to give a short idea of the main direction a policy reform can chose to take. For this it is convenient to consider a simple budget constraint of the pension system which is, for instance, given by

$$(z + \theta)\, W N = b^P N^P .$$

Pension outlays defined as average pension compensations, b^P, multiplied

[2]For instance a search request in 'EconLit' carried out in spring 2000 provides more than 1800 publications since 1993, and the German search system 'WiSo II' reports about 1600 publications since 1993.

by the number of retirees, N^P, are financed by public subsidies and contributions. Subsidies are determined by applying a subsidy rate z to aggregate wage income, while contributions are calculated by levying a rate of contribution θ on the contribution base which again is wage income. The latter is simply defined as the average income W times the number of individuals in the work force, N. Dividing by N and W gives the budget constraint per unit of aggregate wage income which is

$$z + \theta = \pi \left(N^P / N \right), \tag{1.1}$$

where π is the replacement rate of pension benefits in terms of average income and N^P/N is the old age dependency ratio. This equation shows that the government has four degrees of freedom provided it is able to alter all variables, while one variable has to balance the budget. In the case of a benefit defined pension system, e. g. the German pension system, the latter is the rate of contribution θ.

This equation can be used to discuss which are the main lines of reform schemes one should consider. At first, raising z increases the extent of tax or debt financing of the pension system. This is equivalent to a change in the tax base if subsidies are not financed by a payroll tax. A switch to a system which is fully financed by tax can be achieved by setting the subsidy rate to $\pi \left(N^P / N \right)$. This in turns implies a rate of contribution of zero.

The second possibility is to do nothing. This implies an increase in the rate of contribution, θ, as shown by the line CPB in panel (a) of Figure 1.2[3]. In this case the replacement rate stays at its initial level which was about 66% in 1996 in the German case (see the line CPB in panel (b) of Figure 1.2)[4].

Adjusting the replacement rate, π, is the third policy option. We focus again on the German case. If the replacement rate is adjusted so that

[3] The graphs drawn in this figure are the result of the computations presented later on.

[4] This is the replacement rate of an average retiree. The replacement rate publicly discussed in Germany is that of a fictitious retiree (*Eckrentner*), who paid contributions for 45 years, earned an average income in each period, and retires at the age of 65. The replacement rate of this individual was 70.2% in 1996. However, the average retirement age is actually 60 and, thus, the average replacement rate is lower.

Figure 1.2: Problems of the Pension System

a) Rates of contribution b) Replacement rate of net income

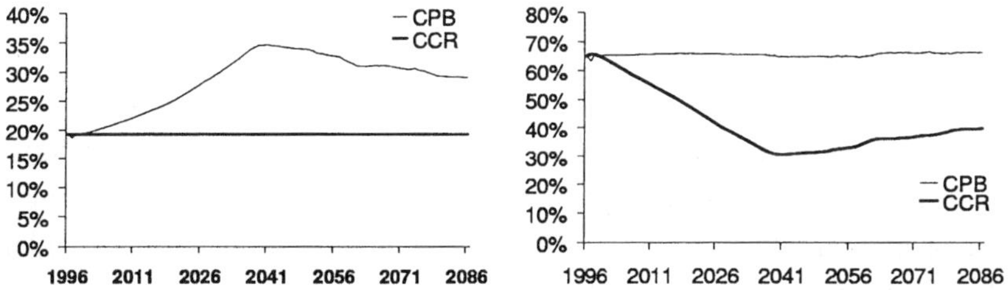

the rate of contribution stays at its initial level of 19.2% and nothing else changes, this causes a decline in the replacement rate from 66% to about 30% in 2041 as shown in panel (b) of Figure 1.2[5]. One can expect that individuals will respond to this reduction in expected benefits by expanding private pension plans. Hence this policy prompts a partial privatization scheme as does each large downward shift of the replacement rate. If the replacement rate is reduced to zero, this scheme constitutes a transition to a fully funded system.

The next variable is the number of retirees. Whether this can actually be influenced directly depends on the specific pension system. For instance the German public pension system includes an insurance against the disability to work or the inability to work in one's own profession. Moreover, the German system has other regulations such as a part time retirement scheme which enables employees to retire earlier. Nonetheless, setting a mandatory retirement age for old age pensions is generally possible. But it is not at all certain that individuals do adjust their retirement age to this mandatory age. There is enough evidence that at least some of the individuals respond to a higher mandatory retirement age by substituting other pension schemes for old age pensions. The fact that the average retirement age in Germany, which was 59.6 in 1996, is below the age of 60, i. e. the retirement age at which pensions are paid to women or unemployed, or 63, i. e. the retirement age for men, demonstrates that the other pension

[5]Again this figures are calculated without considering the second stage of the Pension Act of 1992 which becomes effective in 2001. This is the increase in the retirement age and the introduction of deductions to pension benefits.

schemes are actually used as substitutes for normal pensions. Hence, in order to influence the average retirement age other methods such as using incentives ought to be considered. Therefore Germany has already chosen to introduce deductions when retiring earlier than at the age of 65 and supplements when retirement is postponed beyond the age of 65.

Finally, one can try to increase the number of employees or individuals liable to pay insurance premiums. A relatively direct influence on the number of individuals insured is exerted by immigration policy or extending the obligation to insure oneself in the public pension system. Germany has adopted the latter by including two groups of individuals in the insurance scheme who were not members of the pension system until 1999. These are part time workers earning less than 630 German Marks per month and some of the self employed.

The changes in these five variables include almost all fundamental reform schemes. Hence a comprehensive study of pension policies should discuss alterations in these variables. Consequently the present study deals with pension policies affecting these variables, except the last which however is subject to endogenous changes in the simulations presented below. At first we discuss regulations aimed at raising the average retirement age. Then a full or partial switch to financing by consumption tax is considered. Thereafter we examine changes in the replacement rate in order to allow the rate of contribution of be smoothed. This policy constitutes an introduction of a partially funded system. Finally, further schemes suggesting different degrees of reduction in the replacement rate are explored, such as a transition to a fully funded system or to a flat basic pension scheme.

There is only one reform scheme considered below which cannot be classified according to the temporal budget constraint given above. This is a departure from the pure pay-as-you-go financing. In this proposal the public pension system is allowed to accumulate a capital stock which can be used later on to reduce the adverse effects of aging on the pension system. Such a reform is also examined in this study.

Having chosen the reform schemes to be considered the question arises as to which approach should be applied when examining these policies? To answer this let us look at the variables. Each policy reform scheme affects either taxes, the rate of contribution, the replacement rate, or tries to raise the retirement age and thus alters the tax benefit linkage of the pension system, i. e. the link between contributions and benefits. As the new view of pension systems has made clear almost every change in this tax benefit linkage constitutes a change in the implicit tax rate of the pension system (e. g. Homburg, 1990a). Hence almost every policy alters either explicit or implicit tax rates and, thus, induces changes in individual behavior and efficiency effects. For this reason a micro-founded model should be used. Furthermore these behavioral changes, if large enough, affect the whole economy. At least the latter cannot be excluded in advance and should therefore also be investigated. Moreover, the method should allow the institutions to be accurately modeled so that the different reform schemes can be included. Equally, one should be able to model demographics as well as decisions over the whole lifetime of an individual such as the timing of retiring, and decisions on savings and labor supply. This implies a dynamic general equilibrium model which should be a life cycle or overlapping generations model. Besides it is not possible to use an analytical model since the institutional details are too complex and the signs of the effects of different policies are often ambiguous.

For these reasons we employ a dynamic computable general equilibrium (CGE) analysis in the tradition of Auerbach and Kotlikoff (1987a). This method is an excellent device for examining and evaluating pension policies when seeking to solve the pension crisis of an aging society. Furthermore, we propose and implement some new features and integrate some elements provided by other studies into the basic model of Auerbach and Kotlikoff. Therefore the second task of this study is to develop the method further.

The model includes 58 to 61 cohorts of employees and retirees each living 78 to 81 years. The average life expectancy increases from the age of 78 to 81 within the first 30 years by 0.1 years per period. Since there is also a decrease in the fertility rate the model replicates the aging process as expected to occur in Germany. The model consists of four sectors:

(1) an aggregate production sector producing a homogeneous good which can be used either as a consumption, health, capital, or public good by employing capital and effective labor;

(2) the private households which are represented by a single, representative individual per age cohort;
(3) the Government which collects revenue from a progressive income tax, a consumption tax, capital taxes, and the issue of debt;
(4) the social insurance sector which encompasses the public pension system, aggregate health and long term care insurance, and unemployment insurance, each financed in a pay-as-you-go manner by contributions from individuals, employers, the other social insurance systems and grants from the government.

Individuals decide on their consumption and leisure demand and savings path over their whole working and retirement life. In addition, they can choose their own retirement age. They are however, restricted by the conditions of the labor market and income ceilings on working after retiring. The former determine unemployment, which is understood to be the time an average individual is unemployed per year. Since productivity differs among individuals, which is modeled by a wage profile, the same is true with regard to unemployment, which increases with age. The model is closed by equilibrium conditions of the (restricted) labor market and the capital market. The economy is a closed economy, there are no bequests and no installment costs of capital.

Since we employ this model to examine all policies considered below, the next chapter is devoted to the full specification of the model. There we also provide a brief outline of the German tax and social insurance system. The description of each feature is placed in a separate section in front of the description of the implementation of this particular aspect. Thereafter we examine step by step the different pension policies outlined above. Each chapter starts with a survey of the discussion on the particular reform scheme, which is followed by the presentation of the results of the simulation. The last step is to compare these policies and derive policy recommendations. In addition, we explore the policies likely to be chosen from a political economy point of view, which we define as the 'feasibility' of a reform scheme.

Now, let us summarize the main issues to be considered below: the study attempts to evaluate pension policies by means of a dynamic CGE analysis. This approach enables one to evaluate each policy with respect to welfare, efficiency, redistribution, and the effects on the pension and social insurance system. One can also look at the feasibility of each policy and macroeconomic effects. The final task is to derive policy recommendations by using these criteria. In addition, different innovations or features of the model used below will be evaluated with regard to their usefulness or necessity. Thus, this study also aims at contributing to the further development of the approach chosen.

Chapter 2

The Model

As stated in the introduction this chapter provides the full description of the technical model, which is used in the simulation later on, and of the German institutions which are represented in the model. The parameterizations of the model used to generate the benchmark data base, the data base, and the simulation method are presented in the next chapter.

The simulation model is a modification of the so-called Auerbach-Kotlikoff model or AK model, developed by Auerbach, Kotlikoff, and Skinner (1983), and Auerbach and Kotlikoff (1983b, 1987a, b). In the first section we outline the main structure of the model which is described in detail in the subsequent sections.

2.1 Main Structure of the Model

The AK model allows the transition path and the new steady state induced by a policy reform, for instance alterations in tax rates, taxes, public debt levels, or social insurance to be computed in a life-cycle approach. It is an overlapping generations model with perfect foresight and rational expectations[1]. In addition to the private households, an aggregate production sector, and the government and social insurance system are included.

Individuals maximize their lifetime utility, represented by a CES-utility function, by choosing their consumption and leisure demand, subject to

[1]Other types of expectations are used, for instance, in the CGE analysis performed by BALLARD and GOULDER (1985) or PEREIRA (1988a,b). A full specification of rational expectations in an environment with uncertainty is provided by İMROHOROĞLU, İMROHOROĞLU, JOINES (1995 and 1998), and İMROHOROĞLU (1998).

their lifetime wealth and a time restriction. In our model they also choose their retirement age (see also Hirte, 1998 and 1999a). This is one of the three major innovations compared to the original AK model proposed in this study. This modification allows effects on the individual retirement decision caused by changes in the statutory retirement age and other policy reforms to be examined.

Though a rough approximation to an endogenous retirement decision is included in the traditional AK model, there is a huge difference between this and the approach chosen in our study. In the AK model individuals retire when labor supply reaches zero for the first time, which is the case if the reservation wage exceeds the net wage. Moreover in many studies which use the AK model there is actually a fixed retirement age on the transition path and in the final steady state. However, in reality labor supply is considerably higher than zero in the pre-retirement period. Furthermore not the net wage, which is considered in the AK model, but the *true wage* is the decisive variable for choosing the retirement age. This true wage reflects the effective wage (see below) and all changes in pension benefits, for instance losses in current retirement benefits and future gains, which occur if individuals postpone retiring (see Lazear 1986). If one neglects these effects an alteration of the pension law is unlikely to affect the retirement age. This, however, would be inconsistent with existing empirical evidence suggesting that there is a response to incentives caused by the pension law (see Siddiqui, 1995, 1997a,b and c, and Riphahn and Schmidt, 1997, for Germany)[2].

There are 59 overlapping age cohorts who enter working life at the age of 20. In the initial steady state each identical member[3] of an age cohort lives for 78 years. The last 59 years of his or her life comprise his

[2]There is, however, mixed evidence for the influence of pension benefits on the retirement decision in the U.S. (see the survey of ATKINSON, 1987). Some older studies which estimate the effects of pension benefits in the OECD countries found strong evidence for a significant impact of pension benefits (PECHMAN, AARON and TAUSSIG, 1968, FELDSTEIN, 1977, or MODIGLIANI and STERLING, 1983).

[3]Since we consider identical individuals it is not possible to compute intragenerational distribution effects, as for example has been done by ALTIG et.al. (1997), KOTLIKOFF (1996b), KOTLIKOFF, SMETTERS and WALLISER (1998a, b), FEHR and WIEGARD (1998a, b) and FEHR (1999a).

or her entire working and retirement life. Individuals die with certainty after 78 years of life. This assumption is hardly a shortcoming as can be deduced from the study of Broer and Westerhout (1997). They examine the effects of different treatments of life expectancy: (1) the sudden death assumption, (2) the perpetual youth assumption (Blanchard, 1985), and (3) lifetime expectations dependent on age. According to their findings efficiency effects are very similar under each assumption. Moreover, the assumption of a life expectancy dependent on age provides almost the same intergenerational distribution and labor supply responses as the sudden death assumption. Only the perpetual youth hypothesis causes strong discrepancies in the intergenerational distribution. But as this assumption neglects the effects on labor supply of aging, it is not very useful when discussing pension reforms. For these reasons the use of the sudden death assumption is considered an appropriate simplification[4]. Nonetheless, to obtain a more realistic demographic structure and to examine aging the sudden death assumption is relaxed in the transition period and life expectancy increases. This is modeled by raising the probability of surviving age 78 from zero by 0.1 points per period over the next 30 periods until individuals reach 81[5]. Then individuals die with certainty. Hence length of life is uncertain during the first 30 years of transition, but only with respect to the last year of life.

Another specific feature of the model is that there is no bequest motive. Though there are some specifications of the AK model which use the *joy-of-giving* bequest motive[6] suggested by Yaari (1964), or unintentional bequest (Broer 1999a and b), we omit this to ease computation. The main objection to the Barro-Ricardo specification which assumes an altruistically motivated, operative bequest motive, is that in this setting no intergenerational redistribution occurs. This violates a widely accepted view that social security is a device to redistribute within and across generations (e. g. Boadway, Marchand and Pestieau, 1991, or the review of

---

[4]However if income risks are added to lifetime risk the results can change (see İMROHOROĞLU, İMROHOROĞLU and JOINES 1995).

[5]FEHR (1999c) considers only a strong increase by one year each.

[6]See for example AUERBACH and KOTLIKOFF (1983b, 1984, 1987a, 1992), BROER and WESTERHOUT (1994, 1997), or RAFFELHÜSCHEN and RISA (1995).

Breyer, 1994)[7]. The consequence of the specification chosen in our model is that the resulting amounts of savings and public debt might be too low (see Modigliani, 1988 and Kotlikoff, 1988). Nonetheless one can reconcile this approach with the altruistic bequest motive, as emphasized by Fehr (1999a). This is done by eliminating all intergenerational redistribution effects by means of appropriate intergenerational transfers. As a result only efficiency matters. This method is used in the simulations to compute the pure substitution effects of each reform (see also Fehr, 1999a). In this way both extreme cases – a missing and an altruistic bequest motive – are considered in the simulations. As long as empirical evidence in favor of Ricardian equivalence is ambiguous, we consider this procedure appropriate (see the survey of Seater, 1993).

The production sector is an aggregate production sector, which produces a homogeneous good by using a simple Cobb-Douglas production function and only labor and capital as input. There are no depreciation or installment costs of capital[8]. Then competition ensures that marginal productivity equals unit factor costs. Instead unemployment is introduced via efficiency wages, inducing a modification of the production sector. Though unemployment is usually included in CGE models by means of a union bargaining approach (e. g. Jensen et. al. 1994 and 1996, Jensen 1997, or Sørensen 1997), we employ a rough approximation to an efficiency wage model with quitting costs. The main advantage of our approach is that it allows the derivation of rates of unemployment for each cohort, as well as a joint consumption/leisure decision.

The government collects taxes and issues debt to finance the principal and interest of debt as well as public expenditure. In addition it makes grants to the unemployment insurance (UI) and public pension system. Taxes are a progressive tax on wage income, a tax on capital income, a corporate tax, a tax on pension benefits, and a consumption tax.

Furthermore there is a social insurance system consisting of the public pension system, unemployment insurance, and health and long term

[7]In addition there is a lot of evidence that most bequests are unintentionally rather than altruistically motivated (see the surveys in Rangazas, 1996 and Hurd, 1990).

[8]How this is done is described by Auerbach and Kotlikoff (1987a) or Broer and Westerhout (1997).

care insurance. All expenditure is financed by contributions. The public pension system is approximately identical to the German system (see also Hirte and Weber, 1997a, b). All other social insurance schemes in the model are simpler. For instance, the unemployment insurance system takes into account only short term unemployment. This is the result of the specification of unemployment which rules out knowledge of the history of individual unemployment.

The model is solved for a closed economy. Therefore differences in the results caused by different degrees of capital mobility are neglected. A comparison of different degrees of capital mobility made by Kenc and Perraudin (1997) reveals no differences in the resulting steady states. Other computations by Lassila, Valm and Valonen (1997) have demonstrated that there are differences in the transition paths. But even during the transition, effects on labor supply are very similar. Some differences in the results for pension systems between a closed and a small open economy are provided by Fehr (1999b). However, to reduce the amount of calculation, we neglect the case of a small open economy. Moreover, since population aging is a common feature of the OECD countries, a change in the world interest rate is to be expected. Solving the model for a closed economy provides similar dynamics of the interest rate. In contrast in the case of a small open economy no change in the interest rate would be considered. Hence, implementing a closed economy is in our view the more appropriate approach. Furthermore we focus on the effects of the modeling of unemployment, unemployment insurance, health insurance, and endogenous retirement. Finally, the model is closed by the market clearing conditions for the rationed labor, capital, and goods market. Note that the labor market is only balanced in terms of employed efficient units of labor.

This finishes the description of the basic features of the simulation model used in this study. In the subsequent sections the model is described in more detail. The original AK model as well as many extensions are described in many publications, for instance Auerbach and Kotlikoff (1987a), Bettendorf (1994), Broer and Lassila (1997), and Fehr (1999a). Hence the main features of the AK model are well documented and it is thus not necessary to present all derivations in detail. Some of the modifications used in this book are also represented elsewhere. The tax benefit linkage, the German public pension system, and the increase in the strength of the preference for leisure are completely described in Hirte and Weber (1997a and b) and Hirte (1999c). The modeling of the endogenous retirement decision differs from the procedure proposed by Hirte (1998 and 1999a), but is documented in Hirte (1999c). Nonetheless these innovations are explained with great care below, because they were developed during the creation of the simulation model used in this study. In the following, we also describe the main features of the German fiscal and social insurance system, which are reflected in the model.

2.2 Demographics and Overlapping Generations

In the model only the working and retirement life of individuals is explicitly considered; this lasts 59 periods. Children are subsumed to the utility of the parents. Accordingly the first period of an individual in the model is the first year of his or her working life. Initially there is no uncertainty about the life horizon; people die with certainty after 59 periods or at the age of 78. Hence there are 59 overlapping generations distinguished by age in each year.

Demographics are modeled in a twofold way. First, population growth is considered via birth rates, which can vary from period to period. The rate of growth of population is n_t. It differs between periods, but is constant at initial and final steady state as well as during the last periods of the transition period.

Second, during the transition period an increase in life expectancy is modeled. It is assumed that the probability of surviving age 78 rises from zero by 0.1 points per period over the next 30 periods until individuals reach 81. Then individuals die with certainty.

2.3 Production sector and Unemployment

The production sector is modeled in a very simple way: the aggregate production unit produces a homogeneous good by employing a Cobb-Douglas production function. This good is used as consumption good, investment or capital good, public good, and health good. The only inputs are capital K_s and labor L_s, measured in efficiency units. Hence

$$Y_s = F(L_s, K_s). \tag{2.1}$$

Though this specification rules out a more realistic implementation of depreciation, user costs of capital, and corporate taxes (see Broer and Westerhout, 1997, or Fehr, 1999a), we choose it to simplify matters. Hence changes in capital taxation are not examined and the corporate tax and business tax rates are fixed in the model. This formulation of the production sector facilitates the incorporation of unemployment into the model.

Usually the insider outsider hypothesis developed by Lindbeck and Snower (1988) or a labor market monopolized via unions are used to discuss unemployment in dynamic CGE models (see Blanchard and Kiyotaki, 1987, Jensen et. al., 1994 and 1996, Sørensen, 1997, and Jensen, 1997). In the latter case unions set wages which maximize the utility of their members. Thereafter labor input is chosen by the firms. In these models labor supply is exogenous to individuals and employment is equally shared between employees. After wages are set and the input of labor is chosen, individuals maximize their lifetime utility by choosing their level of consumption while leisure is fixed. Hence labor supply is not endogenous to individuals. Actually this procedure splits the utility maximization process into two stages: first, the maximization of wages, where only the disutility arising from working is taken into account and thus a subutility is considered; and, second, the choice of consumption subject to fixed labor supply. Hence no joint consumption/leisure decision is made.

Though this model allows a discussion of how policy reforms affect employment, efficiency effects generated by responses of labor supply cannot be assessed. It is basically possible to overcome this shortcoming by enlarging the model so that it captures a joint consumption/leisure decision (see Gali, 1996). But then unions' decisions have to be independent of individual utility, i. e. they have to be constructed in an ad-hoc manner. This however is not in accordance with the basic idea of the union bargaining approach. These are the main reasons we refrain from using the insider outsider or union bargaining approach. Instead we choose an approach which can be derived from an efficiency wage model.

Since the seminal papers of Akerlof (1982) and Shapiro and Stiglitz (1984) many specific explanations for the paying of efficiency wages have been published (see Layard, Nickell and Jackman, 1991). Although these theories are all controversial from a theoretical point of view (e. g. Schneider, 1987), and are based on ambiguous empirical evidence, some of them can be included in the model (see Hutton and Ruocco, 1999). Nonetheless most motivations for efficiency wages lead to problems similar to those arising in the union bargaining model discussed above. For example the shirking model developed by Shapiro and Stiglitz also uses a utility specification. Since this can hardly be modeled in a theoretically consistent way together with endogenous labor supply, for the reasons stressed above, we focus on a theory which does not apply utility in determining efficiency wages. This is *retention* or *quitting costs* as the reason for the existence of efficiency wages. This theory allows a joint consumption/leisure decision to be taken into account and, thus, substitution effects related to consumption *and* leisure to be examined.

In a simple model where only the production sector is considered, the use of the efficiency wage approach allows the exact level of unemployment to be derived (see Layard, Nickell and Jackman, 1991, pp. 152-153). However this is not possible for individual unemployment in a more complex framework such as the model used in this study. Therefore a numerical method has to be applied. Such an approach as suggested by Gali (1996) is employed in the following.

Assume there is a variable β determining a wedge between the gross wage, w_s^g, and the unit costs of labor of the firm. For a given β firms choose their demand for labor according to the first order condition which ensures that the wage w_s^g equals the corrected marginal productivity βF_{Ls} (the labor demand curve in Figure 2.1). The resulting wage reflects the deficiency of the matching process in the labor market resulting, for example, from efficiency wages. Individuals take this lower wage into account, i. e. they consider that they are rationed on the labor market. Their restricted labor supply (see W in Figure 2.1) is fully employed. The intersection of the

Figure 2.1: Unemployment and the wage curve

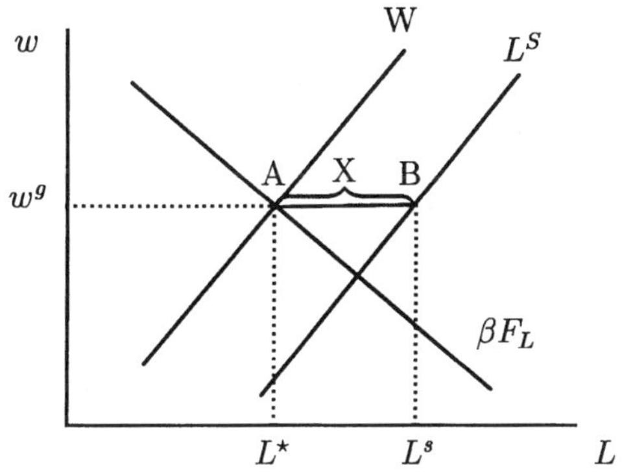

restricted labor supply curve, i. e. the *wage curve*, with the labor demand curve determines employment and the gross wage. Unrestricted labor supply can be computed by setting $\beta = 1$, i. e. by shifting the wage curve to the right (L^S) (see Figure 2.1)[9].

The level of unemployment, X, is determined by the difference between the optimal level of labor supply without rationing, $\beta = 1$, and with rationing, $\beta < 1$.

In the simulation model, the computation of the rate of unemployment is carried out in two stages. First, β is computed. However, the approach used in the model implies a fixed β. One can show that a constant β results, for instance, by adopting an efficiency wage model with quitting costs.

Second, individual rates of unemployment and the overall rate of unemployment are computed. Since individual rates of unemployment can deviate from the average rate of unemployment, individual decisions on

[9]Efficiency wages create a wage curve (BLANCHFLOWER and OSWALD, 1994). Whether such a curve exists in Germany is controversial, even though the majority of estimates provide evidence in favor of the existence of a wage curve in Germany (see the discussion in *Mitteilungen der Arbeitsmarkt und Berufsforschung*, 1996, 1996, with contributions by BLANCHFLOWER and OSWALD 1996, BLIEN 1996b, BELLMAN and BLIEN 1996, and among others MÖLLER, 1996. See in particular the survey provided by BLIEN, 1996a.)

consumption and labor supply are computed as follows: in a first step, private choices are made subject to the rationed labor market, i. e. w_s^g is the gross wage. Thereafter that level of labor supply is determined which is the result of individual decisions when the unit costs of labor, w_s^c, are equal to the gross wage, meaning that there is no restriction in the labor market. The difference between these levels of labor supply determines the individual unemployment level. In this way the choice between consumption and leisure is maintained.

It should be noted that the levels of unemployment are different across cohorts, because the economic situation of each cohort is different due to progressive taxation and the hump-shaped wage profile. Hence individual unemployment deviates from a uniform distribution of unemployment which is assumed, for instance, by Sørensen (1997).

Before discussing the specific approach applied in this study, we derive the general formula for β. Assume there is a sufficiently large number of firms, so that a single firm cannot determine unemployment. Then the profit maximization approach for a representative firm becomes

$$\max \Pi_s = F(L_s, K_s) - w_s^c L_s - r_s^g K_s, \tag{2.2}$$

where Π_s are profits and w_s^c are actual unit labor costs. This is equivalent to

$$\max \Pi_s = F(L_s, K_s) - \left[w_s^g + q(w_s^g, L_s, x_s)\right] L_s - r_s^g K_s,$$

where $q(w_s^g, L_s, x_s)$ is the function representing the quitting costs of labor arising in addition to the wage, w_s^g. We neglect the capital input for the time being. Then the firm chooses the level of its w_s^g and labor input which maximizes profit. Solving this optimization approach constitutes a mark-up on the market-clearing wage.

Maximization leads to

$$\begin{aligned} \frac{\partial \Pi_s}{\partial w_s^g} &= -1 - \frac{q_s}{w_s^g}\varepsilon_w = 0 \\ \frac{\partial \Pi_s}{\partial L_s} &= F_{L_s} - w_s^g - q_s(1+\varepsilon_L) = 0, \end{aligned}$$

and a third condition ensuring that the marginal product of capital is equal to the interest rate. To simplify matters, we present in the following only the maximization with respect to labor demand and wages, while the choice of capital input does not change compared to the basic model. ε_w is the elasticity of q with respect to labor demand. Rearranging and inserting gives the first order condition

$$F_{L_s} = w_s^g/\beta = \frac{\varepsilon_w - 1 - \varepsilon_L}{\varepsilon_w} w_s^g \tag{2.3}$$

and eventually

$$\beta = \frac{\varepsilon_w}{\varepsilon_w - 1 - \varepsilon_L}. \tag{2.4}$$

The mark-up depends on the elasticities of the additional unit labor costs with respect to wages and labor demand. Depending on the specific approach, the elasticities can either be constant or varying with unemployment, unemployment benefits, etc..

Assuming full employment of resources the total interest rate r_s^g is equal to the marginal product of capital

$$F_{K_s} = r_s^g. \tag{2.5}$$

In the following we outline the specific approach used in this study.

Unemployment: Efficiency wages to avoid quitting

Assume firms pay wages above the market clearing level in order to prevent workers from leaving. The size of the mark-up on the market clearing wage depends on the probability of getting another job, expressed by the rate of unemployment, and on the relative wage levels (see Layard, Nickell and Jackman, 1991, pp. 152-153). Consequently both are considered as arguments of the quitting function.

The exact specification of β depends on this quitting function. Following Layard, Nickel and Jackman (1991, p. 152), the quitting rate is defined as a function over the relative wage and the rate of unemployment. Since competition ensures that wages are equal, quittings depend only on unemployment. We use a specification of the quitting function which is derived by analogy from the effort function proposed by Summers (1988). Quittings are defined as

$$q_s = (w_s^g - Q_s)^{-\lambda} = [(1 - \widetilde{\pi}_s^x)\, w_s^g\, x_s]^{-\lambda}, \tag{2.6}$$

where

(2.7) $$Q_s = (1 - x_s)\, w_s^g + x_s\, \widetilde{\pi}_s^x\, w_s^g = \left[1 - x_s\left(1 - \widetilde{\pi}_s^X\right)\right] w_s^g$$

is the average wage expected elsewhere, i. e. the outside opportunity (Layard, Nickell and Jackman 1991, p. 156), $\widetilde{\pi}_s^X$ is the average replacement rate of unemployment benefits with respect to w_s^g, and λ is a response parameter[10]. An individual obtains another job with probability $(1 - x_s)$ and receives unemployment benefits with probability x_s. An increase in unemployment benefits raises the outside opportunity and thus the quitting rate. Note that each cohort has actually another quitting rate on account of differences in net wages. However, provided λ is constant across generations, an average quitting function generates the same aggregate rate of unemployment as aggregating individual quitting functions.

As quitting causes replacement cost w^q the unit labor costs are

$$w_s^c = w_s^g \left\{1 + w^q \left[\left(1 - \widetilde{\pi}_s^X\right) x_s\right]^{-\lambda} \left(w_s^g\right)^{-\lambda-1}\right\}.$$

The elasticities of the additional cost component with respect to wages and labor demand, which is the second expression on the right-hand side, are then given by

$$\varepsilon_w = -\lambda \quad \varepsilon_L = 0.$$

By substituting into (2.4) one obtains

(2.8) $$\beta = \frac{\lambda}{\lambda + 1}.$$

Hence β is a constant proportional factor fully determined by the response parameter of the quitting function, which turns out to equal the elasticity of the quitting function with respect to the wage. Firms face unit labor costs higher than the wage they pay, though this wage might be higher than a market clearing wage when there are no quitting costs.

---

[10]Note that the individuals take the overall rate of unemployment into account instead of the rate of unemployment of their cohort. This assumption is made to simplify the presentation.

2.4 Taxes and Contributions

In this section we turn to the German tax system and describe how the various taxes are modeled. There are four main types of taxes: taxes on capital input, payroll taxes or contributions to the social security systems, income taxes, and consumption taxes.

2.4.1 Capital Taxes

The German Case

Germany levies different types of taxes on business income. They are, for instance, described by BMF (1997). There are two types of taxes on gains from capital: these are the corporate tax (Körperschaftssteuer) and the business tax on earnings of firms (Gewerbeertragssteuer).

The *corporate tax* is a special type of income tax for legal persons such as corporations (AG), private limited companies (GmbH), or partnerships limited by shares (Kommanditgesellschaft auf Aktien, KGaA). The corporate tax rate system is a split rate and full imputation system. The general flat rate on retained earnings was 45% in 1996. This rate is reduced to a uniform tax rate of 30% for distributed profits. The tax liability on dividends is credited against the recipient's liability on personal income tax. To be exact, the tax credit given to the shareholder is added to the dividend that he receives, and his personal income tax is calculated on the basis of this sum. In this way double taxation is avoided. The tax base is the annual income of the firm, which is total income diminished by business expenses. Since the German system allows very generous tax deductions or depreciation allowances, effective tax rates can be considerably lower than the tax rates (see e. g. Schneider, 1990, King and Fullerton, 1984, or Rimbaux, 1996).

The business tax on earnings (Gewerbeertragsssteuer) is a locally levied tax on business profits. It is classified as an indirect tax, since it is not a tax on actual earnings but on the earning capacity of a firm. The tax base is similar to the tax base of the corporate tax, but some deductions granted under the corporation or income tax law are not granted for business taxes. The tax rate is calculated by multiplying the local collection rate (Hebesatz), which on average was about 400% in 1996, by the basic rate (Steuermeßzahl) divided by itself plus one.

Furthermore some other taxes can be classified as taxes on capital. These are the so called 'substance' taxes levied on the capital stock – the 'substance' of a firm – but not on earnings from capital. These are the local business tax on capital (Gewerbekapitalsteuer), levied in the old *Länder* before 1998; the property tax (Grundsteuer) which is also applied to business property, and the net worth tax (Vermögenssteuer) levied on business capital in the old *Länder*, which was abolished in 1997.

Modeling Capital Taxes

In the model we subsume all taxes described above under capital taxes, except the corporate tax on distributed earnings, which is treated as a personal income tax. All capital taxes are assumed to be proportional to the return on capital used in the production sector. The tax liability in period s is

$$T_s^k = \tau_s^k \, r_s \, K_s \, , \tag{2.9}$$

where τ_s^k is the tax rate, r_s is the return after capital taxes or the interest rate, and K_s is the aggregate capital input in the production sector. Using the gross rate of return in period s, r_s^g, the interest rate or net-of-factor-tax return on capital input can be derived giving

$$r_s = r_s^g \, / \, \left(1 + \tau_s^k\right) . \tag{2.10}$$

2.4.2 Payroll Taxes and Contributions to Social Insurance

The German Case

Since 1978 no payroll tax has been levied in Germany. But the contributions to the public pension and unemployment insurance system are collected as taxes on wages and are thus a type of payroll taxes. Following the convention, the term contribution is used since these payments are 'earmarked'. Consequently, we use the term "rate of contribution" instead of "tax rate" in the following. This is to make clear that contributions are like premiums generating claims for future benefits. For example, since the rate of contribution is proportional to income, as described below, there is a strong link between the size of contributions and the size of pension benefits, the so called *tax benefit linkage*. If the linkage is incomplete, the rate of contribution contains a pure tax component, which we call the "net payroll tax" or "implicit tax" of the pension system (Homburg, 1997). It is this implicit tax rate rather than the rate of contribution which causes price distortions (see Homburg, 1990a).

Membership in the social insurance systems is compulsory, except for some groups such as workers whose salaries are below the minimum earnings threshold and civil servants. The latter cannot become unemployed and, consequently, do not pay contributions to unemployment insurance. They also do not contribute to the public pension system, since the government pays their old age pensions out of general taxes. Finally, they are allowed to choose a private health and long term care insurance. Most self employed are also not covered by the social insurance system. Contributions to the public social insurance system are paid in proportion to wage income. However there is a maximum size of contributions. Beyond this threshold the marginal rate of contribution is zero; below this threshold but above the minimum income level the rate of contribution is uniform. Contributions are evenly split between employers and employees. Contributions paid by the employers are not subject to the personal income tax of the employee. But contributions paid by the employees are taxed, except for a small fraction deductible from the income tax base.

Modeling Payroll Taxes and Contributions

As contributions to the social insurance system are levied on wages, they are equivalent to a payroll tax. The rates of contribution are assumed to be proportional to wages and there is no contribution allowance and no upper ceiling on the rates. The latter is due to the fact that in this model average income even of the most productive workers is below the actual upper ceiling of income subject to contribution payments. Hence average and marginal rates of contribution coincide.

Since the rates of contribution are evenly shared between employer and employee and the wage income tax is levied on wages net of contributions of the employer, we distinguish between the two parts of the contributions. The employers pay their contributions out of the gross wage w_s^g. The contribution payment is proportional to the wage, i. e. the gross wage minus the contributions paid by the employer. Technically the contributions paid by the employer are equivalent to a factor tax. As marginal and average rates of contribution coincide, the average wage or net-of-factor-tax wage w_s, is

$$w_s = w_s^g / \left[1 + 0.5 \left(\tau_s^H + \theta_s^P + \theta_s^X\right)\right], \tag{2.11}$$

where θ_s^P and θ_s^X are the rates of contribution of the public pension system and unemployment insurance, and τ_s^H the rate of contribution to health and long term care insurance. The latter is equivalent to a pure payroll tax since health and long term care benefits are independent of the size of contributions. Hence the symbol τ is used instead of θ. For each individual, contributions are paid out of his or her wage income and are proportional to the wage w_s^i. The contribution liability of a member of cohort i is therefore

$$T_s^{J,i} = \theta_s^J \, w_s^i, \qquad \text{where } J \in [P, X], \qquad T_s^{H,i} = \tau_s^H \, w_s^i \tag{2.12}$$

where the index J denotes the specific social insurance system.

2.4.3 Income Taxes

The German Case

The personal income tax in Germany is a comprehensive tax, meaning that it taxes income from different sources. It consists of a wage tax (Lohnsteuer), an assessed income tax (veranlagte Einkommenssteuer), and taxes on capital income which consists of taxes on capital yields (Kapitalertragssteuer) and withholding taxes on capital yields (Zinsabschlagsteuer). Taxes on wages and on capital yields are collected at the source. The assessed income tax is a tax on both the income of the self employed and also the difference between the total tax liability and taxes collected at the source.

Figure 2.2: Marginal and average tax schedules in 1996

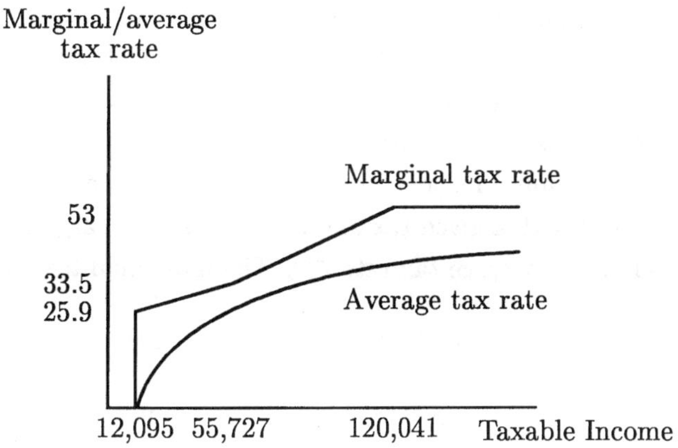

Included in the personal income tax base is the internal yield of the contribution to the pension system, which amounts to 24% of pension benefits for an individual retiring at age 65 in 1996. The part of pension benefits which can be considered as repayment of contributions is exempt from taxation, because contributions are paid out of taxable income during the working life. The income tax base is gross income subject to a wide range of deductions or tax allowances.

The tax rate schedules are shown in Figure 2.2. After computing taxable income a basic tax allowance is deducted, which was 12,095 DM for single persons and 24,191 DM for married couples in 1996. Thereafter the marginal tax rate starts with an initial value of 25.5%, which increases linearly up to 33.5% applied at 55,727 DM of taxable income for single persons or 111,455 DM for married couples. Then the marginal tax rate schedule increases linearly until it reaches its maximum rate of 53% at 120,041 DM or 240,084 DM of taxable income. Beyond this threshold, i. e. in the upper proportional zone, the marginal tax rate remains constant at 53%.

The tax rates on capital yields are 25% on dividend income and 30% on bank interest. There is a tax allowance on capital yields of 6,000 DM for single persons or 12,000 DM for married couples.

Modeling Taxes on Capital Income

To simplify computations, we follow the procedure chosen by Fehr (1999a) and split the comprehensive income tax system into three different taxes. These are taxes on capital income, on wage income, and on internal yields from contributions to the pension system.

The tax on capital income, or capital yield tax, is modeled as a linear progressive tax with a given tax allowance ξ_s^r, a flat marginal tax rate τ_s^r, and an individual average tax rate $\overline{\tau}_s^{r,i}$. The individual tax liability is

$$T_s^{r,i} = \overline{\tau}_s^{r,i}\, r_s\, a_s^i = \tau_s^r \left(r_s\, a_s^i - \xi_s^r\right), \tag{2.13}$$

where a_s^i are accumulated assets of family i in period s. Hence the average tax rate is

$$\overline{\tau}_s^{r,i} = \tau_s^r - \frac{\tau_s^r\, \xi_s^r}{r_s\, a_s^i}. \tag{2.14}$$

Note that according to the full imputation scheme corporate taxes on distributed earnings are subsumed under taxes on capital income.

Modeling Taxes on Labor Income

Taxes on labor income, i. e. the wage tax, are collected from individual gross income. The marginal tax schedule has been described above, where ξ_s^w is the basic tax allowance (see Figure 2.2). The tax liability of an individual is

$$T_s^{w,i} = \overline{\tau}_s^{w,i}\, w_s^i\, l_s^i \tag{2.15}$$

where $\overline{\tau}_s^{w,i}$ is the average tax rate, w_s^i is the individual wage, and l_s^i is the individual working time. However retirees earning less than 630 DM per month are exempt from income taxes. Hence the average and marginal wage tax rates of retirees are zero.

Taxes on Pension Benefits in the Model

The taxes on the internal yields of pension benefits are modeled as taxes on pension benefits, where an additional tax allowance ensures that only

25% of benefits are subject to the income tax. The marginal tax schedule is the same as for the wage tax leading to an individual tax liability of

$$T_s^{b,i} = \overline{\tau}_s^{b,i} \, b_s^{P,i}, \tag{2.16}$$

where $\overline{\tau}_s^{b,i}$ is the average tax rate and $b_s^{P,i}$ are pension benefits.

Using these definitions two distinct net wages and net interest rates can be derived. These are the net wage

$$w_s^{n,i} = w_s^i \left[1 - \overline{\tau}_s^{w,i} - 0.5\left(\tau_s^P + \tau_s^X + \tau_s^H\right)\right] \tag{2.17}$$

and the marginal net wage

$$w_s^{m,i} = w_s^i \left[1 - \tau_s^{w,i} - 0.5\left(\tau_s^P + \tau_s^X + \tau_s^H\right)\right], \tag{2.18}$$

where $\tau_s^{w,i}$ is the individual marginal rate of wage tax. The net interest rate and the marginal net interest rate are

$$r_s^{n,i} = r_s\left(1 - \overline{\tau}_s^{r,i}\right), \qquad r_s^m = r_s\left(1 - \tau_s^r\right). \tag{2.19}$$

2.4.4 Consumption Taxes

The German Case

The value added or turnover tax is collected from the firms, though it is regarded as a tax on consumption. Consequently the tax is explicitly shown in most invoices. In 1996 the tax rate was 15% which has been raised in 1998 to 16%. The tax base is the turnover, but valued added taxes paid on intermediate products are deductible from the tax base.

In addition there are other excise duties levied on the consumption of certain goods, such as the mineral oil duty and the duty on tobacco. These taxes are also collected from the firms, but target private consumption.

Consumption Taxes in the Model

The consumption taxes are proportional to the price of goods, which is normalized to unity. The consumption tax rate in period s is τ_s^c, leading to an individual tax liability of $\tau_s^c \, c_s^i$, where c_s^i is the consumption of individual i in period s.

2.5 Decisions of the Individuals

Each member of a cohort maximizes his or her remaining lifetime utility by choosing a time path of consumption and leisure as well as the retirement age, subject to the intertemporal budget constraint. It is useful to decompose the decision into two stages. In the first stage individuals choose their year of retirement, which is exogenously given in the second stage in which they decide on their time path of labor supply and consumption. Despite this order we present the second decision first.

2.5.1 Consumption, Leisure and Asset Accumulation

The following description of the choice between leisure and consumption is based on Auerbach and Kotlikoff (1987a), Fehr and Ruocco (1997), and Broer and Westerhout (1997). It is based on an exogenously given retirement decision. Individuals retire in period M.

As Yaari (1965) has shown, uncertain lifetime requires a correction of the discount factor. This is reached by considering the probability of survival as a weight in the utility function. In this model the survival rate equals one and thus the hazard rate is zero up to period $J-1$, where J is the last year of life. Hence, the effective and the pure rate of time preference coincide for all but the last year of life. The probability of being alive at age $i-1$, p_s^i, is unity for all years except the last where it lies between zero and unity. In analogy to Broer and Westerhout (1997, p. 114) the probability of living up to age i is $\prod_{h=j}^{i} p_s^h$. In our case this turns out to be p_s^i. Following Broer and Westerhout (1997, p. 114) the representative individual of the cohort aged j at time t maximizes his or her (expected) life time utility which is

$$(2.20) \qquad (E)\,U_t^j = \frac{\gamma}{\gamma-1}\sum_{i=j}^{J}(1+\vartheta)^{j-i}\,p_s^i\left[\left(c_s^i\right)^{\frac{\rho-1}{\rho}} + \alpha^i\left(\ell_s^i\right)^{\frac{\rho-1}{\rho}}\right]^{\frac{\rho(\gamma-1)}{\gamma(\rho-1)}}$$

where c_s^i, ℓ_s^i, and α^i are consumption, leisure, and the strength of the preference for leisure. ρ is the intratemporal and γ the intertemporal elasticity of substitution, and ϑ the pure rate of time preference. The index t denotes the year of reform of the pension system or the year of birth, and s any other period. j and i represent the age of a cohort, where j is the age at the year of reform and i is the age in year s. J is the last year of life. j and i represent the age of a cohort, where j is the age at year of reform and i is the age in year s, where $s = t+i-j$ or $i = j+s-t$.

A specific feature of this study is that the weights of the preference for leisure in the utility function, α^i, depends on age, an approach widely used in labor economics (e. g. Franz, 1996). The values of this parameter are set to approach a reservation wage which increases slowly during working life and faster near retirement age and thereafter. The reason might be that there is "*a gradual deterioration in health*" or a "*loss of interest in the routine of work*" which increase with age (Burtless and Moffitt, 1985, p. 213). This results in the preference for retirement increasing with age as shown by Burtless and Moffitt (1985, p. 230). Individuals spend money on consumption and assets, a_s^i. Income comes from labor and interest earnings, accumulated assets, a_{s-1}^{i-1}, and social security benefits, $b_s^{P,i}$.

Since consumption is proportionally taxed with rate τ_s^c and the price of consumption goods is normalized to unity, consumption expenditure are $(1+\tau_s^c)\ c_s^i$. w_s^i is the wage which equals the average net-of-tax wage times the human capital parameter e^i. The latter reflects the accumulation of human capital at age i, i. e. how many units of 'standard' labor one individual supplies per unit of time in year s. Following Auerbach and Kotlikoff (1987a) e^i depends only on the age of the individual and is exogenously given. This generates a hump-shaped wage profile and is equivalent to an exogenous human capital formation. Perroni (1995) has shown how to endogenize human capital in the AK model. However, since his simulations produce results quite similar to the exogenous human capital approach, human capital is not endogenized in our study.

Since the time of death of the individual is uncertain during the first 30 years of the transition path, individuals die leaving unintended bequests. To rule out bequests we adopt the proposal of Yaari (1965) and introduce a life insurance. As there is no uncertainty at the aggregate level, the insurer can fully insure against the risk of the insured living longer than average. Given full competition in the insurance sector the annuity paid in the last year of life to an individual who lives longer than average is $(1-p_s^i)/p_s^i$

times his or her private assets. These are financed by collecting the estate of all other individuals, which is $(1-p_s^i)\,a_{s-1}^{i-1}$. Accordingly the temporal budget constraint or wealth accumulation equation is

$$(2.21)\quad (1+\tau_s^c)\,c_s^i + a_s^i = w_s^{n,i}\left(h-\ell_s^i\right) + b_s^{X,i} + \left(1-\overline{\tau}_s^{b,i} - 0.5\,\tau_s^H\right) b_s^{P,i} + \left(1+r_s^{n,i}\right)\frac{1}{p_s^i}\,a_{s-1}^{i-1},$$

where h is time endowment, $b_s^{X,i}$ are unemployment benefits, $\overline{\tau}_s^{b,i}$ is the individual average tax rate on pension benefits $b_s^{P,i}$, and τ_s^H is the rate of contribution of pensioners to health and long term care insurance, half of which is paid by the pensioners. If the insurance is fair aggregate wealth equals aggregate expenditure. Assuming initial financial wealth is equal to zero, aggregation over time yields the intertemporal budget constraint

$$(2.22)\qquad \sum_{i=j}^{J} R_s^{n,i}\left[(1+\tau_s^c)\,c_s^i + w_s^{n,i}\,\ell_s^i\right] = W_t^j .$$

The present value of remaining lifetime consumption of goods and leisure equals the remaining lifetime resources, W_t^j. The latter is the present discounted value of future resources net of taxes plus pension benefits

$$(2.23)\quad W_t^j = \sum_{i=j}^{M-1} R_s^{n,i}\left(w_s^{n,i}\,h + b_s^{X,i}\right) + \sum_{i=M}^{J} R_s^{n,i}\left[w_s^{n,i}\,h + \left(1-\overline{\tau}_s^{b,i} - 0.5\,\tau_s^H\right) b_s^{P,i}\right],$$

where pension benefits $b_s^{P,i}$ are positive only after retirement, providing the number of years spent working exceeds the number of years required to qualify for pension benefits. Unemployment benefits are zero after retirement, i. e. for $s \geq M$. The discount factor is

$$R_s^{n,i} = \begin{cases} 1 & \text{if } s = t \\ p_s^i \prod_{\nu=t+1}^{s}\left(1+r_\nu^{n,h}\right)^{-1} & \text{if } s > t \end{cases}$$

and depends on the probability of being alive at age i.

Maximizing (expected) utility subject to the budget constraint, a time restriction, and a constraint of an upper ceiling of working after retiring, leads to

$$\ell_s^i = \left(\alpha_s^i\right)^\rho \left(\frac{1+\tau_s^c}{w_s^{a,i}}\right)^\rho c_s^i, \tag{2.24}$$

where $w_s^{a,i}$ is the reservation wage defined as

$$w_s^{a,i} = w_s^{e,i} + w_s^{\mu,i}, \tag{2.25}$$

with $w_s^{e,i}$ as effective wage and

$$w_s^{\mu,i} = \eta \, p_s^i \, R_s^m \, \mu_s^i$$

as the shadow price of leisure, which is greater than zero if the time restriction is binding. η is the Lagrange multiplier of the intertemporal budget constraint, and R_s^m is the marginal discount factor, defined as

$$R_s^{m,i} = \begin{cases} 1 & \text{if } s = t \\ \prod_{\nu=t+1}^{s} \left(1 + r_\nu^{m,h}\right)^{-1} & \text{if } s > t \end{cases}.$$

The effective wage is then the reservation wage minus the shadow wage, or the sum of the marginal net wage and the wage components of social insurance

$$w_s^{e,i} = w_s^{m,i} + \left(\phi_s^{X,i} + \phi_s^{P,i}\right) w_s^i. \tag{2.26}$$

The wage components are defined as the present value of the marginal change in future unemployment, $\phi_s^{X,i}$, and pension benefits, $\phi_s^{P,i}$, per unit of wage if labor supply is marginally increased (see equations (2.36) on page 44 and (2.40) on page 47).

Solving (2.22) and (2.24) for c_s^i yields the demand function for consumption in the first year of working life

$$c_t^j = \Gamma_t^j \, W_t^j, \tag{2.27}$$

where

$$\Gamma_t^j = \left[\left(1+\tau_t^c\right)^\gamma \sum_{i=j}^{J} R_s^{n,i} \left(R_s^m\right)^{-\gamma} \left(1+\tau_s^c\right)^{1-\gamma} \left(\zeta_s^i\right)^{\frac{\rho-1}{\gamma-\rho}} \left(\frac{\zeta_s^i}{\zeta_t^j}\right) (1+\vartheta)^{\gamma(i-j)} \right]^{-1}$$

and

$$\zeta_s^i = \left[1 + \left(\alpha_s^i\right)^\rho \left(\frac{w_s^{a,i}}{1+\tau_s^c}\right)^{1-\rho}\right]^{\frac{\gamma-\rho}{\rho-1}}.$$

The demand for consumption in the first year depends on the present value of lifetime wealth, W_t^j, and the marginal propensity to consume out of total wealth which increases with age, Γ_s^j. The marginal propensity depends on the ratio of the reservation wage $w_s^{a,i}$ to the price of goods, the rate of time preference, and the discount factor.

The shadow price is computed by using (2.24) and (2.25), where $\ell_s^i = h$, and solving for $w_s^{\mu,i}$ (see Auerbach and Kotlikoff, 1987a). This yields

$$w_s^{\mu,i} = \begin{cases} 0 & \text{if } \ell_s^i < h \\ \left(1+\tau_s^c\right) \alpha_s^i \left(\dfrac{c_s^i}{h}\right)^{1/\rho} - w_s^{e,i} & \text{if } \ell_s^i = h. \end{cases} \tag{2.28}$$

Note that labor supply is restricted to the number of working hours allowed after retirement. Hence the shadow wage $w_s^{\mu,i}$ can be negative, if individuals want to work more than is allowed after retirement. It is positive if the time restriction is binding.

2.5.2 *Retirement decision*

Let us give an intuitive basis for the retirement decision. Assume labor supply is exogenously given but the retirement decision is endogenous. Then the time endowment can be neglected in the decision and one obtains the following explanations.

Individuals who choose to work in a period might lose pension benefits in this period, but they might gain additional or higher benefits in the future. Though these effects are not represented in the effective wage, individuals consider them in their decision making. Adding this implicit net loss in pension benefits accruing if individuals do not retire to the effective wage income generates the *true wage* income (Lazear , 1986). If the reservation wage income exceeds this true wage income, individuals retire; otherwise they work.

Knowing this true wage, the retirement decision can be derived. Technically the decision problem is solved in two stages: first the optimal consumption and leisure demand is derived, given the retirement age; second,

Figure 2.3: Retirement decision

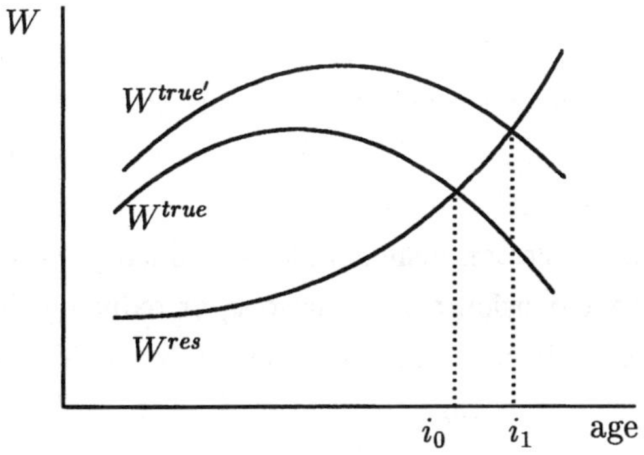

by using these demands the indirect utility function can be maximized to obtain the optimal retirement age. Such a decision has been analyzed in the literature, but only for fixed labor supply (Burtless and Moffitt, 1985, Genosko, 1985, or Breyer 1990). The reason is that considering endogenous labor supply and working after retiring complicate the model. In principle, the optimal retirement decision can be found in a model where labor supply is also endogenous.

Franz (1996) illustrates this decision by using a drawing where the true wage and the reservation wage of retirement with respect to age are shown. The intersection of these curves determines the optimal retirement age. We reproduce his drawing in Figure 2.3.

The true wage or true labor income in the setting used in the present study is defined as

$$\begin{aligned} W_s^{true,i} &= \left(w_s^{n,i} l_s^i - w_s^i l_s^{P,i} + b_s^{X,i}\right) + \left(\overline{\phi}_s^{P,i} w_s^i l_s^i - b_s^{P,i}\right) \\ &= \overline{w}_s^{e,i} l_s^i - w_s^i l_s^{P,i} - b_s^{P,i}. \end{aligned} \tag{2.29}$$

The true wage is the sum of the excess of net wage income and unemployment benefits if not retired over wage income when retired plus the change in the present value of current and future unemployment and pension benefits when working. As the decision is whether to work or retire average variables are used. Then $\overline{\phi}_s^{P,i}$ represents the change in the present value of future pension benefits per unit of effective labor when working an additional unit of time. The individuals who decide against retiring earn labor income, receive unemployment benefits, and are entitled to receive higher pension benefits during retirement since their contribution period is lengthened so that they collect additional personal earning points. In contrast, they forego labor income which they would earn if they work during the first period of retirement, $w_s^i l_s^{P,i}$, and pension benefits they would receive if they retire in the period under consideration. The use of this definition shows that raising the tax benefit linkage, reducing the wage tax, cutting the size of current pension compensations, or reducing the income ceiling for working after retiring, all increase the true wage. This is reflected in an upward shift of the true wage curve from W^{true} to $W^{true'}$. Since this shifts the intersection to the right individuals prefer retiring later. The change in the true wage induces two effects. An income effect occurs which depends on the action chosen to affect the true wage. If income grows individuals become richer and the preference for retiring increases and vice versa. On the other hand, a higher true wage raises the relative price of retiring, which is defined as the opportunity costs of retiring or the income an individual sacrifices when retiring. Hence retiring becomes more expensive and the preferred retirement age increases. Usually, the substitution effect dominates (Genosko, 1985).

The decision in our model is more complex than is suggested by the explanation provided above. The reason is that labor supply is endogenous. Therefore changes in wealth depend not on labor supply before and after retiring but on the change in the value of the time endowment. On account of the time restriction on working after retiring, at most the restricted time can be transformed into working income. Hence, this time restriction on working after retiring has to be valued by the net wage for working after retiring. The residual time endowment cannot be used for working. Therefore the shadow wage of labor supply is the appropriate value for each unit of the residual time endowment. Retirement does not reduce the time endowment, but only changes the monetary value of this time endowment. This value of the time endowment has to be considered when determining the optimal retirement period. Fortunately, it coincides with the true wage as defined above (equation (2.29)).

The transition from work to retirement also changes the price of leisure. The price of the amount of leisure which does not exceed the time restriction is the shadow price of labor. The price of the residual amount of leisure is the net wage. The difference between the change in the value of the time endowment and the costs of leisure are exactly equal to the change in income as defined by (2.29). For this reason, the illustration in Franz (1996) is also appropriate for a model with endogenous labor supply. Hence, the true wage could be used to determine the optimal retirement age (see Hirte, 1999b). However, since time is discrete using the true wage produces instabilities in the computation, so that the following approach is more useful.

Despite this problem the decision can also be decomposed into a decision about consumption and leisure and a decision about the retirement age. Individuals time their retirement so that utility is maximized. As utility can be directly calculated in the simulation, we 'simply' compute utility for different retirement decisions in each iteration.[11] The retirement age is then fixed as the year of retirement which provides the highest utility. Accordingly, the retirement decision is modeled in three stages:

(1) compute life-time decisions for alternative years of retirement;
(2) determine the year of retirement; this is the year providing the highest lifetime utility[12];
(3) determine the consumption/leisure path given the year of retirement.

One can also illustrate the decision in the discrete time setting by using Figure 2.4. To simplify matters we assume that neither the true wage income nor the reservation wage income are affected by considering a discrete time setting where the unit of time is one year. Given these assumptions Figure 2.4 shows that the age of retirement chosen usually deviates from

[11] Actually, this is not as simple as it looks. It consumes about 1/3 of all computation time.

[12] We do not adopt the approach used in Hirte (1999a) who explicitly considers the true wage. Though it is in line with the theoretical approach it can result in an ambiguous retirement decision. This means that in some iterations individuals jump between two retirement ages due to strong changes in the budget constraint. Computing utility allows utility across iterations to be compared and thus an unambiguous retirement age to be determined.

Figure 2.4: Retirement decision within a discrete time setting

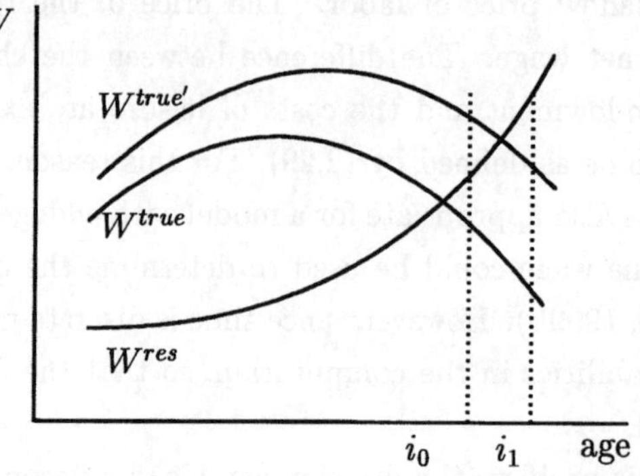

the retirement age individuals prefer in a continuous time setting. In the example shown in this figure the intersection of the true and the reservation wage income is to the left of the chosen retirement age. Since the intersection is not an age at which one can chose to retire, individuals retire either before or after this age, e. g. at i_0, depending on the utility the ages provide. If the true wage income increases, the incentive to retire later increases. Whether this incentive is high enough to make individuals retire later depends on the utility at the relevant adjacent points on the age axis. In Figure 2.4 we suppose that the retirement age increases to i_1. This shows that not all changes in the true wage income are high enough to affect the retirement decision.

2.6 The Social Insurance System

2.6.1 Health and Long Term Care Insurance

The German Health and Long Term Care Insurance

The German health and long term care insurance system consists of public insurance (*Gesetzliche Krankenversicherung* and *Gesetzliche Pflegeversicherung*) and private insurance corporations. Membership in the public system is mandatory for employees earning less than 75% of the income ceiling of the public pension system. All other employees as well as all self employed persons and civil servants are free to choose a private insurance, though health and long term care insurance is compulsory for all groups. The system is financed by contributions in a pay-as-you-go manner. Contributions to the public insurance system are payroll taxes paid equally by employers and employees. If individuals are unemployed, unemployment insurance pays the contributions according to the former income of the unemployed person. Pensioners are also members of the health insurance system. Half the contributions are paid by themselves and the other half by the public pension system. Spouses without income and children of a member of the public insurance are insured free.

The public health insurance pays the medical costs directly. This is independent of the size of the contributions paid by the members. However, in response to the financial problems more and more of these costs, for instance dentures and prescriptions, are paid partially by the members when they are ill. Moreover, health insurance pays benefits which comprise death benefits, sickness cash benefits if individuals are sick for more than six weeks, and temporary maternal salary paid six weeks before and eight weeks after the birth.

The long term care insurance provides cash payments to relatives who look after persons needing care at home, and also pays directly for professional care. The persons needing care are divided into three groups which determine the size of allowances of long term care: group I consists of persons needing care only once a day; group II of persons needing care three times a day; and group III of persons needing continuous care. Cash benefits to private individuals providing care amount to 400 DM for group I, 800 DM for group II, and 1300 DM for group III in 1996. The amount paid increases to 750, 1800 or 2800 DM for professional services. Since only persons belonging to group III need stationary care, 2800 DM is also the payment for stationary care. These payments are below the actual costs of long term care because individuals are supposed to contribute to their long term care costs.

Health and Long Term Care Insurance in the Model

In the model all employees are members of the consolidated health and long term care insurance, and pay contributions as payroll taxes with the aggregate rate of contribution τ_s^H, while health and long term care allowances are granted as goods $c^{H,i}$ to the member of cohort i. The consumption of these goods is assumed to be independent of individual decisions but increases with the age of the individual, though it does not change with time. The budget constraint of the health and long term care insurance is

$$\sum_{i=1}^{J} c^{H,i} N_s^i = \sum_{i=1}^{J} \tau_s^H w_s^i l^i N_s^i + P_s^H + X_s^H \tag{2.30}$$

where the right hand side includes contributions paid out of labor income, pension benefits, and by unemployment insurance, X_s^H.

2.6.2 The Public Pension System

The German Public Pension System

The German public pension system is a defined benefit system since benefits are computed according to certain rules while the rate of contribution is set so that revenue equals contributions in each period. Hence the German system is financed in a pay-as-you-go way. In the following we describe the rules valid in 1996. This includes most regulations of the Pension Act of 1992, all those which became effective before 1996. One of the main regulations stipulated in the Pension Act of 1992 (Rentenreformgesetz 92) was the change from gross to net wage adjustment of pension benefits. All these regulations are subsumed in the following under 'Part I of the Pension Act of 1992', while the regulations which become effective after 1996 are denoted as 'Part II'. The regulations encompassed in Part II are discussed in section 6.5.2 on page 125. They include the introduction of deductions for early retirement. These regulations are not considered in the benchmark case.

The monthly size of pension benefits b^P of a newly retired individual is computed according to the pension equation

$$b^P = e^{P,M} \times a^F \times a^R.$$

Pension benefits depend on the personal earning points, $e^{P,M}$, a factor which depends on the type of the pension, a^F, and the current pension value, a^R. $e^{P,M}$ and a^F are personal factors while a^R is a general factor which determines the average size of the pension. It is the monthly pension which an average employee receives after paying contributions for one year. The current pension value is adjusted yearly according to the change in net income and in net pension benefits.

The individual components of the pension formula are the *personal earning points*, $e^{P,M}$, and the *pension type factor* a^F. Personal earning points are the sum of all pension credits an individual accumulates during his working life. They are based on contribution periods and exempt periods. The value of the personal earning points for one year is insured income for a calendar year during which contributions have been paid, as a proportion of the average income of all insured persons. Times of unemployment are also counted provided individuals received unemployment benefits. According to this formula the personal earning points increase with the length of the working life. For example, if the individual earns 120% of the average wage income in a period, he or she collects 1.2 earning points for this period. Hence an individual working 45 years and earning the average wage income in each period, collects 45 earning points. In addition personal earning points can be credited for exempt periods. For instance, up to seven years of schooling and military service are also counted as time spent working and are weighted with 75% of average income. A similar rule applies to child care, for which one year can be counted, weighted with 0.75 earning points.

Furthermore there is a guaranteed minimum of earning points. During the first four years spent working, the earning points are increased to 0.9 points if the relative wage income is lower. If a retiree has collected on average less than 0.75 points per year, his earning points are increased to 0.75 points per year. This determines a minimum benefit level per year of membership in the pension system. These rules have been changed in the German Pensions Act of 1992, which is described later on.

Note that there are different qualifying periods, for instance, 35 years of contributions and exempt periods are required for men to qualify for long service pensions. These can be paid to men after their 63th year of life, and to women, unemployed, and disabled persons after their 60th year of life. The qualifying period for women and unemployed is only 15 years.

There are different types of pension which determine the benefits. In the case of normal retirement or retirement on medical grounds the benefits are computed as described above. If retirement is due to occupational disability, i. e. the inability to work in one's own profession on medical grounds, the benefits are reduced. Another type of benefits are widow's and orphan's annuities which are also lower than ordinary benefits.

Retirees are allowed to work after retiring provided the monthly salary is below 630 DM between retirement and their 65th year of life. Beyond this age working is not restricted.

Benefits are financed according to a pay-as-you-go system by current revenue from a payroll tax and grants from the national government. The grants should finance the so called non-insurance benefits which are based on years of schooling, military service, child care, and pensions of persons resettled from eastern Europe and of inhabitants of the former GDR (for more details see, e. g., Smith, 1994, and van Essen, 1994). Revenue collected by the payroll tax is provided partly by employers and employees and by unemployment insurance of all unemployed persons receiving unemployment benefits. The pension system pays also allowances toward the costs of rehabilitation and half of the contributions of retirees to the health and long term care insurance.

The Public Pension System in the Model

The implementation is largely based on the German system described above with some modifications. It has the following features.

The level of benefits $b_s^{P,i}$ of an individual aged i in year s is computed according to the pension equation

$$b_s^{P,i} = e_t^{P,M} \times a_s^R \ , \tag{2.31}$$

where $e_t^{P,M}$ are aggregate earning points, which determine the difference between individual and average benefits for an individual born in period t, and a_s^R is the current pension value.

The current pension value, a_s^R, determines the monetary value of one unit of the personal earning points, i. e. the pension an average earner receives per month – in the model per year – of working. To be exact, a_s^R changes over time according to

$$a_s^R = a_{s-1}^R \times \frac{BE_{s-1}}{BE_{s-2}} \times \frac{NQ_{s-1}}{NQ_{s-2}} \times \frac{RQ_{s-2}}{RQ_{s-1}} \tag{2.32}$$

where NQ_{s-1}, NQ_{s-2} are the ratios of average net wage to average wage income, RQ_{s-2}, RQ_{s-1} are the ratios of average net to average gross pension benefits, and BE_{s-1}, BE_{s-2} are the average wage incomes of all individuals not retired in the last two years, i. e.

$$BE_s = \left(\sum_{i=1}^{M-1} w_s^i l_s^i N_s^i\right) \Big/ \left(\sum_{i=1}^{M-1} N_s^i\right) . \tag{2.33}$$

Hence equation (2.32) states that the current pension value grows if wage income increases, or the difference between wage income and net wage income decreases over time. For example an increase in the wage tax rate reduces NQ and thus a^R and the average level of benefits. Additionally, a_s^R decreases if the net pension level increases, for instance caused by changes in the rate of contribution to health insurance.

The essential factor in equation (2.32) is $e_t^{P,M}$, the personal earning points. They depend on the relative size of the insured income and the number of months in which contributions were made to the pension system. Thus the individual benefit multiplier relates contributions to pension benefits: the longer the contribution period, the more earning points are collected; the higher the wage income, i. e. the contribution base, of an individual compared to the average wage income, BE_s, in each period of payment of contributions, the higher the pension benefits of this individual. The individual earning points reflect the principle of equivalence in the German pension system, i. e. different contributions produce different pension benefits. The formula for $e_t^{P,M}$ for an individual born in period t and retired in period M is

$$e_t^{P,M} = \sum_{i=1}^{M-1} \frac{w_s^i l_s^i}{BE_s} + E_t^{P,M}, \qquad s = t + i - 1, \tag{2.34}$$

where $E_t^{P,i}$ are additional earning points of cohort M credited for exempt periods such as education or vocational training, military service, or caring for children. In the simulation only four years of schooling are taken into account.

The contributions to the pension system are paid by a payroll tax with the rate of contribution θ_s^P for the individual wage w_s^i. Each additional unit of labor increases pension benefits. Hence one can derive a marginal rate of pension benefits and, thus, the *implicit tax rate of the pension system*

$$\tau_s^{P,i} = \theta_s^P - \phi_s^{P,i}, \tag{2.35}$$

where $\phi_s^{P,i}$ is the *marginal rate of pension benefits* or the marginal tax benefit linkage (see Appendix)

$$\phi_s^{P,i} = \frac{1}{BE_s} \sum_{\nu=M}^{J} R_k^{m,\nu} \, a_k^R \left(1 - \tau_k^{b,\nu} - 0.5\,\tau_k^H\right), \tag{2.36}$$

where $R_k^{m,\nu}$ is the marginal discount factor and $\tau_k^{b,\nu}$ is the marginal tax rate on pension benefits. The marginal rate of pension benefits can be derived by differentiating the present value of pension benefits with respect to labor supply. The implicit tax rate depends on the rate of contribution θ_s^P, average wage income, the individual marginal discount factor, the current pension value, and the aggregate tax on pension benefits. An increase in the current pension value reduces the implicit tax rate of the pension system, while an increase in the rate of contribution to health insurance increases this tax rate.

Since the internal rate of return of the public pension system is below the interest rate – there is a small population and no productivity growth – the marginal tax benefit linkage, $\phi_s^{P,i}$, is the lower the younger the individual. It increases with age until age 60 but declines thereafter since the number of remaining retirement years decreases.

Retirees are allowed to work after retirement though earnings are restricted to 630 DM until age 65. Until 1999 these earning were also exempt from contribution payments to social insurance.

As there is a pay-as-you-go system and the public pension system is not allowed to issue debt, the budget equation of the public pension system is

$$\sum_{i=M}^{J} b_s^{P,i} N_s^i + G_s^P + 0.5 P_s^H = \sum_{i=1}^{M-1} \theta_s^P w_s^i l_s^i N_s^i + X_s^P + Z_s^P, \tag{2.37}$$

where N_s^i is the number of individuals in cohort i, G_s^P is the consumption of the pension system, P_s^H are the contributions paid to health and long term care insurance computed according to

$$P_s^H = \sum_{i=M}^{J} 0.5\, \tau_s^H\, b_s^{P,i} N_s^i,$$

X_s^P are contributions paid by unemployment insurance, and Z_s^P are grants from the government.

2.6.3 Unemployment Insurance

The German Unemployment Insurance System

All employees earning more than a minimum income must contribute to the German unemployment insurance system. As mentioned above there is an upper ceiling to the size of contributions, which are collected according to a proportional wage tax until the maximum size of contributions is reached. Beyond this threshold the marginal tax rate becomes zero. The rate of contribution is determined by the government, which is also responsible for financing all remaining deficits of the Federal Bureau of Labor (***Bundesanstalt für Arbeit***), the executive of the unemployment insurance system. In addition the Federal Government provides unemployment assistance for the long term unemployed, which is financed out of the government budget. All revenues of the Federal Bureau of Labor are used in an pay-as-you-go way to finance unemployment benefits, unemployment maintenance paid during periods of vocational training when unemployed, and other programs for the unemployed such as programs for promoting employment (*Arbeitsbeschaffungsmaßnahmen*).

Persons qualify for unemployment benefits if they fulfill some conditions such as a sufficiently long period of recent employment, which is at least 12 months of employment subject to compulsory contributions to unemployment insurance during the last three years, and that the cause of unemployment is that the individual has been laid off. This means for example that individuals unemployed directly after studying do not receive unemployment benefits.

The size of unemployment benefits is proportional to the adjusted average weekly net income in the year preceding the current spell of unemployment. This adjusted net income is the wage income corrected by a wage tax and a rate of contribution, both computed as average for all employees subject to compulsory membership of unemployment insurance. In 1996 unemployed persons with children received 67% of this net income, unemployed persons without a child 63%, which has been reduced to 60% in 1998. The size of unemployment maintenance is slightly higher in order to encourage an unemployed person to attend vocational training.

After a period of 6 to 32 months, depending on age and the aggregate length of all working years during the last 7 years, unemployment benefits change into unemployment assistance. The latter is about 57% of net income for an unemployed person with child and 50% if there is no child. In 1996 individuals qualified for unemployment benefits who were younger than 42 years received unemployment benefits for at least 6 and at most 12 months. The maximum length of the period of receiving unemployment benefits increased to 18 months if the individual was older than 42 but younger than 44 years; it increased to 22 months for individuals aged between 44 and 49 years and to 26 months for individuals aged between 49 and 54 years. Beyond the age of 54 years this maximum length increased to 32 months. In 1998 all thresholds have been raised by three years so that the group older than 57 is entitled to receive unemployment benefits for at most 32 months.

Unemployed individuals can retire at the age of 60. The receipt of unemployment benefits is postponed or interrupted if the unemployed person has left his or her job, has broken off a vocational training, or is not willing to accept offers of employment. Before April 1999 severance pay, diminished by an allowance dependent on age, was taken into account in determining the size of unemployment benefits. In this case unemployment benefits have been reduced by 50% until the severance pay has been used up.

Contributions to health and long term care insurance and the pension system are also covered by unemployment insurance. These are computed according to the assessed net wage of an unemployed person.

Modeling Unemployment Insurance

In the simulation model the history of individual unemployment is not known. Furthermore the shortest period is one year. Both restrictions rule out the consideration of most specific arrangements of the German unemployment insurance system. Therefore some simplifying assumptions are needed. First, we assume that each unemployed person whose cohort contributed to unemployment insurance in the previous year receives unemployment benefits during his or her period of unemployment. Second, we assume that unemployment benefits are proportional to the current income of an employed member of the cohort. Both assumptions determine unemployment benefits to be

$$b_s^{X,i} = x_s^i \, \pi_s^X \, w_s^{n,i} \, l_s^i \tag{2.38}$$

where π_s^X is the replacement rate and x_s^i is the rate of unemployment of the individual, which determines the proportion of the year an individual is unemployed. The individual rate of unemployment is defined as

$$x_s^i = \frac{l_s^{g,i} - l_s^i}{l_s^i} \tag{2.39}$$

where $l_s^{g,i}$ is labor supply under full employment.

Contributions to unemployment insurance constitute claims on unemployment benefits, and thus generate a tax benefit linkage. However, as the receipt of unemployment benefits is restricted to individuals who have paid contributions in the previous period, we assume that current employment entitles them to receive unemployment benefits only in the next year. This simplification is consistent with the lack of knowledge of the individual working and unemployment history.

Again one can derive a marginal rate of benefits, $\phi_s^{X,i}$ (see Appendix), which is approximately equal to

$$\phi_s^{X,i} \approx x_{s+1}^{i+1} \left(\frac{\pi_{s+1}^X}{1 + r_{s+1}^m} \frac{w_s^{n,i}}{w_s^i} + 0.8 \, \phi_s^{P,i} \right), \tag{2.40}$$

where $\tau_s^{w,i}$ is the marginal rate of wage tax of individual i and θ_s^{SI} is the aggregate rate of contribution to social insurance. Note that it is also taken into account that recipients of unemployment benefits are entitled to receive pension benefits (see (2.43)). The marginal rate of unemployment benefits is the sum of the present value of future unemployment and pension benefits, because times of unemployment also produce claims for pension benefits. The *implicit tax rate of unemployment insurance* is then

$$\tau_s^{X,i} = \theta_s^X - \phi_s^{X,i}. \tag{2.41}$$

In the model members of the youngest cohort unemployed in the first year of their working life do not qualify for unemployment benefits. This matches the German rule where individuals are only entitled to receive unemployment benefits after twelve months of working. In addition it is assumed that the marginal rate of unemployment benefits of a member of the oldest working cohort is 50% of the marginal rate of unemployment benefits of the preceding cohort. Though it is not really consistent with the unit of time chosen in the model, this assumption reduces instabilities otherwise caused by the strong change in the tax benefit linkage.

As the unemployment insurance system is not allowed to run a deficit or surplus, the budget has to be balanced in each period. This gives the temporal budget constraint

$$\sum_{i=1}^{M-1} b_s^{X,i} N_s^i + X_s^P + X_s^H = \sum_{\nu=1}^{M-1} \theta_s^X \, w_s^i l_s^i \, N_s^i + Z_s^X, \tag{2.42}$$

where Z_s^X are grants from the government and

$$X_s^P = \sum_{i=1}^{M-1} \theta_s^P \, x_s^i \, w_s^{n,i} \, l_s^i \, N_s^i \qquad X_s^H = \sum_{i=1}^{M-1} \tau_s^H \, x_s^i \, w_s^{n,i} \, l_s^i \, N_s^i$$

are contributions to the other parts of the social insurance system paid by unemployment insurance. These contributions are computed according to the net income of cohort i, where the appropriate net wage is computed by using the average of the average wage tax rate, $\bar{\bar{\tau}}_s^w$, giving

$$\overline{w}_s^{n,i} = \left[1 - \bar{\bar{\tau}}_s^w - 0.5\left(\theta_s^P - \theta_s^X - \tau_s^H\right)\right] w_s^i. \tag{2.43}$$

2.7 The Government Sector

The government collects taxes and issues debt to finance the principal and interest of previous debt as well as public expenditure. In addition it makes grants to unemployment insurance and the public pension system. The grants to unemployment insurance are represented by Z_s^X and the grants to the public pension system are represented by Z_s^P. D_s is public debt at time s, G_s is public expenditure, and T_s overall tax revenue. Then the temporal budget constraint of the government is

$$G_s + (1 + r_s)\, D_{s-1} + Z_s^X + Z_s^P = T_s + D_s. \tag{2.44}$$

Tax revenue is

$$\begin{aligned} T_s &= T_s^k + T_s^r + T_s^w + T_s^b + T_s^c \\ &= \tau_s^k\, r_s\, K_s + \overline{\tau}_s^r\, r_s\, A_{s-1} + \overline{\tau}_s^{w,i}\, w_s\, L_s + \overline{\tau}_s^{b,i}\, B_s^P + \tau_s^c\, C_s, \end{aligned}$$

where A_{s-1} are aggregate assets, L_s is aggregate labor input, B_s^p are aggregate pension benefits, and C_s is aggregate consumption. The grants to unemployment insurance and the pension system are a fixed share of the expenditure of these systems.

Integrating forward and using the No-Ponzi-Game condition

$$\lim_{T \to \infty} R_T\, D_T = 0$$

gives the intertemporal budget constraint

$$D_0 = \sum_{s=1}^{\infty} R_s \left(T_s - G_s - Z_s^X - Z_s^P\right), \tag{2.45}$$

where

$$R_s = \prod_{h=1}^{s} (1 + r)^{-1}.$$

Initial public debt must be equal to the present value of the primary surplus. Since G_s is exogenous and D_s is positive, permanent tax reductions are only feasible if grants to the social insurance system are also permanently reduced.

2.8 Equilibrium Conditions

If all decisions are consistent with maximization of utility and profits, a balanced growth equilibrium requires that all budget constraints are satisfied and all markets are cleared. These constitutes a set of equilibrium conditions which have to be satisfied in general equilibrium. The budget constraints are the intertemporal budget constraints of the individuals (2.22), the intertemporal budget constraint of the government (2.45), and all temporal budget constraints of the public pension system (2.37), the health and long term care insurance system (2.30), and the unemployment insurance system (2.42). The market clearing conditions required are the condition of balanced markets for goods, labor, and capital. However due to Walras' law, one of these conditions could be omitted.

The market for goods is cleared if production equals demand, i. e.

$$Y_s = C_s + C_s^H + C_s^P + G_s + G_s^P + I_s + V_s, \tag{2.46}$$

where

$$V_s = (w_s^c - w_s^g)\, L_s$$

are intermediate goods which are caused by labor input.

An "equilibrium"in the labor market requires that

$$L_s^d = \sum_{i=1}^{M-1} e_s^i\, l_s^i\, N_s^i.$$

Note that this condition refers to labor measured in efficiency units and to labor supply rationed by efficiency wages. Consequently there is an equilibrium rate of unemployment.

Finally, the capital market has to be cleared in each period. This condition can be written as

$$A_s = D_s + K_{s+1}. \tag{2.47}$$

Private assets are equal to public debt plus the aggregate capital stock.

Having completed the description of the economic model the next task is to determine the data base and some parameters, then to calibrate and compute the initial steady state or the benchmark equilibrium. These steps are described in the next chapter.

Chapter 3

Database and Simulation Method

In order to perform some simulations with the model presented above, the data base and the values of the parameters must be determined. Since all equilibrium conditions of the simulation model ought to be satisfied, one cannot simply take all data from the national accounts. Furthermore some parameters must be chosen. As there are only a few estimates of the significant parameters, and hardly any using the functions applied in the model, the "true" values are not known. Hence some assumptions must be made. Usually, the remaining parameters are endogenously computed by using the data base and exogenously chosen parameter values, so that the simulation replicates the benchmark data base[1]. This method for determining parameter values and the benchmark data base is known as *calibration*. It is a shortcut to the correct method, which is an econometric estimation of all the data and parameters (see Jorgensen, 1984). The shortcomings of calibration include the lack of tests of the model specification, and the need to make many guesstimates instead of econometric estimates. However, the discussion on the usefulness of calibration and its problems made clear that it is a convenient shortcut to the parameterization of the model (see Lau, 1984). Therefore we follow the common procedure and calibrate the parameters.

As Fehr (1999a, p. 57) notes, the use of a single production sector facilitates the process of creating a data base for a dynamic CGE study.

[1]See MANSUR and WHALLEY (1984) for a static CGE model, ST.-HILAIRE and WHALLEY (1983) for an interregional static CGE model, or FULLERTON and ROGERS (1993) for a dynamic CGE analysis. The generation of a data base for an interregional static CGE model for Germany is described in HIRTE (1996).

In this case it is not necessary to determine the whole data base before using the simulation model to calibrate the parameter values. Instead the choice of some data, almost all the parameters, and the tax and rates of contribution, allows the consistent data base to be computed by using the simulation model. The basic data and parameter values are assigned so that the resulting initial steady state reflects some macroeconomic facts of the economy in the year taken as a starting point. This procedure considerably simplifies the generation of the benchmark data base, but it creates a problem for sensitivity analyses. The evaluation of the reliability and robustness of the results requires the parameter values to be varied. This however implies a new calculation of the data base, which changes with changes in the parameter values. The main advantage of this method is that the affects of modifications of the model, for instance omitting unemployment, can be examined in the sensitivity analysis. This is not possible in a CGE analysis where the data base is computed before the parameter values.

The parameter values and basic data chosen in this study and the data base computed as an initial steady state are described below. Since Fehr (1999a) provides an survey of the literature on the estimation of parameters, we focus only on some points and on the values chosen in our study.

3.1 Parameterization and Basic Data

Despite the break in the data caused by German unification, we do not choose the year 1989, as in other accompanying studies (see Hirte and Weber, 1997b, or Hirte, 1998 and 1999a), but 1996 as the base year to ensure topicality.

3.1.1 Production Sector and Unemployment

The *elasticity of substitution between capital and labor* is unity because a Cobb-Douglas production technology is used.

$$F(K,L) = \Phi\, K^{\psi}\, L^{1-\psi}.$$

The scale parameter, Φ, and the share parameter, ψ, are computed to match the given gross interest rate, capital and labor input, and output, yielding $\Phi = 1.114$ and $\psi = 0.2610868$. Though the values of the capital stock, labor input, output, gross wage, and interest rate are required to determine the parameters, they are endogenously computed in the simulation model. The parameterization of the Cobb-Douglas function ensures that the gross wage and interest rate match the chosen values if capital stock and labor input are endogenously determined so that they are equal to the values from national accounts. Hence these data are exogenously given though they are endogenously recalculated in the simulation. However, as the simulation almost exactly reproduces the given values it can be considered as a replication check.

Another variable given is the aggregate labor input which is assumed to equal aggregate labor costs, which were 1902,7 $\times 10^9$ DM in 1996 according to the national accounts. Here the gross wage is normalized to unity. Furthermore output, 2734,8 $\times 10^9$ DM, defined as turnover or national income plus business taxes,[2] as well as overall capital income (832,1 $\times 10^9$ DM) are given. Since the price index is also normalized to unity, the net domestic product is equivalent to the aggregate output. The gross rate of interest, r_s^g, is assumed to equal the average of the gross real rate of return on equity used in industry (Institut der Deutschen Wirtschaft, 1998, p. 72) and the real rate of return of bonds grossed-up by the capital tax rate of the last ten years, yielding a gross real rate of interest of 8.895%. The rate of interest, i. e. the after-factor-tax rate of interest, r is 8.03%. Using these data and the capital tax rate the aggregate capital stock can be computed by solving $Y = w^g L + r^g K$ for K.

The most important parameter for determining unemployment is the *mark-up* β. β is constant and equal to $\lambda / (1 + \lambda)$ in the retention model. Reproducing the rate of unemployment of 1996 which was 11.5% requires λ to equal 3.983 giving β equals 0.8.

[2]Note that the costs of quitting are not included in this definition. These costs add up to about 18% of GDP as defined in this study.

Figure 3.1: Wage profile

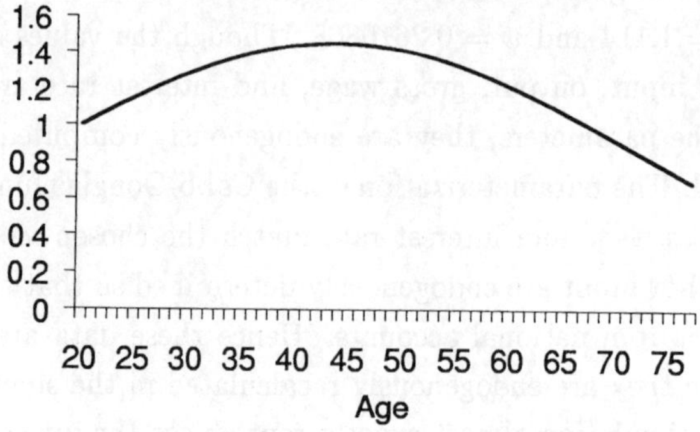

3.1.2 Household Parameters

Some household parameters are set to the same values as chosen by Fehr (1999a). Since he summarizes the literature on the estimation of the crucial parameters, we concentrate upon the most relevant sources.

Strength of the preference for leisure. As noted above a specific feature of our model is the age dependency of the strength of the preference for leisure, α^i. It is assumed to be time-invariant but to increase with the age of the cohort. α^i is 1.5, a value chosen in most dynamic CGE studies, but increases between the 60th and the 69th year of life by 0.05 per year to 2.0 where it remains for the rest of life.

The value of the *time endowment* h is chosen to ensure that individual labor supply equals aggregate labor supply in terms of efficiency units not actual units of time. Hence, deviating from Fullerton and Rogers (1993), we do not focus on the actual number of working hours per year. Since aggregate labor supply in this study equals the total wage bill of the national accounts if the unit labor costs are normalized to unity, total time endowment is also a normalized parameter set to 74.143. Depending on the values chosen for α^i labor supply is between 32% and 47% of the time endowment.

Human capital is exogenously fixed as suggested by Auerbach and Kotlikoff (1987a). e^i increases with age at a decreasing rate and decreases after a peak in the middle of the working and retirement life. The human capital

Table 3.1: Population growth rates

t	n	t	n	t	n	t	n
1996	0.85	2006	-0.13	2016	3.38	2026	-1.00
1997	-6.93	2007	1.92	2017	-0.70	2027	-1.00
1998	-5.07	2008	4.11	2018	-9.03	2028	-1.00
1999	-10.51	2009	-0.82	2019	-3.69	2029	-0.50
2000	-10.26	2010	0.17	2020	-2.60	2030	-0.50
2001	-2.70	2011	-3.63	2021	-3.97	2031	-0.50
2002	-3.07	2012	-11.03	2022	-1.13	2032	-0.50
2003	1.52	2013	13.01	2023	3.35	2033	-0.50
2004	0.15	2014	3.54	2024	-1.00	2034	-0.30
2005	0.15	2015	0.74	2025	-1.00	2035	-0.30

Source: STATISTISCHES BUNDESAMT (1996) and own calculations.

parameter creates a hump-shaped wage profile. The values of the parameters of the human capital function $e^i = a_1 + a_2 i + a_3 i^2$ are $a_1 = 4.47$, $a_2 = 0.033$ and $a_3 = -0.00067$. The resulting wage profile peaks after 24 years of working (see curve AK in Figure 3.1)[3]. The model is normalized so that the wage of an individual of cohort i is equal to unity.

The rate of time preference. The study of Hansen and Singleton (1982) provides a value of 0.1 whereas Lawrance (1991) estimated a value of ϑ ranging from 0.01 to 0.04 for different income classes. Due to the lack of studies for Germany we rely on these studies and set ϑ to 0.01.

The elasticity of substitution between leisure and consumption, i. e. the intratemporal elasticity of substitution ρ is set to 0.8 which is close to the value of 0.83 provided by Ghez and Becker (1975).

The intertemporal elasticity of substitution γ is set to 0.3 mainly to generate more realistic data. This value lies between the estimates for Germany of Flaig (1988) who proposes a value between 0.4 and 0.75, and Hansen (1996) who finds evidence that γ is approximately zero. The surveys of Fehr (1999a, p. 58-59) and Elmendorf (1996) show that there are many other estimates of this elasticity ranging from 0.1 to 0.76.

[3] In other studies we used a wage profile which decreases slower ($a_2 = 0.034$ and $a_3 = -0.00058$), which is a rough approximation to the wage profile curves provided by FRANZ (1996, p. 82). This curve peaks after 30 years of working (see HIRTE and WEBER, 1997b, and Hirte, 1999b).

Table 3.2: Demographics in Germany and in the model

	Statist.Bundesamt[a]		Interminist. AG[b]		This study	
Year	∑Pop.[c] Mill.	Old age[d] %	∑Pop. Mill.	Old age %	∑Pop. Mill.	Old age %
1996	82.8	37.0	82.8	37.0	82.9	36.9
2000	83.7	41.5	82.2	40.8	83.6	38.2
2005	83.8	43.5	81.8	44.5	83.8	41.3
2010	83.4	44.1	81.0	44.8	83.8	44.6
2015	82.5	46.8	79.9	47.9	83.4	48.5
2020	81.2	51.6	78.4	53.1	82.9	53.1
2025	79.5	60.1	76.6	62.6	82.2	59.2
2030	77.4	67.9	74.3	73.2	81.1	63.3
2035	75.1	68.5	71.7	76.6	79.0	74.0
2040	72.4	67.8	68.8	76.4	76.8	78.6
2045		67.9		77.6		76.6
2050		69.7		80.2		74.7

[a]National Bureau of Statistics (Statistisches Bundesamt, 1994).
[b]Interministerielle Arbeitsgruppe (Wissenschaftlicher Beirat, 1998, p. 6).
[c]Total Population.
[d]Old age dependency ratio.

3.1.3 Other Parameters and Variables

Other parameters exogenously given are population growth, tax rates, and replacement rates. The level of most tax rates or tax allowances are chosen so that the tax revenue approximately matches actual tax revenue in 1996.

The *population growth rate* in the initial steady state is set to 0.85%. This value ensures that the initial population structure is approximately equal to the data given by the National Bureau of Statistics (Statistisches Bundesamt, 1994) and the Advisory Board at the Ministry of Economics (Wissenschaftlicher Beirat, 1998). The rates of commencement of employment in subsequent years are equal to the rates of change of the size of the cohorts who are in 1996 younger than 30 years. This defines the changes in the size of the youngest cohorts for the years 1997 to 2025[4]. Thereafter the birth rates converge to the long term rate, which is set to -0.3%. Applying

[4]In this way the population decline is delayed, since cohorts initially between 20 and 30 years old have positive growth rates, while they already have negative growth rates in reality. Nonetheless this assumption is necessary for the computation. This is the reason why population decline is delayed in this study.

this assumption provides the birth rates given in Table 3.1.

As a result the old age dependency ratio, i. e. the ratio of retirees to employees, increases from 0.36 to 0.76 in 2045, while the figures suggested by the Statistisches Bundesamt (1994) or the Wissenschaftlicher Beirat (1998, p. 6) are 0.37 and 0.67 or 0.77. The size of the youngest working cohort in the initial steady state is computed as 1,372,425 individuals. Overall population is 82,877,638.

Life expectancy is initially set to 78 years. It is the sum of the 19 years of childhood, 40 years of working life and the length of the retirement life which is assumed to be 19 years. While the average length of retirement of a man is only 16.5 years in 1996, the average length of retirement of a woman is 22.9 years. The choice of 19 years is below the mean of both values, since not all retirees are married. In addition it is assumed that life expectancy increases from 78 to 81. Starting with 1997 the average life expectancy increases by 0.1 years per year until it reaches 81 years in 2037. The main figures are compared to the figures given by the Wissenschaftlicher Beirat (1998, p. 6) in Table 3.2. It shows that population growth rates and the assumed increase in life expectancy leads to a pattern of population similar to that forecast in both studies.

Consumption taxes. The consumption tax rate is set to 22.2%, a value ensuring that computed tax revenue amounts to the actual revenue from various consumption taxes in 1996.

Taxes on capital input. Aggregating corporate taxes on retained earnings, business taxes, property taxes, and the net worth tax, gives the revenue of taxes on capital input. Though there are no data available on revenue from corporate tax on retained earnings, they can assessed as suggested by Fehr (1999a, p. 69). The corporate tax rate on distributed earnings is 30%. As these earnings are distributed as dividends the tax base approximately matches the tax base of the capital income tax. The tax rate of the latter is 25%. Using this information the tax receipts from the corporate tax on distributed earnings can be calculated. As capital is proportionally taxed in the model, the capital tax rate is obtained by dividing the capital stock by the actual tax revenue, leading to a tax rate of 10.76%.

Figure 3.2: Health and long term care consumption

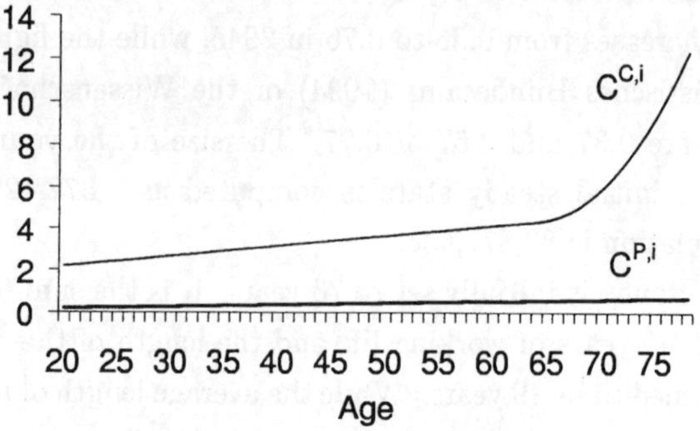

Tax on capital income. Income from capital income is subject to a linear progressive tax. The marginal tax rate is 30%. The tax allowance is set to 18,900 DM, which is between the average deduction of 7,000 DM of the lowest income class and 40,000 DM of the top income class. These values ensure that computed tax revenue matches actual tax revenue.

Wage and pension taxes. Labor income and the return on pension contributions are taxed according to the income tax schedule (see Figure 2.2 on page 27). The share of pension benefits subject to income tax is set to 25%. Tax allowances are set to 9,960 DM. This ensures that the wage tax revenue almost equals the wage tax revenue in 1996.[5]

To compute *health* and *long term consumption per capita*, we use the data for aggregate cohorts given in Eckerle and Oczipka (1998, p. 86). These data are well approximated by the function for aggregate health, $C^{C,i}$, and long term care expenditure, $C^{P,i}$ (see Figure 3.2)

$$c^{H,i} = C^{C,i} + C^{P,i} = a_1^H + a_2^H\, i + a_3^H\, i^2 + a_1^P + a_2^P\, i$$

where $a_1^H = 2.96154$, $a_2^H = 0.0669$, and $a_3^H = 0$ for individuals younger than 65 and $a_3^H = 0.05155$ for individuals aged 65 or older, and $a_1^P = 0.2383$ and $a_2^P = 0.01166$. The average rate of contribution is $\tau^H = 14.24\%$, compared to the actual rate of 14.55%.

[5]The tax allowance is below the basic tax allowance of the German system (12,056 DM). This is due to the equivalence of population and labor force, while in reality the male labor force contains 55 % of the male population and of female labor force contains 40% of the female population.

Public expenditure as well as public debt are computed endogenously in the initial steady state. But some parameters of the public pension and the unemployment insurance system have to be specified. Though *grants to unemployment insurance* are actually about 30% of all contributions, they are assumed to be 5.6% at the initial steady state. The reason for this choice is that this allows the endogenously computed rate of contribution, τ_s^X, to match its real counterpart which is 6.5% of wage income. As mentioned above the rate of contribution is assumed to be flat.

The *replacement rate of unemployment benefits* is 67% of the previous net income which corresponds to the replacement rate of unemployed persons with children in 1996.

The *replacement rate of public pension benefits*, π_s^P, is 70.1% for individuals whose contribution period is 45 years. In the model, it is assumed that working life is 40 years and that in addition four years of schooling are credited when computing pension benefits. Hence individuals, who on average work only 40 years, are treated as though they have worked for 44 years. Following the German pension regulations, it is assumed that 0.75 earning points per year of schooling is included in the pension formula. However due to periods of unemployment where earning points are below average income, pension benefits reach only 65.41% of the gross income of a fully employed average earner.

Consumption of the public pension system, G_s^P, is exogenously given as 45.2 Mill. DM. This is the sum of all expenditure of the public pension system minus contributions to health and long term care insurance and pension benefits. These expenditures include the costs of administration, expenditure for rehabilitation and other expenditures in 1996 (see Eckerle and Oczipka, 1998).

3.2 Initial Steady State

The initial steady state can be computed by using all exogenously given data and parameter values (see Table 3.3).

Table 3.3: Parameters and basic data

Parameter	Symbol	Value
Production sector		
Unit labor cost	w^g	1
Gross interest rate	r^g	8.895
Interest rate	r	8.03%
Capital stock	K	9455.8
Labor input	L_d	1902.7
Output	Y	2743.8
Scale parameter	Φ	1.114
Share parameter	ψ	0.2610868
Unemployment		
Rate of unemployment	x	11.5%
Response parameter for quitting	λ	3.983
Policy variables		
Member of cohort born in $t = 0$	N_s^1	1.372 Mill
Population	$\sum N$	82.877 Mill.
Replacement rate of pension benefits	π_s^P	70.1%
Replacement rate of UI-benefits	π_s^X	67.0%
Consumption tax rate	τ^c	22.2%
Capital tax rate	τ^k	10.76%
Marginal rate of capital income tax	τ^r	30.0%
Marginal rates of wage tax	$\tau^w = \tau^b$	25.0%...33.0%...53.0%
Tax allowance for capital income tax	ξ^r	18,900 DM
Tax allowance for wage tax	$\xi^w = \xi^p$	9,960 DM
Private households		
Time endowment	h	74.143
Strength of the preference for leisure	α^i	1.5 ... 2.0
Intertemporal elasticity of substitution	γ	0.3
Intratemporal elasticity of substitution	ρ	0.8
Pure rate of time preference	ϑ	0.01

Table 3.4: Data of the social insurance system

Variable	Symbol	Model 1996	Germany 1996[a]
Pension system			
Age of retirement M	60	60	
Length of retirement	$J-M$	19	16.5-22.1
Rate of contribution	τ^P	19.2	19.2
Old age dependency ratio		36.9	37.0
Grants in % of GDP	(Z^P)	1.6	1.6
Replacement rate after 45 years of working	π^P	70.1	70.1
Pension benefits in % of GDP	(B^P)	11.9	11.9
Public goods in % of GDP	(G^P)	1.5	1.5
Unemployment insurance (UI)			
Rate of unemployment	x	11.5	11.5
Rate of contribution	τ^X	6.5	6.5
Replacement rate after 1 year of working	π^X	67.0	67.0
Grants to UI in % GDP	(Z^X)	0.2	0.4
UI-benefits in % of GDP	(B^X)	3.5	3.3[b]
Health and long term care insurance			
Rate of contribution	τ^H	14.24	14.55
Health expenditure in % of GDP	(C^H)	9.0	8.3
Aggregate expenditure on long term care	C^N	26.1	21.2

[a]Sources: BA (1997), ECKERLE and OCZIPKA (1998), VDR (1999), Wiss. Beirat (1998).

[b]All expenditure of the Federal Bureau of Labor (Bundesanstalt für Arbeit).

3.2.1 Macroeconomic Data

In Table 3.5 the values computed are compared to the actual data of 1996 which are taken from the national accounts (see Statistisches Bundesamt, 1997 and 1998). Tax rates and parameters are chosen so that some basic facts are reproduced in the benchmark data base. These are, for instance, the rate of unemployment, which was 11.5% in 1996, the average retirement age (41th year of the working life which is age 60), or the rate of contribution to unemployment insurance (6.5%). Additionally tax allowances and tax rates are chosen to generate tax revenues similar to actual revenues as described above.

In discussing the data one should bear in mind that the data base is not necessarily identical to data from the national accounts, because the theoretical model deviates from the method applied in constructing the national accounts. It is therefore for the modeler to decide which data should be matched and hence are considered as crucial. We chose to accept large deviations only when necessary, i. e. if they cannot be avoided due to differences in the theoretical models used to generate the data.

Tables 3.4 and 3.5 show that most variables almost match their actual counterpart. This is especially true for the unemployment parameters – the rate of unemployment, unemployment benefits, and the rate of contribution to the unemployment system. Furthermore, the total wage bill and the capital cost are equal to the actual values. The output used in the simulations differs from the Gross Domestic Product (GDP) of the national accounts on account of net transfers abroad, depreciation, as well as subsidies and some production taxes, which are all omitted in the simulation. The marginal rate of wage tax amounts to 29.8% while the average rate of wage tax is 19.4%, a value not too different to the average rate of income tax of 21% assessed by the OECD (1998, p. 104). Nonetheless wage tax revenue is equal to actual revenue which is also the case for tax revenue from the capital income and corporate taxes. The average rate of capital income tax is 2.66%.

The figures in Table 3.5 show some noticeable differences between computed and real data. The first are investment outlays, which are only 27.5% of their real value. One reason for this deviation is the superficial modeling of the investment decision. Another reason is that the burden of unification is not replicated in the model. Further deviations can be found in subsidies to the public pension system and unemployment insurance. The first is due to the so-called non-insurance benefits[6] and widow's or orphan's annuities, which are not taken into account in the simulation model. The only exceptions are exempt periods credited for vocational training. And finally, private consumption exceeds and public debt is below its real value. Both are the result of the superficial modeling of investment and could be caused by the missing bequest motive.

[6]Non-insurance benefits are for example benefits paid for years of military service, schooling or rearing children. BERTHOLD and THODE (1996) estimate that these benefits, as far as they are financed by contributions, amounts to 38 $\times 10^9$ DM in 1994.

Table 3.5: Comparing macrodata with national account

Variable	Symbol	Model 1996	Germany 1996[a]
Expenditure (in % of NDP)[b]			
Private consumption	$C + T^c + C^H$	75.2	66.0
Public good consumption	$G + G^P$	22.2	22.8
Net investment	I	2.6	9.5
Exports - imports		0.0	1.7
Saving rate (in % of NDP)		3.01	8.6
Value added (in % of NDP)			
Total wage bill	$w^g\, L$	61.0	61.1
Total capital cost (+ business taxes)	$r^g\, K$	27.0	27.2
Indirect taxes minus subsidies[c]	T^c	12.0	11.2
Net domestic product in bill. DM	$Y - V + T^c$	3118.7	3089.0
Public budget in % of NDP			
Interest payments	$r\, D$	3.9	4.2
Grants to unemployment insurance		0.2	0.4
Grants to the pension system		1.6	1.6
Public gross debt	D	48.1	67.7
Tax revenue	T	26.0	26.3
Consumption taxes	T^c	12.0	12.1
Capital taxes	T^k	1.5	1.5
Corporate and business taxes	T^r	2.6	2.6
Labor income taxes	T^{w+b}	9.8	9.9

[a]Source: STATISTISCHES BUNDESAMT (1997 and 1998).
[b]Net domestic product = GDP - depreciation.
[c]Indirect taxes - business taxes - subsidies + net transfers from abroad.

3.2.2 *Individual Data*

Let us now turn to data on individuals. We discuss three variables below.

Individual Unemployment

The rates of unemployment of different cohorts in Germany in 1996 (ANBA, 1997) show a pattern similar to the computed rates of unemployment (see Table 3.6).

The increase in the rate of unemployment between the youngest and oldest cohort is reflected in the model; it is caused by differences in the economic situation such as the wage profile. Despite some differences be-

Table 3.6: Rates of unemployment

Age	Computed	Germany 1996[a]
20-25[b]	9.67%	9.30%
26-30	9.66%	11.30%
31-35	9.96%	13.00%
36-40	10.57%	11.70%
41-45	11.56%	10.30%
46-50	13.06%	9.50%
51-55	15.32%	9.60%
56-60	17.93%	19.40%

[a]ANBA(1997)
[b]Age 21-25 in Germany 1996.

tween the computed values and the actual values, Table 3.6 shows that the modeling of unemployment produces far better results than a uniform distribution of unemployment which is assumed by Sørensen (1997).

Implicit Tax of the Public Pension System

As argued above, the German public pension system creates a positive tax benefit linkage. Individuals currently paying contributions expect to receive pension benefits in the future. Provided current pension law remains unchanged the implicit tax rate τ^P decreases with age until the individual reaches retirement. This implicit tax rate is plotted in Figure 3.3 for each age and compared to the rate of contribution which is 10.17%. Since the present value of future benefits is the lower the younger the individual, the implicit tax rate decreases with age. The difference between the rate of contribution and the implicit tax rate is the tax benefit linkage. It is based on the assumption that individuals who work before the age of 60 retire with 60. But for individuals older than 59 the tax benefit linkage is fictional; it is computed for the case that the individuals work in the year considered and retire in the next period. Therefore after retirement at age 60 the implicit tax rate increases, since the number of retirement years is reduced with time.

The implicit tax rate of the pension system can also be used to compare a fully funded pension system with the compulsory public pension system. In the first system contributions earn the market rate of interest.

Figure 3.3: Tax benefit linkage of the German pension system

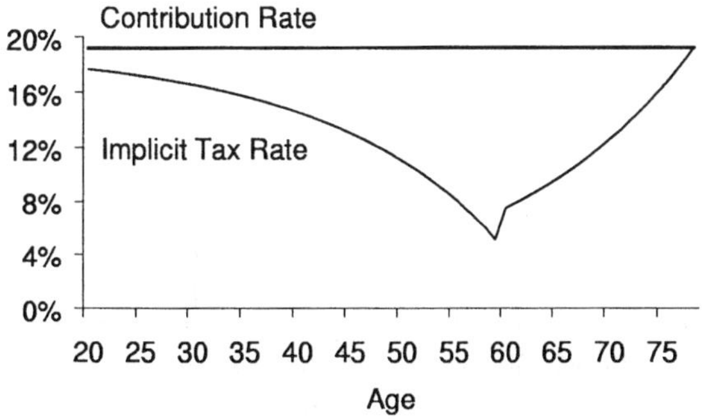

A compulsory public pension system is actuarially fair if it pays the same internal rate of return. This induces an implicit tax rate of zero. However as Figure 3.3 shows, the implicit tax rate of the pension system is positive – it is 13.93% on average – and, thus, the internal rate of return of the compulsory public pension system is below the market rate of interest[7]. The net rate of contribution is 5.99% on average. This is very low for two reasons. First, there is no economic growth, and thus the internal rate of return or the tax benefit linkage is lower than in reality. Second, by computing the implicit tax rate only net pension benefits are considered, since contributions of retirees to health and long term care insurance are pure tax rates.

As long as the implicit tax rate of the pension system is below the rate of contribution, the public pension system has a positive internal rate of return. According to Hirte (1999b) the internal rate of return of the German public pension system of an individual retiring in 1996 was 2.5% on average. Calculating the internal rate of return of an individual retiring in initial steady state provides a value of 0.9%. Since we do not consider economic growth, the difference is entirely due to differences in the growth rates and, thus, growth in wages and pension benefits.

[7]A calculation of the implicit tax rate for different income groups and men and women can be found in Hirte(2000c)

Figure 3.4: Tax benefit linkage of the German UI system

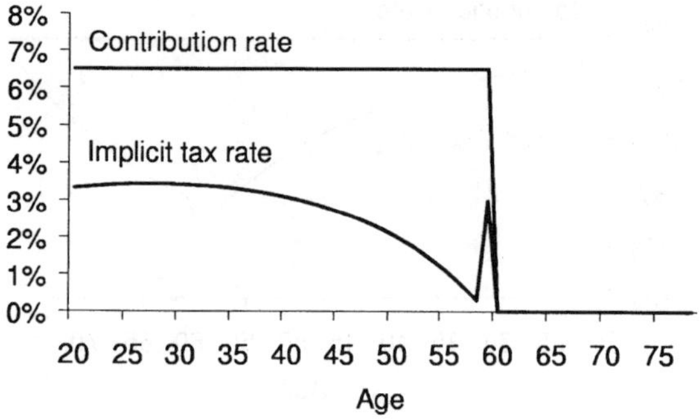

Implicit Tax of Unemployment Insurance

Since the probability of being unemployed in the next period for an individual of cohort i is x_s^i, the individual rate of unemployment, individuals expect to receive unemployment benefits with the same probability. This constitutes a tax benefit linkage between contributions to unemployment insurance and benefits. Figure 3.4 shows that this tax benefit linkage is positive for all cohorts before retirement. The net rate of contribution is below the rate of contribution. As the individual rate of unemployment increases with age, the present value of future unemployment benefits increases, causing a decrease in the net rate of contribution. Due to the extremely high individual rate of unemployment near retirement, the net rate of contribution becomes negative for individuals aged 54 to 59. Note that in this figure individuals older than 60 are assumed to be retirees and thus neither pay contributions nor receive unemployment benefits. The average rate of implicit tax of unemployment insurance amounts to 1.99%, hence unemployment insurance is also not actuarially fair on average.

This finishes the description and construction of the benchmark data base. In the next section we describe the method of computation.

3.3 Simulation method

As is known from many studies, for instance Auerbach and Kotlikoff (1987a) or Bettendorf (1994), there are different methods to obtain the solution for a perfect foresight equilibrium in the life cycle framework described above. A simple but efficient method is the so-called Gauss-Seidel algorithm, an iterative solution technique. It is, for instance, used by Auerbach and Kotlikoff (1987a) and in a more sophisticated version by Keuschnigg (1991).

Using initial guesses of the capital stock, tax rates, the interest rate, and wages for all periods, all other variables are computed. These variables are employed to update the capital stock, tax rates, interest rates, and wages. These are in turn used to recalculate all other variables in the next iteration, and so on. In the end all "prices"should converge to their equilibrium values, ensuring that all equilibrium conditions are satisfied. Though this procedure usually converges to a steady state equilibrium, neither stability nor uniqueness are theoretically ensured without further examination (see Kehoe and Levine, 1990). However we refer to Laitner (1990) who has computed the eigenvalues of a linearized version of the basic AK model for different combinations of parameters. His results suggest that there is uniqueness in this type of model. Therefore we do not further discuss this point and turn now to a detailed description of the computational approach.

Given the values of the parameters and basic data the effects of a policy reform or economic shock are computed in three steps: first, the initial steady state, second, the final steady state and, third, the transition path between the initial and final steady states are computed. The basic procedure is the same in all stages of the simulation. There are some differences in the number of periods to be solved for and the initial guesses.

In all the steps initial guesses of the capital stock, labor input, tax rates, rates of contribution, the shadow wage of leisure, the retirement age, and individual and overall rates of unemployment are made. Using these guesses marginal productivities, unit costs of labor, the gross rate of interest, the gross wage, formula (2.11), and the interest rate (2.10) are computed. Given these variables the algorithm solves for all individual variables, starting with the computation of individual wages and net wages, (2.17) and (2.18), individual net interest rates (2.19), and the reservation wage (2.25). Then the retirement age is computed; this requires the computation of pension benefits for each year considered, new implicit taxes, leisure and consumption. Thereafter unemployment (2.38), pension benefits (2.31), and the corresponding tax benefit linkages, (2.41) or (2.35) are calculated, followed by the computation of tax bases and the present value of income (2.23). These are used in the next step to determine consumption (2.27), leisure (2.24), savings and labor supply. Next, average and marginal tax rates and the shadow wage (2.28) are computed. Then the algorithm enters a loop where unemployment is determined. After multiplying all wages and benefits by β to generate the clearing wages of the labor market, the reservation wage, consumption, leisure, savings, and the shadow wage of the unrestricted labor market are computed. The algorithm leaves this loop when the change in unrestricted leisure between two iterations has converged to almost zero. Then individual unemployment is determined as the difference between unrestricted and restricted leisure demands (2.39). Eventually unemployment is aggregated to find the overall rate of unemployment, and all wages and benefits are reset by dividing by β. This finishes the computation of all individual variables in the first iteration.

The remaining task is to aggregate individual variables to overall consumption, assets, labor supply, unemployment benefits, health and long term care benefits, and pension benefits. Using these values, output (2.46), public debt defined as a fixed proportion of output, and the capital stock are computed (2.47). Next all public budget variables as well as the variables of the public pension, health and long term care, and unemployment insurance are determined. These are revenues from different taxes, (2.9), (2.13), (2.15), and (2.16), revenue from contributions, grants, aggregate benefits, and contributions of unemployment insurance to the pension sector and health and long term care insurance.

Then the public budget (2.44), the budget of unemployment insurance (2.42), the budget of health and long term care insurance (2.30), and the budget of the pension system (2.37) are calculated. In the last step in this iteration the rates of contribution and a particular tax rate are recalculated so that they balance these budgets. The tax rate, the rates of contribution, and the new capital stock per capita are then compared to their previous values. If they deviate the next iteration starts and the updated values are used as starting values. After some iterations, about 200 in the calculation of the initial steady state, the deviations between the starting values and the updated values of the rates of contribution vanish and equilibrium is reached. To ensure that all equilibrium conditions are satisfied, the equilibrium of the market for goods is checked at the end of each iteration. If the final solution also satisfies this the algorithm terminates.

Since in all reform projects discussed below the final steady state does not depend on the transition path, the final steady state can be computed exactly as the initial steady state. In this case we use the results of the initial steady state as starting values for the final steady state.

The most time consuming step is the determination of the transition path following a policy reform. Here it is assumed that individuals are initially ignorant of a policy reform or economic shock which takes place in year one or thereafter. To find the transition path all computations have to be made for at least 230 periods, and an equal number of tax rates, rates of contribution, and capital stocks have to converge. Furthermore for each cohort and each period the equilibrium values of leisure, consumption, the retirement age, and the shadow wage have to be found. Note that the individuals born before year one suffer a time inconsistency. They all have to determine new consumption and labor supply paths for their remaining life time. This is an additional task in stage three of the computation. Individuals living near the final steady state use the values of the final steady state computed in step two. This requires a second modification of the original algorithm. In order to increase the efficiency of the algorithm starting values are used which lie between the values computed in the initial and final steady state. Despite the huge number of calculations necessary in each iteration, solutions for most policy reforms can be found within a range of time lasting from 20 minutes to one hour.

Chapter 4

Tax Incidence

The main aim of this chapter is to present the methodology which is extensively used to understand and interpret the results of the simulations. The main procedure is the decomposition into income effects and excess burden, as proposed by Keuschnigg (1992 and 1994) and developed for use in the AK model by Fehr (1996). In the following we present the derivation of this decomposition, which is closely related to Fehr (1999a). Then we give some hypotheses on economic effects caused by changes in the policy variables of the model. These are to a large part results of other simulation studies. We start with a short description of the method used to determine excess burden and tax incidence which is suggested by Keuschnigg (1994) and Fehr (1996).

4.1 Excess Burden and Tax Incidence

Dynamic effects of a fiscal reform can be explored in different frameworks. In a traditional Ramsey model (see e. g. Blanchard and Fischer, 1989) where individuals have an infinite horizon as well as in the Barro model (Barro, 1974) with an operative bequest motive, which implies an infinite horizon of an altruistically linked family, intergenerational redistribution is excluded and welfare changes occur only due to efficiency effects. However this is true only if individuals are homogeneous, which is also assumed throughout this study. Each deviation from the operative bequest motive generates redistribution between cohorts. Consequently redistribution as well as efficiency effects occur in this study, both affecting individual welfare. In order to discuss both effects welfare changes are decomposed into efficiency and income effects. Although there are many studies deriving these effects analytically, in a complex model like the one used in this study, such a decomposition requires simulation.

Of course, to isolate efficiency effects all income effects have to be neutralized by compensations. Such a compensation scheme has been introduced in the AK model by Auerbach and Kotlikoff (1987a). They employ a lump sum redistribution agency, which redistributes between cohorts so that the cohorts currently alive are utility compensated whereas all welfare gains or losses are shifted into the future[1]. Though this allows a general assessment of the aggregate efficiency effects of a fiscal policy reform, efficiency effects experienced by specific cohorts cannot be assessed. To determine these effects a compensation mechanism is needed which neutralizes all *individual* income and redistribution but not the efficiency effects. Keuschnigg(1992 and 1994) has shown in general how the economic effects of a tax reform can be decomposed into excess burden and income effects in a dynamic life cycle model. Fehr (1996), Fehr and Ruocco (1997), Fehr and Wiegard (1998 a, b, c, 1999), or Fehr (1999a) have extended this approach to assess excess burden and redistribution effects numerically.

In order to decompose the effects, the individual tax burdens, which include net contributions to the social security system, have to be computed. Once these are known excess burden and income effects can be determined. How this is done is shown below. To simplify matters we assume throughout this section that there are only two generations each living for two periods. Population and human capital are normalized to unity so that each generation consists only of one representative member and both generations living in a period earn the same wage. Following Fehr (1999a) we derive the tax and contribution burden of the generations in a first step. Thereafter the welfare effects are decomposed into income and efficiency effects.

[1] A similar approach was used by RAFFELHÜSCHEN (1993) to explore the effects of a transition from a PAYGO to a fully funded system.

4.1.1 *Tax and Contribution Burden*

The model used below is the same as presented above (see chapter 2), except that we consider only two generations the number of whose members is normalized to unity, a homogeneous gross wage, and a lifetime horizon of two periods. The base year is period t; hence all effects ought to be derived for individuals old in period t and individuals young in period s for all $s \geq t$.

Tax Burden of the Individual Old in Period t

Assume individuals are allowed to work when old but wage income is exempt from wage taxation or contributions to the social insurance system. This meets the German case except that working is restricted for pensioners aged between 60 and 65.

Then the temporal budget constraint of the individual who is old in period t is given by

$$(4.1) \quad \left(1+\tau_t^c\right) c_{ot} = w_t^g \left(h - \ell_{ot}\right) + \frac{1+r_{ot}^n}{p_{yt-1}} a_{t-1} + \left(1 - \bar{\tau}_{ot}^b - 0.5\, \tau_s^H\right) b_{ot}^P ,$$

where the index o denotes "old". Replacing private assets by using the equilibrium condition of the capital market, (2.47) on page 50, and rearranging gives

$$c_{ot} - w_t^g \left(h - \ell_{ot}\right) - \frac{1+r_t}{p_{yt-1}} \left(D_{t-1} + D_{t-1}^f\right) - \frac{1+r_t^g}{p_{yt-1}} K_t = -\tau_t^c c_{ot}$$
$$- \bar{\tau}_{ot}^{r,i} \frac{r_t}{p_{yt-1}} \left(D_{t-1} + K_t\right) - \tau_t^k \frac{r_t}{p_{yt-1}} K_t + \left(1 - \bar{\tau}_{ot}^b - 0.5\, \tau_s^H\right) b_{ot}^P$$

from (2.11) on page 26, (2.10) on page 24, (2.17) on page 29, and (2.19) on page 29. Note that aggregate foreign assets, D_{t-1}^f, are actually zero in the closed economy. Nonetheless, considering D_{t-1}^f is convenient since it alleviates the consolidation of the temporal budget constraints. It is useful to define net tax liabilities of the individual old in period t

$$\widetilde{T}_{ot} = T_{ot}^c + T_{ot}^r + T_{ot}^k + T_{ot}^b ,$$

and net social insurance benefits of the same individual

$$P_{ot} = \left(1 - 0.5\, \tau_s^H\right) b_{ot}^P .$$

By using these definitions we obtain

$$c_{ot} - w_t^g (h - \ell_{ot}) - \frac{1+r_t}{p_{yt-1}} \left(D_{t-1} + D_{t-1}^f \right) - \frac{1+r_t^g}{p_{yt-1}} K_t = -\widetilde{T}_{ot} + P_{ot}.$$

According to Kotlikoff (1993) tax revenues can be redefined to include public debt. This leads to

$$c_{ot} - w_t^g (h - \ell_{ot}) - \frac{1+r_t}{p_{yt-1}} D_{t-1}^f - \frac{1+r_t^g}{p_{yt-1}} K_t = -T_{ot} + P_{ot}, \tag{4.2}$$

where

$$T_{ot} = \widetilde{T}_{ot} - \frac{1+r_t}{p_{yt-1}} D_{t-1}.$$

The right hand side of equation (4.2) represents the total tax and net contribution burden of the individual old in period t. His or her net payments to the government include tax liabilities minus principal and interest he or she receives for buying public debt issues when young. The latter are raised by payments of life insurance.

Tax Burden of an Individual Young in Period s, $s \geq t$

The temporal budget constraint of an individual young in period s who is not certain whether he or she will survive his or her youth is for all $s \geq t$ (see (2.21) on page 32)

$$(1 + \tau_s^c)\, c_{ys} + a_{ys} = w_{ys}^n (h - \ell_{ys}) + b_{ys}^X,$$

where the index y denotes 'young'. The budget constraint of the first period can be transformed into

$$c_{ys} - w_s^g (h - \ell_{ys}) + a_{ys} = -\tau_s^c c_{ys} - \\ \left(\overline{\tau}_{ys}^w + \theta_s^P + \theta_s^X + \tau_s^H\right) w_s (h - \ell_{ys}) + b_{ys}^X.$$

Again, using the capital market condition (2.47) on page 50 and inserting tax liabilities which include public debt issues and net social insurance benefits

$$T_{ys} = T_{ys}^w + T_{ys}^c + D_s,$$
$$P_{ys} = \left(\theta_s^X + \theta_s^P + \tau_s^H\right) w_s (h - \ell_{ys}) - b_{ys}^X,$$

gives

$$c_{ys} - w_s^g (h - \ell_{ys}) + K_{s+1} + D_s^f = -T_{ys} + P_{ys}.$$

After consolidating the budget constraints of the individual young in s and old in $s+1$ (4.2) one obtains the intertemporal budget constraint

$$\begin{aligned}(4.3)\quad c_{ys} + \frac{p_{ys}}{1+r_{s+1}} c_{os+1} &= w_s^g (h - \ell_{ys}) + \frac{p_{ys}}{1+r_{s+1}} w_{s+1}^g (h - \ell_{os+1}) \\ &+ \frac{r_{s+1}^g - r_{s+1}}{1+r_{s+1}} K_{s+1} - T_{ys} + P_{ys} - \frac{p_{ys}}{1+r_{s+1}} (T_{os+1} - P_{os+1}).\end{aligned}$$

Using the definitions of T_{ot}, T_{ys}, and T_{os+1}, and inserting the budget constraints of the social insurance system (2.30) on page 40, (2.37) on page 44, and (2.42) on page 48 into

$$C_s^H + G_s^P + Z_s^P + Z_s^X = P_{ys} + P_{os}$$

one can rewrite the government budget constraint (2.44) on page 49 as

$$(4.4)\qquad G_s + G_s^P + C_s^H = T_{os} + T_{ys} - P_{ys} - P_{os}.$$

Public expenditure is equal to the aggregate tax burden redefined to include public debt minus aggregate net social insurance benefits.

4.1.2 Decomposing Welfare Effects

Following Fehr (1999a), the marginal welfare effects or changes in utility of the individuals can be decomposed into income effects and excess burden. To derive this decomposition the first order conditions of utility maximization and the partial derivatives of the budget constraints derived above are inserted into the total differential of the utility function. If in addition one uses the equilibrium condition of the capital market and the other budget constraints, the resulting normalized change in marginal utility expresses all welfare effects occurring in the simulation model. We derive these welfare effects below. As above we begin with the individual old in the period of departure.

Since an individual lives for only two periods, the utility function of an individual born in period s is given by

$$(4.5)\qquad U_s = u(c_{ys}, \ell_{ys}) + p_{ys}\, u(c_{os+1}, \ell_{os+1}).$$

Utility Effects of the Individual Old in Period t

Totally differentiating the utility function of an individual old in period t yields

$$dU_{t-1} = \frac{\partial u}{\partial c_{ot}}\, dc_{ot} + \frac{\partial u}{\partial \ell_{ot}}\, d\ell_{ot}. \tag{4.6}$$

By inserting the first order conditions of utility maximization subject to the temporal budget constraint (4.2) this becomes

$$\frac{dU_{t-1}}{\eta_{t-1}} = (1+\tau_t^c)\; dc_{ot} + w_t^g\; d\ell_{ot}, \tag{4.7}$$

where η_{t-1} is the marginal utility of wealth for the individual born in period $t-1$. The total differential of the budget constraint (4.2) is

$$dc_{ot} + w_t^g\, d\ell_{ot} = (h - \ell_{ot})\; dw_t^g + \frac{K_t}{p_{yt-1}}\, dr_t^g + \frac{1+r_t^g}{p_{yt-1}}\, dK_t - dT_{ot} + dP_{ot}.$$

Inserting into (4.7) and rearranging gives the normalized change in utility change

$$\frac{dU_{t-1}}{\eta_{t-1}} = \Delta W_{ot} - \Delta T_{ot} + \Delta P_{ot} + \Delta EB_{ot}, \tag{4.8}$$

where

$$\Delta W_{ot} = (h - \ell_{ot})\; dw_t^g + \frac{1}{p_{yt-1}}\, K_t\, dr_t^g, \tag{4.9}$$

$$\Delta T_{ot} = dT_{ot}, \qquad \Delta P_{ot} = dP_{ot}, \tag{4.10}$$

and

$$\Delta EB_{ot} = \tau_t^c\, dc_{ot} + \frac{1+r_t^g}{p_{yt-1}}\, dK_t.$$

The normalized utility change of the individual old in period t is composed of four components: the change in factor income, ΔW_{ot}, the change in his or her aggregate tax burden, ΔT_{ot}, the change in net social insurance benefits, ΔP_{ot}, and the change in his or her economic behavior. If all income effects are neutralized the latter is equivalent to the change in excess burden, ΔEB_{ot}. However dK_t equals zero since savings decisions cannot be changed. Hence

$$\Delta EB_{ot} = \tau_t^c\, dc_{ot}. \tag{4.11}$$

4.1.3 Utility Effects of Individuals Born in Period s

The welfare changes of all other individuals can also be decomposed into these three components. As before we start by totally differentiating the utility function (4.5) of an individual born in period s, resulting in

$$(4.12)\quad dU_s = \frac{\partial u}{\partial c_{ys}}\, dc_{ys} + \frac{\partial u}{\partial \ell_{ys}}\, d\ell_{ys} + p_{ys}\,\frac{\partial u}{\partial c_{os+1}}\, dc_{os+1} + p_{ys}\frac{\partial u}{\partial \ell_{os+1}}\, d\ell_{os+1}.$$

By using the first order conditions for utility maximization this equation can be transformed into the normalized change in utility

$$(4.13)\quad \begin{aligned} \frac{dU_s}{\eta_s} &= dc_{ys} + \frac{p_{ys}}{1+r_{s+1}}\, dc_{os+1} + w_s^g\, d\ell_{ys} + \frac{p_{ys}}{1+r_{s+1}}\, w_{s+1}^g\, d\ell_{os+1} \\ &+ \tau_s^c dc_{ys} + \left[\frac{\left(1+\tau_{s+1}^c\right)\left(1+r_{s+1}\right)}{1+r_{s+1}^m} - 1\right] \frac{p_{ys}}{1+r_{s+1}}\, dc_{os+1} \\ &- \left(\tau_{ys}^w + \tau_{ys}^X + \tau_{ys}^P + \tau_{ys}^H\right) w_s\, d\ell_{ys} + \\ &+ \left(\frac{1+r_{s+1}}{1+r_{s+1}^m} - 1\right) \frac{p_{ys}}{1+r_{s+1}}\, w_{s+1}^g\, d\ell_{os+1}. \end{aligned}$$

Inserting the total differential of the budget constraint (4.3) yields

$$\frac{dU_s}{\eta_s} = \Delta W_s - \Delta T_s + \Delta P_s + \Delta EB_s.$$

The normalized change in utility consists of changes in factor income, changes in aggregate tax burden, changes in net social insurance benefits, and changes in economic behavior. Changes in factor income induced by changes in the gross factor prices are, since $h - \ell_{ys} = l_{ys}$,

$$(4.14)\quad \Delta W_s = l_{ys}\, dw_s^g + \frac{p_{ys}}{1+r_{s+1}}\, l_{os+1}\, dw_{s+1}^g + \frac{1}{1+r_{s+1}}\, K_{s+1}\, dr_{s+1}^g,$$

Changes in net tax burden and social insurance benefits are

$$(4.15)\quad \Delta T_s = dT_{ys} + \frac{p_{ys}}{1+r_{s+1}}\, dT_{os+1},$$

$$(4.16)\quad \Delta P_s = dP_{ys} + \frac{p_{ys}}{1+r_{s+1}}\, dP_{os+1}.$$

and the change in tax revenue caused by changes in individual behavior is

$$\text{(4.17)}\quad \Delta EB_s = \tau_s^c\, dc_{ys} + \left[\frac{\left(1+\tau_{s+1}^c\right)\left(1+r_{s+1}\right)}{1+r_{s+1}^m} - 1\right] \frac{p_{ys}}{1+r_{s+1}} dc_{os+1}$$
$$- \left(\tau_s^w + \tau_{ys}^X + \tau_{ys}^P + \tau_{ys}^H\right) w_s\, d\ell_{ys}$$
$$+ \left(\frac{1+r_{s+1}}{1+r_{s+1}^m} - 1\right) \frac{p_{ys}}{1+r_{s+1}} w_{s+1}^g\, d\ell_{os+1}$$
$$+ \frac{1}{1+r_{s+1}} \tau_{s+1}^k\, r_{s+1} dK_{s+1}.$$

Note that despite the notation ΔEB_s expresses changes in economic behavior. ΔEB_s is equivalent to excess burden only if individuals are compensated for all income effects.

Since in the simulation time is discrete, the derivations of efficiency and redistribution effects is not exact if the retirement age changes. Nonetheless there is as yet no better method. Therefore this decomposition is used as an approximation to the true effects.

4.1.4 Computing Efficiency Effects

In order to compute the pure efficiency effects all income effects have to be neutralized. As mentioned above, calculating individual efficiency effects requires each individual to be compensated for his or her income effects. As suggested by Fehr (1996), we introduce a redistribution agency which determines lump sum transfers according to

$$\text{(4.18)}\quad Tr_{os} = \Delta W_{os} - \Delta T_{os}$$

$$\text{(4.19)}\quad Tr_{ys} = \Delta W_{ys} - \Delta T_{ys}.$$

These transfers are really neutral if and only if aggregate transfers in each period amount to zero. Otherwise the compensation scheme does not completely neutralize intertemporal redistribution. Whether this condition is satisfied can be examined as follows (see Fehr, 1999a, p. 89). Totally differentiating the aggregate public budget constraint in the case without a population shock (4.4) gives

$$dG + dG^P + dC^H + dC^P = dT_{os} + dT_{ys} - dP_{os} - dP_{ys} = 0,$$

since G and G^P are fixed per capita, and C^H and C^P do not change without changes in population. Note that not the change across periods is considered but rather the change caused by a policy reform within a period. Hence, provided there is no population shock, this equation holds.

Changes in factor income can be derived by using the Euler equation together with the assumptions on competition, yielding

$$F(K_s, L_s) - V_s = F_{K_s} K_s + F_{L_s} L_s - V_s = r_s^g K_s + w_s^c L_s - V_s.$$

Total differentiation gives

$$K_s \, dr_s^g + L_s \, dw_s^g = 0$$

where profit maximization ensures that for given factor prices changes in factor costs equal changes in turnover.

Since the (rationed) labor market equilibrium requires

$$L_s = (h - \ell_{ys}) + (h - \ell_{os})$$

one obtains eventually

$$Tr_{os} + Tr_{ys} = 0.$$

Hence compensation transfers in each period s add up to zero and, thus, all income effects are eliminated by these transfers.

After neutralizing income effects all remaining welfare changes are due only to substitution effects. These are expressed by ΔEB after compensation. As mentioned above these substitution effects are equivalent to the results in the Barro world with an operative bequest motive. Hence the computation of excess burden also provides the results of a life cycle model with altruistically linked individuals and an operative bequest motive.

However, this decomposition is only correct for infinitely small changes. If one examines discrete fiscal policy reforms, the total effect can be computed by performing the policy reform in small steps and integrating the resulting welfare changes (see Fehr and Kotlikoff, 1996, or Fehr, 1999a, p. 90). However, since changes in individual retirement decisions are always discrete changes, even implementing policy reforms in more than one step can be expected to produce results not much better than using one step. Therefore changes in aggregate excess burden as calculated in the simulation can deviate from changes in welfare, though theoretically they must be equal. Nonetheless, the simulations show that the differences are large only in some cases. Even in these cases the true efficiency effects should at least have the same sign as the effects calculated and should have approximately the same size. This is clear from aggregating income and efficiency effects and evaluating the deviation from changes in utility for each cohort in the simulations presented below.

Distribution and efficiency effects of a fiscal policy reform can be explored by performing simulations and applying the methods described in this section. These simulations also affect the macroeconomic variables, which are capital accumulation, labor supply, output, wages, interest rates, or unemployment. It is therefore useful to make some introductory remarks on the main effects of such changes.

4.2 Basic Effects of Tax Changes

We first describe the effects which occur in the simple model introduced in the previous section. Then we review the results of some simulation studies of the overall effects caused by the whole tax system.

4.2.1 Partial Equilibrium Effects

Since in most policy reforms one distorting tax is substituted for another distorting tax, the efficiency effects of such a reform depend on the relative strength of the distortions. These relative distortions can be examined by performing simulation studies. The first comprehensive study of such experiments in the AK model is Auerbach and Kotlikoff (1987a). Though many other studies have also provided results allowing different taxes to be compared, we refer on Auerbach and Kotlikoff (1987a) for the time being. They also provide some explanations of the distortionary and income effects of the different taxes.

Income Effects

As shown above income effects are caused by changes in the size of factor income and net liabilities to the public and social insurance system.

Though there can be considerable income effects for individuals or cohorts, aggregate income effects must add up to zero. But even in this case intergenerational redistribution effects occur. One can illustrate these effects for specific policy reforms by applying the formulae derived above.

Assume for simplicity that there are only two generations, the elder does not work, and there are no general equilibrium effects on factor prices. As shown above, the net tax liabilities of an individual and the net social insurance benefits of the elder generation are given by

$$T_{ot} = \tau_t^c c_o + \left(\overline{\tau}_{ot}^r + \tau_t^k\right) \frac{r_t}{p_{yt-1}} K_t - \frac{1 + r_{ot}^n}{p_{yt-1}} D_{t-1} + \overline{\tau}_{ot}^b b_{ot}^P, \tag{4.20}$$

$$P_{ot} = \left(1 - 0.5\,\tau_s^H\right) b_{ot}^P. \tag{4.21}$$

Income effects are expressed by changes in these variables (see (4.10) on page 76). Moreover, equations (4.20) and (4.21) show that the wage and implicit taxes are the only taxes which do not affect the wealth of the elderly. They also show that any rise in consumption, capital income, corporate or capital income taxes, or contributions to health insurance increases, ceteris paribus, tax liabilities. A rise in the replacement rates of unemployment insurance or the pension system has the opposite effect. Hence any switch from a wage or implicit tax to another equal yield tax increases tax liabilities. An increase in the replacement rate causes the opposite effect. In addition, since the elderly are already retired, there is no indirect effect on income via changes in the retirement decision.

Now, consider the income effects of the younger generation. The net tax liabilities of this generation are given by

$$\begin{aligned} T_s = \tau_s^c c_{ys} + \overline{\tau}_{ys}^w w_s (h - \ell_{ys}) + \frac{p_{ys}}{1 + r_{s+1}} \left(\tau_{s+1}^c c_{os+1} + \overline{\tau}_{os+1}^b b_{os+1}^P\right) \\ + \frac{1}{1 + r_{s+1}} \overline{\tau}_{os+1}^r r_{s+1} D_s + \frac{1}{1 + r_{s+1}} \left(\overline{\tau}_{os+1}^r + \tau_{s+1}^k\right) r_{s+1} K_{s+1}. \end{aligned} \tag{4.22}$$

Using $\overline{\tau}^P$ for the average implicit tax rate of the pension system and $\overline{\tau}^X$ for the average implicit tax rate of unemployment insurance, net social insurance benefits, (4.16), of the younger generation can be rewritten as

$$P_s = \left(\overline{\tau}^P + \overline{\tau}^X + \tau_s^H\right) w_s (h - \ell_{ys}). \tag{4.23}$$

Net tax liabilities and net social insurance benefits, and thus wealth, of the currently young as well as all subsequent generations depend on all taxes. Hence any tax increase reduces the aggregate consumption possibilities of the younger generation. Of course, individual wealth is affected by net, not by gross, transfers from the social insurance system.

As Auerbach and Kotlikoff (1987a) have shown, a switch from wage to an equal yield consumption tax causes a redistribution away from the currently old to the currently young and all subsequent generations. Since the elder generation has to pay higher consumption taxes its tax liability increases allowing the tax liabilities of the younger and all subsequent generations to fall. If the tax reform does not change revenues, the present value of the gains to the younger and subsequent generations equals the loss to the first generation of the elderly. This argument applies also to a switch from wage tax to consumption tax financing of the social insurance system which does not change revenues. Such a reform has been carried out in Germany.

Equations (4.22) and (4.23) can be used to derive exactly the changes in the components of individual income effects caused by changes in taxation or other policy measures (see (4.10) and (4.15)). For instance, an equal yield rise of the consumption tax raises the consumption tax payments by the elderly. But the consumption tax liabilities of the younger individuals are not reduced by exactly this amount, since indirect effects also change other components of net tax liabilities of the younger individuals. Totally differentiating equations (4.22) and (4.15) with respect to the consumption tax rate shows that all other explicit and implicit taxes are affected by higher consumption taxes due to alterations in consumption, savings, and leisure demand.

Equations (4.22) and (4.23) can also be solved for effects caused by changes in the pension law which alter the retirement decision. For instance, raising the retirement age leads to a loss in current pension benefits while future benefits increase. Furthermore labor supply, consumption, and savings change and, thus, the corresponding tax liabilities.

One can also derive some income effects arising from changes in factor prices. If the elder generation does not work, any increase in gross wages increases the wealth of the younger and subsequent generations. On the other hand, an increase in the gross interest rate only raises the wealth of the elder generation.

Substitution Effects

The magnitude of the efficiency effects of the individuals can be calculated by determining ΔEB_{ot} (see equation (4.11)) and ΔEB_{ys} (see (4.17)).

Since in the model the comprehensive income tax is implemented as a combination of a wage tax, a tax on pension benefits, and a tax on capital income, the different components of the income tax are explicitly taken into account. The wage tax corresponds to the payroll tax component of the income tax; the tax on capital income corresponds to the capital income tax component.

A *wage tax* distorts the intratemporal leisure/consumption decision. The implicit taxes of unemployment insurance or the pension system are equivalent to a payroll tax and thus cause the same distortions as the wage tax. If the tax rates are the same in all periods, no intertemporal substitution effects arise during the working life. However, due to retirement some intertemporal substitution effects occur between the working and retirement life[2]. In addition, in our case the level of the implicit tax rate depends on age. Therefore some intertemporal substitution effects occur during working life. Since the implicit tax rate decreases with time, the price of leisure increases and leisure when young is substituted for leisure later on.

These equations also show that *taxes on capital income* affect the discount rate and distort the intertemporal decisions between all periods. The same is true of taxes on capital input which drive a wedge between the marginal product of capital, r^g, and the interest rate r.

A *consumption tax* distorts the choice between consumption and leisure, both within and across periods. Hence it has also a payroll tax component. If working is allowed after retirement, (4.11) gives the changes in

---

[2]If individual are permitted to work after retirement, which is the case in Germany, substitution effects between working before and after retirement can also occur (see BURTLESS and MOFFITT, 1985, or AN, 1993).

excess burden. Then the payroll component of the consumption tax also applies to retirement and adversely affects efficiency. If working is not allowed, ΔEB_{os} becomes zero. Then no efficiency effects occur for the elderly, since individuals cannot respond to higher consumption taxation. However, the consumption tax induces additional distortions if the tax rate varies with time. If it is constant with time, no intertemporal distortions occur. This is the lump sum component of the consumption tax. If in an experiment the decision between consumption and leisure is altered, the net effect of these distortions on the path of consumption of wealth accumulation cannot be derived uniquely (see Sandmo, 1985, p. 278).

In addition to these complex interactions the effects described above entail many other effects in a general equilibrium model not considered up to now. Hence simulations are needed to examine most policy reforms in this complex environment. We give a short overview of some of the results found in other studies.

4.2.2 General Equilibrium Effects

Auerbach and Kotlikoff (1987a) have found the following results by simulation: for tax changes which do not alter revenue, income and consumption taxes raise welfare more than a wage tax. Moreover a consumption tax is the most efficient alternative to the payroll tax. Whether these findings can be exploited depends on the nature of the policy reform considered. For example, if a reform changes revenue the results of Auerbach and Kotlikoff (1987a) might no longer hold. The simulation of such a reform in which the German PAYGO system is abolished by replacing the implicit pension tax by a consumption tax and compensating changes in utility, is described in Hirte and Weber (1997b). In this case additional compensation transfers to the pensioners increase the tax revenue needed. Then the consumption tax rate increases more than in an experiment which leaves revenue unchanged. This, together with a positive tax benefit linkage, changes the results and the consumption tax reduces welfare compared to the implicit pension tax.

In addition to consumption taxes several other taxes also levied in Germany are likely sources of distortions. A large number of simulation studies have examined distortions caused by these taxes arising in models of other countries and some have explored the efficiency losses caused by the German fiscal system. The main findings of these studies are summarized below to give an idea of the efficiency losses of distortionary taxation which are to be expected in the simulations in this study.

Some studies have assessed the welfare losses caused by distortionary taxation. These are the studies of Ballard et. al. (1985), Fullerton and Rogers (1993) and Jorgenson and Yun (1993), which all examine the effects of the U.S. tax system, and the study of Fehr (1999a), who examines the efficiency losses of the German tax system.

By using a static CGE model of the Shoven-Whalley type, Ballard et. al. (1985) computed a welfare loss of between 13% and 24% of aggregate tax revenue. A similar figure, 18%, has been computed by Jorgenson and Yun (1993) in a dynamic model with a representative consumer. Fullerton and Rogers (1993, p. 150) also employ a dynamic model which however is an overlapping generations model where individuals have myopic expectations. According to their findings aggregate efficiency losses are about 1.3% of the present value of aggregate lifetime income. But, as emphasized by Fehr (1999a, p. 92), their study captures only a part of the intertemporal distortions due to the assumption of myopic expectations.

Fehr (1999a) examines the efficiency and distribution effects of the German tax and public pension system. His simulation model is the AK model adjusted to the German system. By replacing all taxes by a tax on the value of the time endowment, which is a non-distorting tax, he computed the welfare and distribution effects for five income groups and 55 generations. The overall change in excess burden amounts to 34.2% of overall tax revenue (Fehr, 1999a, p. 111) or 3.4% of the present value of all remaining lifetime resources in a model with installment costs of capital (Fehr, 1999a, p. 108). This increases to 3.5% if no adjustment costs of capital are considered. Except for the oldest generation, which suffers large welfare losses due to this hypothetical reform, all other generations gain. The gains are the higher, the higher the relative income. This outcome might be caused by the progressive income tax. Fehr also examines the effects of each specific tax. The results show that the capital income tax and the corporate tax induce the largest excess burden compared to their tax revenue. His results suggest that the excess burden of these taxes amounts to more than 90% of the corresponding tax revenue (Fehr, 1999a, p. 111). These figures are considerably higher than in the studies for the U.S. system cited above.

In addition to the general incidence of the tax system one can compute the incidence of the pension system and public debt. Following Raffelhüschen (1993), Fehr (1999a and b) performs a transition to a fully funded system, in which he assumes that the current PAYGO system is phased out and pensions are financed by a lump sum tax after the year of reform. As is clear from Fenge (1995), the efficiency effects of this reform are not caused by the choice of the pension system, but are entirely due to the tax reform implemented in the experiment. Therefore Fehr (1999a) actually performs a tax reform, while his choice of the pension system does not matter. He calculates the effects of substituting a tax on the time endowment for the payroll tax. Since the payroll tax is the only source of efficiency losses of the pension system in such a model, abolishing this tax should generate efficiency gains. This is theoretically shown by Breyer and Straub (1989). Fehr (1999a, p. 115) finds that the overall excess burden of the payroll tax adds up to 1.03% of aggregate remaining life time income. Only the oldest cohorts suffer small welfare losses due to higher excess burden. One should, however, note that Fehr does not take the tax benefit linkage into account. He assumes that the rate of contribution is a pure payroll tax. Hence the efficiency gains computed in his experiment are too high.

We do not discuss this in more detail at this point. A more extensive discussion of the different effects can be found below. In the next chapter we explore the effects of a population decline as is taking place in Germany. This is also the benchmark case which is used in all subsequent simulations to be compared to the results of policy reforms.

Chapter 5

The Impact of Aging on the Economy

The strong aging trend expected to take place in Germany not only affects the pension system but also other branches of the social insurance system and other macroeconomic variables. To obtain an impression of the consequences of aging, we perform some simulations which constitute the benchmark path for all subsequent simulations. They are used to demonstrate the main techniques and show the pure economic effects of aging without any policy reform.

The benchmark case also shows the economic consequences of an aging population which is about to happen in Germany. The growth rates of population used here have already been discussed above, showing that after the "initial steady state"[1] an adverse shock to population growth takes place. This shock represents the end of the baby boom during the late sixties. In addition life expectancy increases which strengthens the aging trend. As the base year in this study is 1996, the fall in population growth is considered to start in 1976, which represents a delay of ten years compared to reality. Nonetheless the effects of this decline can be examined. This is done in the last section of this chapter.

[1] Actually the year 1996 does not represent a steady state since the population change had already started 20 years earlier. Nevertheless we compute the initial situation as a steady state. This is necessary to solve the CGE model. Therefore any policy changes taking place in 1996 can also be thought of as a shock occurring in a steady state.

5.1 *Effects of Aging in other Studies*

To give a first impression of the likely outcomes of a population decline, we describe some of the results of other studies.

A decline in population growth leads to aging. The effects of this on a PAYGO system are widely discussed (for example Hagemann and Nicoletti, 1989, Jensen and Nielsen, 1993, Meijdam and Verbon, 1997, Broer, 1999a). In a defined benefit system the rate of contribution increases due to aging. This entails a reduction in the internal rate of return of current and future employees, whereas the internal rate remains unchanged for current pensioners. Hence the implicit tax rate increases and individuals reduce labor supply and increase savings to offset the losses in pension benefits[2]. However, as shown by Hu (1991) a rise in life expectancy implies a postponement of retirement. The effect of a decline in population growth on the retirement age is however ambiguous. This effect can lower the adverse effects of aging on the implicit tax rate. Whether these effects also occur in a model with endogenous labor supply remains to be examined.

Moreover overall labor productivity changes. In the first year after the shock labor productivity increases because the youngest generations, who are less productive than the average employee, become relatively smaller. Thereafter labor productivity decreases since elder employees are less productive than the average.

These effects alter macroeconomic variables. If the labor force ages aggregate labor supply is expected to decrease. This implies higher wages. The general pattern of asset accumulation in the life cycle model is that older individuals reduce their assets while younger accumulate assets. As a consequence aging reduces the capital stock per capita and the overall capital stock, leading to higher interest rates. Due to lower factor inputs output per capita as well as overall output decreases. Some of these effects are examined, for instance, in a dynamic CGE analysis by Chauveau and Loufir (1997). Furthermore, since public expenditure per capita is assumed to be constant, the consumption tax rate must be raised to offset lower receipts from taxes on wages and capital income.

[2]Other effects as, for example, a change in labor mobility and flexibility as suggested by HAGEMANN and NICOLETTI (1989) are outside the range of this study.

Accordingly utility decreases in the long term while short term effects can differ considerably from the long term effects (Meijdam and Verbon, 1997). According to a study by Cutler et. al. (1991), the short term effects depend on whether aging is expected or not. In the first case consumption possibilities increase in the short term and decrease in the long term while they decrease in the second case. These results are derived by using a Ramsey model with infinite time horizon. Meijdam and Verbon (1997, p. 30) show that in an overlapping generations model changes in consumption possibilities depend "*not so much on the fact whether aging is expected or not but on the size of the existing PAYG-scheme. In particular, if this size is relatively small, ..., aging should initially lead to rising consumption possibilities for young as well as old individuals.*"

Another effect is the increase in individual utility due to the increase in life expectancy. Whether this effect is sufficiently large to compensate for the adverse effects of aging on tax rates, the rate of contribution, and pension benefits is uncertain.

There are some CGE studies discussing aging in Germany. Among them are the papers of Buslei and Kraus (1996) who only consider a constant decrease in population growth, Hirte (1999a), who examines the effects of a decline in population growth with varying population growth rates, and the study of Fehr (1999c), who also simulates a raise in life expectancy. The latter two studies found an initial increase in employment and savings, since both increase until individuals reach middle age. As the youngest cohort is initially the largest, both variables increase until these cohorts grow old. Then both variables decrease. In addition the wage tax rate and rate of contribution to the public pension system increase. According to Hirte (1999a) individuals become worse off from year one of the transition compared to the initial equilibrium, i. e. to a situation without a population decline.

An additional effect of aging is the decrease in the internal rate of return. As the old age dependency ratio, i. e. the ratio of pensioners to the labor force, will increase during the next 40 years in Germany, the current pension formula leads to higher implicit taxation and a lower internal rate of return of the public pension system. This is also the outcome of the

Table 5.1: Internal rate of return of the German public pension system

Cohort retiring in	Eitenmüller (1996) nominal	Schnabel (1998) real	Hirte (1999b) real
1980	–	–	5.0%
1990	–	3.5%	3.5%
2000	6.3%	2.0%	1.6%
2010	5.4%	1.1%	0.6%
2020	5.0%	0.8%	-0.3%
2030	4.5%	0.2%	–
2040	3.7%	0.0%	–

studies of Eitenmüller (1996), Schnabel (1998), and Hirte (1999b) who compute the internal rates of return of the German public pension system[3]. The results of these three studies are compared for married men in Table 5.1. While Eitenmüller (1996) computed only the nominal internal rate of return, Schnabel (1998) and Hirte (1999b) calculated the real rates of return.

The differences between the first and the other studies are stronger than the inflation rate. This is caused by the more sophisticated computations and assumptions of the latter studies. As the average retirement age is about 60 a cohort born in 1930 is defined as cohort 1990 which is its retirement age. This allows a comparison of the results of Eitenmüller (1996) and Schnabel (1998), who define cohorts by the year of birth, with the results of Hirte (1999b), who defines cohorts according to the retirement age. Table 5.1 shows that the rate of return declines in all the studies. For the cohort 2040 Schnabel expects a zero rate of return, implying that interest income which exceeds the real implicit debt level is completely taxed away.

The results of Hirte (1999b) are the most pessimistic since married men retiring in 2020 yield a negative internal rate of return. This is mainly caused by assuming a smaller increase in life expectancy than assumed by Schnabel (1998). All studies suggest that the internal rate of return

[3]Similar computations were carried out by Börsch-Supan and Schnabel (1998) and the Deutsches Institut für Altersvorsorge (1998 and 1999a).

declines with time. Hence, individuals will be higher taxed in the future and their implicit tax rate will increase. The simulations of the population decline performed in the present study should replicate these findings. Let us now turn to these simulations.

5.2 Results of the Simulation

We present the results of our simulations of the population shock below. Note, again, that the rise in the mandatory retirement age which will become effective as of 2001 are not considered in these simulations, though it is part of the Pension Act of 1992. Therefore the figures are more pessimistic than most forecasts which take it into account. Figures 5.1, 5.2, and 5.3 show the social insurance and macroeconomic variables resulting in the benchmark case.

The bold curve marked "Benchmark"in panel (a) of Figure 5.1 depicts the old age dependency ratio in the benchmark case. This is expected to increase from currently 0.37 to approximately 0.79 in 2041. Thereafter it decreases to reach a long term level of 0.60. While a single retiree is financed by 2.7 employees in 1996, this ratio decreases to 1.27 in 2041. These numbers are also close to the forecast of Schmähl (1994). In his study the ratio of individuals aged 60 and more to individuals aged 20 to 60 increases from 0.35 in 1991 to 0.73 in 2039. The two other curves stand for changes in the old age dependency ratio caused by the decline in population growth rates – curve "Decline" – and the increase in life expectancy – curve "Lifetime". They are computed by performing simulations in which life expectancy is constant or population growth is fixed. This decomposition of the overall effects is also carried out for all other variables. It shows that changes in life expectancy matter, even though the decline in the growth rates accounts for most of the effects.

The rise in the old age dependency ratio implies an increase in the rate of contribution to the pension system from currently 19.2% to almost 35% in 2041 (see panel (b) of Figure 5.1). 3 percentage points of this change originate from longer lifetime.

The implicit tax rate reflects a similar pattern as documented in the second panel of Figure 5.1. As the pension formula of the German pension

Figure 5.1: Benchmark case: social insurance variables

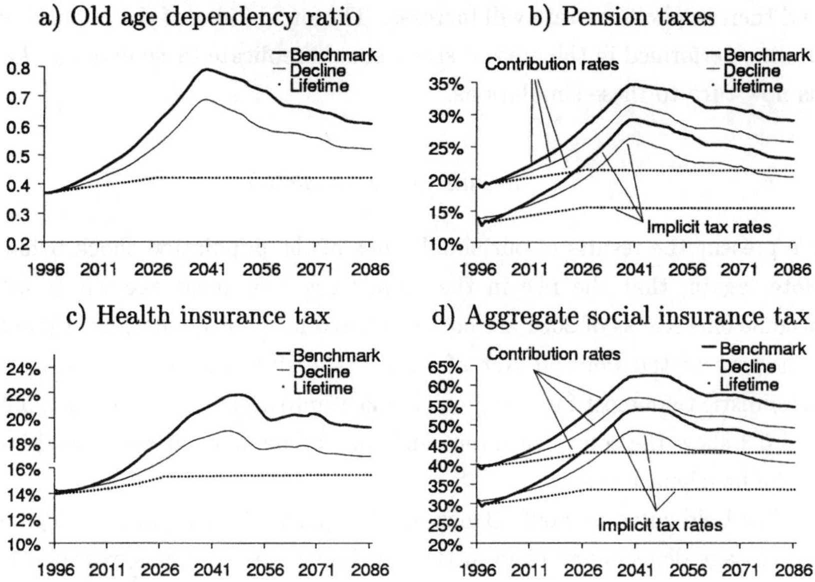

system ensures that the replacement rate with respect to net wages is approximately constant, the increase in the rate of contribution is almost fully taken up by a rise in the implicit tax rate. In other words: while the net rate of benefits does not change, the tax burden of the working population increases.

As health and long term care expenditure increase with age, the rate of contribution also increases – from 14% to about 22% (see panel (c) of Figure 5.1). Though aging causes higher health expenditure for the elderly, expenditure for the younger cohorts decrease because of the diminishing size of these cohorts. Therefore health expenditure and the rate of contribution[4] peak about 12 years later than the expenditure of the pension system.

The aggregate rate of contribution increases from initially 40% to about 62% in the 2040s, and reaches about 54% in the long term (see panel (d) of Figure 5.1). Most of these changes are due to the reduction in the birth

[4]Note that we subsume long term care under health in the following.

Figure 5.2: Benchmark case: labor market

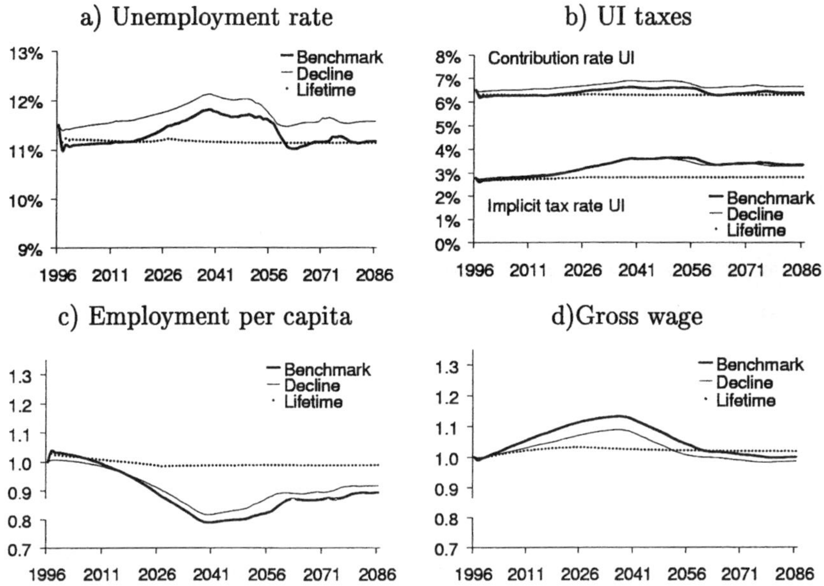

rate, as a comparison with the curve "Decline"shows. The implicit tax rate shows a similar pattern though it is about 9% lower. Hence aging also implies a strong increase in the implicit tax rate.

The aggregate rate of contribution and the aggregate rate of implicit tax also depend on unemployment which is plotted in the first panel of Figure 5.2. It decreases initially but exceeds its initial level between the years 2035 and 2050. In the long term it is 11.1%. The main cause of the fall in the rate of unemployment in the first two years is the increase in longevity (see the curve "Decline"in the last panel of Figure 5.1)[5]. Individuals reduce consumption and raise labor supply to built up resources for their longer lifetime. As the younger cohorts, whose lifetime increases the most, are initially larger than the elder working cohorts and have lower rates of unemployment, the rise in labor supply results in higher employment per capita and an immediate drop in the rate of unemployment. It is only

[5]Since in reality individuals have known in 1996 and before that life expectancy increases, these initial effects are specific to the simulation.

Figure 5.3: Benchmark case: capital and consumption

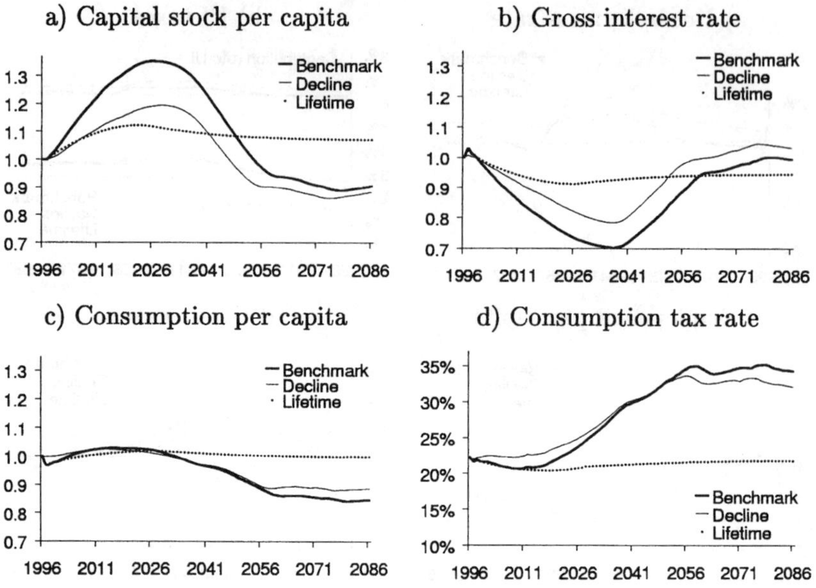

after some periods that the decline in population growth rates starts to dominate the '*lifetime effect*' on the rate of unemployment, at least during the time of the strongest change in population growth. Then the initially young cohorts enter the last third of their working life and experience a strong increase in unemployment. At this time the cohorts with relatively lower rates of unemployment, i.e. the youngest cohorts, are considerably smaller than the middle-aged cohorts. Consequently the aggregate rate of unemployment increases. These changes in the rate of unemployment are reflected in alterations of the rate of contribution to unemployment insurance and its implicit tax rate (see panel (b) of Figure 5.2). While an increase in unemployment raises the tax benefit linkage, the increase in the old age dependency ratio increases the burden imposed on unemployment insurance by contributions to the pension system and health insurance and, thus, lowers the tax benefit linkage. The curve of the implicit tax rate of unemployment insurance in panel (b) of Figure 5.2 reveals that the latter effects are stronger, and, thus, the implicit tax rate increases more than the rate of contribution to unemployment insurance.

Since the participation rate, i. e. the fraction of the total lifetime spent working, of a cohort decreases with age, total employment declines (see panel (c) of Figure 5.2). However, during the first years after the shock labor productivity increases because the youngest generations, who are less productive than the average worker, become relatively smaller while the number of middle-aged individuals increases. As productivity is higher during middle age, overall employment, which is measured in efficiency units, increases. In addition individuals increase their labor supply due to the increase in longevity. However, since the population decline is reduced in the long term, employment as well as individual labor supply exceed their minimum levels in the long term, where they are about 10% below the initial levels (see panel (c) of Figure 5.2). The gross wage responds to the strong decrease in employment and grows until the minimum employment level is reached. In the long term it returns to its initial level (see panel (d) of Figure 5.2).

The general pattern of asset accumulation, plotted in the first panel of Figure 5.3, in the life cycle model is that older individuals reduce their assets while younger accumulate assets. Consequently, assets increase until retirement is reached. Then they decline so as to reach zero at the time of death. Hence aging also reduces the capital stock per capita and the aggregate capital stock leading to higher interest rates in the long term as shown in panel (b) of Figure 5.3. However, capital accumulation increases in the short term because the middle-aged generations, who are the strongest savers, increase in number (see curve "Decline"in panel (a) of Figure 5.3). Moreover individuals accumulate assets as provisions for their longer lifetime. It is for this reason that an increase in life expectancy strengthens capital accumulation (see curve "Lifetime"in panel (a) of Figure 5.3). These effects are called the *savings effect* of aging. They are strong immediately after the start of an adverse population shock. About two decades later the middle-aged generation form the largest group in the population while a further two decades later the elderly become the largest group and the capital stock declines. Accordingly, the interest rate decreases during the first four post-shock decades and decreases thereafter (see panel (b) of Figure 5.3). In the long term population growth and thus

Table 5.2: Internal rate of return of the German public pension

Cohort retiring in	Population shock[a]	Schnabel (1998)[b]
1990	–	3.5%
1996	1.3%	
2000	1.3%	2.0%
2010	1.4%	1.1%
2020	1.1%	0.8%
2030	0.5%	0.2%
2040	-0.4%	0.0%
2050	-0.8%	
2060	-0.9%	
∞	-0.3%	

[a]Without the Pension Act of 1992.
[b]After the Pension Act of 1992.

the capital stock per capita and the interest rate become stable again.

The strong capital accumulation allows the consumption per capita to rise during the first three decades, until the decline in employment and, later on, the declining capital stock reduce the consumption per capita (see panel (c) of Figure 5.3).

Furthermore since public expenditures per capita are assumed to be constant, the consumption tax rate must be raised in the long term to offset lower receipts of the taxes on wage and capital income and the decline in consumption per capita (see panel (d) of Figure 5.3). The higher levels of output and consumption per capita allow the consumption tax rate to be reduced by about 1.6 percentage points only during the first two decades. Thereafter it increases to more than 35% before it converges to the long term level of 31.3%.

As a result of the changes in the rate of contribution and implicit tax, the internal real rate of return of the public pension system decreases (see Table 5.2). Starting with a value of 1.3% for the cohort retiring in 1996, i. e. the cohort 1996, it decreases to 1.1% for the cohort 2020, and reaches -0.9 when the cohort 2060 retires. The difference to the study of Schnabel (1998) is the absolute value of the internal rate of return, while the time pattern is similar in both studies. The main reasons for the deviations are that neither economic growth nor inflation occur in this study despite changes in the consumption tax rate.

5.3 Sensitivity Analysis

To examine the effects of the new features of the model we perform some simulations, each of a different modification of the main model. The cases considered are: (1) the model without unemployment and unemployment insurance, (2) the model without health insurance, (3) a higher elasticity of the retirement age. The last is achieved by raising the strength of the preference for leisure, α, at a slower rate. While in the basic parameterizations of the model α grows by 0.05 per year from age 60 to age 70 and stays constant thereafter, it grows from age 43 to 47 by 0.04 and from 68 to 74 by 0.05 per year in this modification. This raises the propensity to postpone the retirement age if the true wage increases compared to the benchmark case.

Table 5.3 reports the values of some variables computed in these different modifications. '∞' denotes the final steady state. The figures document that many variables already deviate from the base case in the base year. This is the result of the adjustment of the data base to the changes in the model or parameter values.

Consider the results shown in columns 'No UI' of Table 5.3 which document the results of the specification *without unemployment.* Since unemployment insurance (UI) pays contributions to the pension system, omitting unemployment insurance raises the implicit tax rate of the pension system. The contributions to the pension system which are paid by unemployment insurance create claims on pension benefits not based on individual contributions to the pension system. In contrast, the aggregate rate of implicit tax is lower without unemployment since the implicit tax rate of unemployment insurance is zero. Consequently, aggregate contributions are also lower. Despite these changes the rate of contribution to the pension system almost matches the rate in the base case. Large deviations from the base case are also reported for consumption, the capital stock, and the consumption tax rate. For instance the capital stock per capita is 26% above its base year level in 2045 while it is only 22% higher in the

Table 5.3: Benchmark case: sensitivity analysis – macro effects

Year of birth	Base Case	No UI[a]	No HI[b]	Low α[c]	Base Case	No UI	No HI	Low α
	Old age dependency ratio				Unemployment rate: x			
1996	0.37	0.37	0.37	0.37	11.5	–	11.5	11.5
1997	0.37	0.37	0.37	0.37	11.0	–	11.2	10.9
2001	0.38	0.38	0.38	0.38	11.2	–	11.2	11.0
2041	0.79	0.79	0.79	0.79	11.8	–	11.3	11.7
∞	0.60	0.60	0.60	0.60	11.2	–	11.1	11.1
	Consumption tax rate: τ^c				Pension contr. rate: θ^P			
1996	22.2	21.7	17.3	22.2	19.2	19.2	19.2	19.2
1997	21.7	21.6	17.3	21.4	18.6	18.7	18.7	18.6
2001	21.6	21.4	17.3	21.1	19.7	19.6	19.7	19.7
2041	30.0	26.7	20.9	29.8	34.7	34.5	34.9	34.7
∞	31.3	30.0	21.9	29.4	28.6	28.5	28.4	28.5
	Implicit pension tax: τ^P				Aggregate contr. rate: θ^{SI}			
1996	13.9	14.7	13.2	14.0	40.0	34.2	25.7	40.0
1997	12.7	13.5	11.3	12.6	38.6	33.4	24.9	38.6
2001	13.8	14.4	12.3	13.7	39.9	34.3	25.9	39.9
2041	29.2	29.9	27.9	29.0	61.7	55.2	41.5	61.7
∞	22.7	23.4	21.1	22.5	53.8	48.2	34.7	53.6
	Aggregate implicit tax: τ^{SI}				Employment per capita			
1996	31.0	29.7	15.4	31.1	1.00	1.00	1.00	1.00
1997	29.2	28.1	13.4	29.1	1.04	1.04	1.03	1.04
2001	30.5	29.2	14.5	30.5	1.03	1.03	1.02	1.03
2041	53.2	50.6	30.9	53.1	0.79	0.80	0.81	0.79
∞	44.8	43.1	23.7	44.5	0.89	0.90	0.90	0.90
	Capital stock per capita				Consumption per capita			
1996	1.00	1.00	1.00	1.00	1.00	1.00	1.00	1.00
1997	1.00	1.00	1.00	1.0	0.97	0.96	0.97	0.97
2001	1.06	1.05	1.06	1.06	0.99	0.99	0.99	0.99
2041	1.22	1.26	1.23	1.24	0.97	1.00	1.02	0.96
∞	0.98	1.07	1.05	1.01	0.89	0.90	0.97	0.90

[a]No unemployment and no unemployment insurance.
[b]No health insurance.
[c]Slower increase in the strength of the preference for leisure.

base case. Even larger is the difference in the long term: the capital stock per capita is 7% higher without unemployment but 2% lower with unemployment compared to the initial level. On account of both a lower rate of contribution and a lower rate of implicit tax, consumption and savings can be relatively higher under the 'No UI' scenario.

The next case is 'No HI', the simulation *without health insurance.* Contributions to the health system are considered as pure taxes if individuals work at least one hour more than they have to work to become mandatory members of health insurance. Consequently, the aggregate rate of implicit tax is considerably lower than in the benchmark case. This difference is even stronger in the future. This raises employment per capita above the benchmark level. Furthermore a lower implicit tax rate induces higher income. As contributions to health insurance are higher when working than during retirement, the income gain is spread across the lifetime by raising savings and, thus, accelerating capital accumulation. Finally, higher income increases consumption per capita which is 102% of its initial level in 2041 and 97% in the long term, while the corresponding figures are 97% and 89% in the benchmark case.

Finally, consider the simulation of a *higher elasticity of the retirement age* ('Low α'). Apparently, aging causes no change in the retirement age. The reason is that the new age pattern of the weight of leisure in the utility function lowers the increase in consumption in the early part of retirement, but accelerates the increase in consumption at the end of life. This stimulates asset accumulation and the capital stock per capita in the medium and long term. Consequently, the consumption tax rate is below its benchmark level.

In this chapter we have presented the effects of aging. These results are used as the benchmark case in the remaining chapters. Since the population decline is the common feature of all following simulations, one can derive the effects of a policy reform by comparing them to this benchmark case.

Chapter 6

Raising the Retirement Age

One way to reduce the financial problems of the PAYGO financed public pension system seems to be a rise in the average retirement age. This reduces the length of the retirement life while raising the length of the working life. Therefore we examine in this chapter policies aimed at raising the retirement age. After a short introduction, welfare and redistribution effects as well as the impact on the public pension system of two measures are explored by simulation. The discussion focuses on incentives since a pure change of the minimum or mandatory retirement age is not very effective as long as invalidity or disability pensions can be substituted for normal retirement. Since Germany begins in 2001 to introduce incentives for postponing retirement, a large part of this chapter deals with the German Pension Act of 1992.

6.1 Introductory Remarks

As outlined in the first two chapters, the severe crisis facing the PAYGO public pension systems in most OECD countries will be mainly caused by the dramatic increase in the old age dependency ratio, i. e. the ratio of the number of pensioners to the labor force, which is expected to peak about 2040. Among the policy options available, raising the minimum or mandatory retirement age seems to be one of the most promising measures to reduce this increase in the old age dependency ratio and, thus, the rate of contribution to the pension system. Consequently some countries like the U.S. and Germany have already enacted such measures and others, for instance Japan or Italy, are discussing them. The U.S. reform of 1983 enacted an increase in the standard retirement age from 65 to 66 by 2009, and further to 67 by 2027. The German Pension Act of 1992 contains a mix of two reform schemes: an increase in the minimum retirement age for women and unemployed persons and an increase in the statutory retirement age accompanied by deductions from pension benefits if individuals choose early retirement.

Nevertheless positive effects of such a reform on the budget of the pension system, as claimed for instance by Schmähl (1990), are not as certain as one might think. Neither are the signs of welfare and redistribution effects. There is, for instance, some evidence that such a reform cannot achieve an increase in the average retirement age in the U.S. (Burtless and Moffitt, 1985), but can cause a slight increase in Germany (Börsch-Supan, 1991, 1992, 1998a, and Siddiqui, 1995, 1997a, b, and c)[1]. The prospect of success of such measures mainly depends on whether they influence individual retirement decisions. If, for example, disability retirement can be substituted for normal retirement, raising the minimum retirement age would be entirely ineffective. If, instead, the statutory retirement age is raised additional measures are needed to rule out early retirement. These can be deductions from pension benefits if individuals retire before the age of statutory retirement. However, actual deductions can be too low to discourage individuals from early retirement. This is emphasized by Schmähl (1990), Genosko (1993), and Schmidt (1995), who think that the deductions levied in Germany are actually too low because they are below their actuarial levels [2]. To overcome these problems, Breyer, Kifmann and Stolte (1997) suggest that individuals should be rewarded for raising their retirement age above the current level. By granting supplements to pension benefits, incentives are created inducing later retirement. Unfortu-

[1]That the pension decision is very volatile with respect to changes in the regulations of pensions is shown by Börsch-Supan (1992), Schmidt (1995), Riphahn and Schmidt (1997) and Siddiqui (1997a and b).

[2]The Pension Act of 1992 introduces a reduction in pension benefits amounting to 3.6% of pension benefits for each year retirement takes place before the age of 65. Assume an individual, whose average life expectancy is 78 years, retires only one year earlier. Assume contributions are unchanged, despite a shorter working life. Then the level of pension benefits has to be reduced by about 1/14 or 7.14%. This is the lower bound of an actuarially fair reduction rate.

nately, as they show in the same paper, this measure increases the financial problems of the pension system. From this they conclude that a rise in the retirement age does not reduce the problems of public pension systems and is therefore not a useful policy option. But this point of view is also questioned. In Hirte (1999a) we show that their results depend on the assumption that actuarial compensation is granted. This, however, provides overcompensation and is the reason for their pessimistic findings. Moreover, it is possible to design compensation schemes which create incentives to raise the retirement age and simultaneously improve the situation of the pension system.

This is the current state of the debate on the chances and risks of policy reforms which aim to raise the retirement age. There are three possible measures to achieve this: raising the minimum retirement age, raising the statutory retirement age, or creating incentives to encourage individuals to postpone retirement. We examine these options by discussing the following questions: what are the likely effects of each measure on the pension system? What are the welfare implications? And, what are the redistribution effects? However, before turning to the simulations, we give a short overview of the likely effects of each reform scheme.

Raising the minimum retirement age unambiguously lowers the old age dependency ratio. Of course, this is only true if there is no perfect substitute for normal retirement. This particular condition is violated in the German case, were all members of the public pension system are also insured against disability and invalidity. But, despite thorough health checks required before receiving disability pensions, disability or invalidity retirement is an option for a large part of the labor force. This is obvious from the following data. While the minimum retirement age for normal pensions is 63 for men and 60 for the unemployed and women, the average retirement age in 1996 was 59.6. Accordingly, disability and invalidity retirement seem to be substitutes for normal retirement. Therefore a pure increase in the minimum age for normal retirement is unlikely to induce a significant rise in the average retirement age. For this reason we do not calculate the effects of this measure. Even if disability pensions are considerably lower than old age pensions the effect of an increase in the minimum retirement age is thought to be very small in the German case. Moreover, the Pension Act of 1992 enacted that early retirement is accompanied by deductions from the pension benefits. These deductions have a similar effect as a rise in the minimum retirement age and relatively lower disability and invalidity pensions. Therefore we consider an examination of the German Pension Act of 1992 as sufficient and do not explicitly examine a rise in the minimum retirement age.

The second measure is a *rise in the statutory retirement age* accompanied by deductions from the pension level which are levied if individuals retire earlier. If individuals are allowed to retire before the statutory retirement age, an increase in this age does not on its own induce any effects. Therefore the introduction of deductions is necessary. Then the central question about the efficacy of this instrument is the extent of the deductions. If individuals are risk-neutral and deductions are actuarially neutral, they are indifferent between retiring at the statutory retirement age and retiring earlier. In this case the present value of pension benefits is independent of the retirement age. If deductions are marginally increased above their actuarial level, risk-neutral individuals will postpone retirement, and the average retirement age will increase. However, as we have emphasized in Hirte (1999a), if individuals are risk-averse, which is usually assumed, there is no need for deductions to be actuarially neutral. We will discuss this point in more detail in the next section. At any rate, deductions, even if not actuarially fair, reduce pension benefits due to either a shorter length of retirement or a reduced level of pension benefits. Therefore they ease the crisis of the pension system even if the average retirement age does not change. The welfare implications are also clear: as individuals receive the benefit level they would receive without reform if and only if they retire later, i. e. at the statutory retirement age, all individuals lose. However for the currently young and for future cohorts these losses are overcompensated by efficiency and income gains due to lower implicit taxation and lower contribution payments. Therefore welfare and income effects have the same sign as that induced by a rise in the minimum retirement age.

Obviously, both a rise in the minimum retirement age and a rise of the statutory retirement age accompanied by deductions have the same outcome: provided there are no perfect substitutes for normal retirement or deductions are high enough, both alternatives reduce the financial problems of the public pension system. In addition, both generate welfare gains and induce a redistribution away from the generation who is middle-aged at the year of reform, to all young and future cohorts.

The introduction of *incentives* to induce an increase in the retirement age without changes in the statutory or minimum retirement age has less clear implications. Though Breyer, Kifmann and Stolte (1997) claim to have shown that compensating individuals for postponing retirement increases the problems of the PAYGO system if there is negative population growth, they have actually proven this only for actuarial supplements (see Hirte, 1999a and below). Under certain circumstances supplements can be lower and might reduce the problems of the pension system, as we have argued in Hirte (1999a). This is at least true if population decline is moderate. Then a Pareto improving supplement scheme can be found. Hence the implications depend on whether such a scheme exists or not. If not welfare decreases, while at least one cohort loses. If there is a Pareto improving scheme, welfare increases and at least one cohort gains. However, in both cases the sign of income and individual efficiency effects depends on the specific supplement scheme.

We present these arguments in the next section, and examine whether such a Pareto improving alternative also exists if a strong population decline is considered, as forecast for Germany. Then, we evaluate the rules of the German Pension Act of 1992 concerning the retirement age.

6.2 Incentives for Raising the Retirement Age

This section deals with incentives to induce individuals to voluntarily increase their age of retirement. Since such a measure does not impose strong constraints on the retirement decision, inefficiencies should be considerably lower than for direct measures such as raising the minimum or statutory retirement age. In the former case individuals are free to choose their retirement age. However, to encourage individuals to retire later compensations are needed. These can be provided by means of supplements to pension benefits, if individuals postpone retirement beyond the initial level. Since supplements impose an additional burden on the pension system, while postponing retirement reduces expenditure, two opposite effects occur. A mitigation of the pension crisis by using incentives is only possible if supplements can be set to such a level that the latter effect dominates. If such a scheme ensures that each cohort retires later or is exactly indifferent whether to do so, it is, ceteris paribus, also Pareto improving. Therefore one has to search for an incentive scheme which mitigates the pension crisis by inducing later retirement by supplement rates which are neither too high nor too low.

The first paper to address this issue is that of Breyer, Kifmann and Stolte (1997). They show that a rise in the retirement age reached by actuarially fair supplements worsens the financial situation of a public pension system in the long term if there is negative population growth. As a result the rate of contribution increases after a temporary decline to a level above the initial rate. Like Schmähl (1990), Genosko (1993) or Schmidt (1995), they state that actuarial compensations are required to achieve a rise in the retirement age. An actuarial supplement to pension benefits ensures that the present value of net pension benefits remains unchanged despite a lengthening of the working life. From this they deduce that individuals are becoming indifferent towards their age of retirement. However, such a supplement scheme imposes additional burdens on future cohorts since contributions grow with population – assuming zero per capita growth and full employment – whereas compensation payments grow with the market rate of interest. As population growth is below the interest rate the rate of contribution has to increase in the long term. Hence the PAYGO system is enlarged and welfare losses arise. Consequently Breyer, Kifmann and Stolte (1997) infer that a rise in the retirement age cannot help to alleviate the financial problems of a PAYGO system facing a population decline. Such a rise produces an intergenerational redistribution from the younger to the older cohorts. Though not done by Breyer, Kifmann and Stolte, one can draw the following conclusion which is discussed in detail below: that current generations are fully compensated for postponing their retirement age whereas future generations are worse off. Hence a rise in the retirement age is, ceteris paribus, Pareto inferior.

This reasoning is not fully correct as we have pointed out in Hirte (1999a). In fact, indifference towards the retirement age occurs if and only if individuals are compensated for changes in utility. If individuals are risk-neutral this is equivalent to actuarial compensation and the results of Breyer, Kifmann and Stolte hold. If however individuals are risk-averse, which is most likely, compensation for changes in utility requires a lower present value of pension benefits than actuarial compensation. This implies a relatively lower rate of contribution and lower burdens for future cohorts. Moreover it is not even clear whether welfare changes are actually negative. If they are this incentive scheme is also Pareto inferior and the results of Breyer, Kifmann and Stolte can be considered as a rough approximation to the true effects. Otherwise a Pareto improving rise in the retirement age accompanied by a reduction in the rate of contribution is feasible, and the results of Breyer, Kifmann and Stolte are misleading. In the latter case the German discussion about the appropriate level of supplements, for instance Börsch-Supan (1991), also focuses on the wrong variable. However, if compensation for changes in utility is the optimal compensation scheme, the change in the rate of contribution and the welfare effects of this compensation scheme have to be examined.

The analysis is carried out as follows: first we show how the simulation model has to be changed to include the supplement rate; then we replicate the argument of Hirte (1999a) in a more detailed fashion and demonstrate that actuarial supplements actually provide overcompensation. Therefore the burden imposed on the PAYGO system is lower than computed by Breyer, Kifmann and Stolte (1997). This creates the opportunity to devise a compensation scheme which avoids a Pareto inferior increase in the retirement age. We use the simulation model to search for such a scheme. This is appropriate because welfare effects of a rise in the retirement age depend not only on changes in the rate of contribution but also on repercussion effects on factor prices, tax rates, etc..

6.3 Adjusting the Model

Assume that a supplement factor θ_s^{π}, e.g. 0.06, is granted for each year retirement is postponed beyond a basic retirement age $\overline{M}_s$. If the same factor is levied as a deduction if individuals retire earlier, an individual supplement rate $\theta_s^{z,i}$ can be computed as

$$\theta_s^{z,i} = \theta_s^{\pi} \left(M_s^i - \overline{M}_s\right). \tag{6.1}$$

If, for instance, the basic retirement age is 65 but individuals retire at 70, the supplement rate is 30%. According to equation (2.31) on page 42 the new pension level is

$$b_s^{P,i} = \left(1 + \theta_s^{z,i}\right) \times e_t^{P,M} \times a_s^R.$$

As the marginal tax benefit linkage is now $\left(1 + \theta_s^{z,i}\right) \phi_s^{P,i}$ the implicit tax rate of the pension system, equation (2.35) on page 44, becomes

$$\tau_s^{P,i} = \theta_s^P - \left(1 + \theta_s^{z,i}\right) \phi_s^{P,i}. \tag{6.2}$$

These are the most important changes in the model induced by supplements.

6.4 Actuarial supplements

As a first step a simple diagram is used to demonstrate the basic idea of our reasoning (see also Hirte, 1999a). In order to simplify matters we assume for the time being that there is no wage tax and no unemployment system. Assume the representative individual consumes a composite commodity c, whose price is normalized to unity, and leisure ℓ. In addition, he or she has to decide in period t whether to work or retire. If the individual chooses to work, he or she earns the effective wage, w^e, which corresponds to the market wage corrected by the implicit tax rate (6.2), which is without supplements

$$w^e = w \left[1 - \left(\theta^P - \phi_s^{P,i}\right)\right].$$

This effective wage determines the slope of the budget constraint. Since we assume that there is no non-labor income in addition to pension benefits, the budget constraint in the case of working is given by the line AA in Figure 6.1[3]. If the individual chooses retirement he or she receives pension

[3]Note that working now increases future pension benefits. The present value of this increase generates non-labor income shifting the budget line upwards. Taking this into account does not change our reasoning. To simplify matters we omit it.

Figure 6.1: Actuarial versus utility compensation

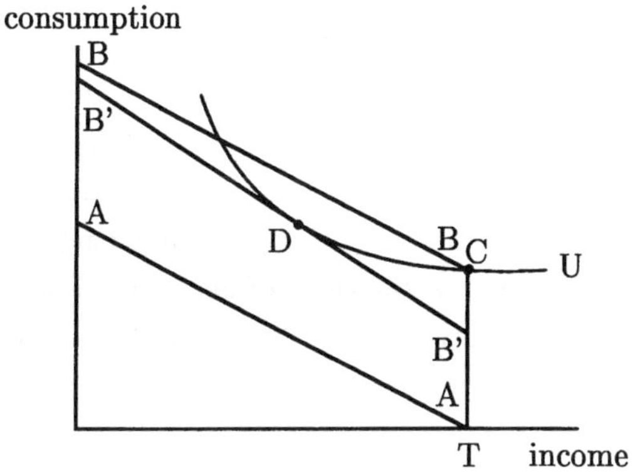

benefits CT. In this situation a risk-averse individual facing indifference curves of type U chooses retirement, i. e. point C.

Now assume that an actuarial supplement on future retirement benefits is granted if the individual chooses not to retire in the current period. This is the case discussed by Breyer, Kifmann and Stolte (1997). An actuarial supplement which ensures that the present value of the induced change in future pension benefits is exactly equal to the pension benefits foregone in the current period, i. e. it is exactly equal to TC. Since this supplement or compensation is independent of current wages but endogenously computed it shifts the budget line to BB. This line is parallel to AA since despite any change in labor supply the present value of future benefits remains unchanged, and the difference between the budget lines is exactly equal to TC. The individual receives a wage depending on current labor supply plus compensation for the loss in current pension benefits. The burden for the PAYGO system is given by TC and is independent of the decision of the individual. Because TC is unchanged an increase in the retirement age does not reduce the financial problems of the pension system. However it is obvious that a postponement of retirement can be accomplished by granting utility compensation instead of actuarial compensation, provided the utility function is concave.

In the case of utility compensation the new budget line $B'B'$ is below BB and the transfers are lower than TC. Note that the slope of the budget line $B'B'$ is larger than the slope of BB. The reason is that the supplement rate, θ^z, reduces the implicit tax rate if future pension benefits depend on the level of current labor supply. Thus the effective wage becomes $w_s^e = w_s \left\{1 - \left[\theta_s^P - (1 + \theta_s^z)\, \phi_s^P\right]\right\}$. In addition there is a level effect, shifting the original budget line upward. This effect is caused by changes in future pension benefits due to all non-marginal effects, such as the lengthening of the working life. Since the difference between $B'B'$ and BB is less than TC, the present value of net pension benefits is reduced, which eases the financial problems of the pension system without lowering utility. This supports our view that actuarial compensation is not appropriate for evaluating the usefulness of supplement rates. Whether this is also true in a more complex environment where repercussions are explicitly taken into account and a life cycle model is considered is examined in the next sections.

6.4.1 Simulations and Results

Utility versus actuarial compensation

As we have emphasized supplements required to compensate individuals can be below actuarial supplements. To examine whether this is sufficient to avoid welfare losses compared to a situation without policy reform we have performed some simulations. We have already presented a similar simulation study (Hirte, 1999a). However, in that paper the year 1989 was chosen as the starting year and population growth rates were considerably lower, since they were computed according to the excess of births over deaths while neither migration nor changes in longevity were considered. As explained in the previous chapter, population growth in this study includes all changes in population accruing until 1996. This also implies that growth rates are absolutely higher compared to Hirte (1999a) for all generations alive during the initial year, which is 1996 in this study. This difference might matter. Breyer, Kifmann and Stolte (1997) have shown that the change from positive to negative population growth is the threshold between positive and negative effects on the pension system. In our study supplements are below the actuarial supplements used by Breyer, Kifmann and Stolte (1997). Therefore the adverse effects of a population decline must be stronger than in their study to dominate the results. Whether the very strong population decline expected for Germany is strong enough could not be decided without simulations.

Note that in the following we use constant supplement rates (see also Hirte, 1998). In another paper we have examined supplement rates which vary with time but are constant for individuals (see Hirte, 1999a). There we found many supplement schemes which induce a Pareto improvement compared to the situation without any policy reform, also for various values of the parameters. However, in the current study it turned out that we could not find a Pareto superior supplement scheme. This is due to the absolutely higher population growth rates. Accordingly the result of Breyer, Kifmann and Stolte (1997) seems to hold when population growth rates are very high. Obviously, the difference between actuarially fair compensation and utility compensation is not sufficiently high to overcome the adverse effects of the strong aging trend. Nonetheless, the threshold for the impossibility of a Pareto improving rise in the retirement age is not a negative population growth as suggested by Breyer, Kifmann and Stolte (1997). Rather it is a fast population decline, while a slow population decline allows a Pareto improving way to raise the retirement age to be determined (Hirte, 1999a).

Nonetheless we present the result of a simulation to show the effects caused by such a reform. We examine a reform where the supplement rate is set to 7%. The reform begins after 5 years, i. e. in 2000, but is already announced in 1996. This scheme is chosen because it ensures that each cohort postpones retirement by at least one year.

6.4.2 Effects on the Pension System

The supplement scheme presented above induces individuals in all periods to retire at least one year later. This reduces the old age dependency ratio below the benchmark ratio as shown in panel (a) of Figure 6.2.

Due to the lower old age dependency ratio, the rate of contribution and implicit tax are also relatively lower, but only in the short term (see panel (b) of Figure 6.2). The immediate increase in the retirement age implies

Figure 6.2: Supplements only: social insurance variables

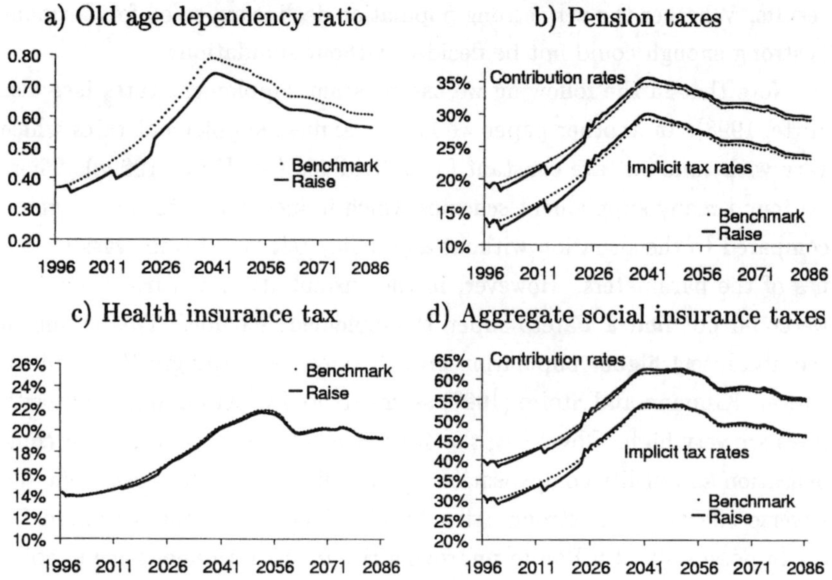

an instantaneous reduction in the rate of contribution since no individual retires during the period of reform. Beginning with the second period all newly retiring individuals receive supplements plus a higher benefit level on account of the increased length of their working life. This imposes a huge burden on the labor force which is added to the burden induced by the population decline. Therefore the rate of contribution as well as the implicit tax rate start to rise faster than in the benchmark case though both remain below their benchmark levels. However as time goes by the rising number of pensioners receiving supplements increases the expenditure of the pension system. For this reason the rate of contribution exceeds the rate in the case without reform after 2019. Hence this supplement scheme does provide a small improvement which is restricted to the first twenty years, compared to the situation without reform. The result of these effects is that the rise in the average retirement age induced by utility compensating supplements does not reduce the financial problems of the PAYGO system. It only provides a transitory reduction in the rate of contribution. Apparently, the supplement rate required to achieve a postponement of

Table 6.1: Supplements only: internal rate of return of the German pension system

Cohort retiring in	Benchm.	Raising	Schnabel (1998)
1996	1.28%	1.27%	3.5%
2000	1.43%	1.29%	2.0%
2010	1.39%	1.46%	1.1%
2020	1.09%	1.18%	0.8%
2030	0.55%	0.61%	0.2%
2040	-0.34%	-0.26%	0.0%
2050	-0.72%	-0.67%	
2060	-0.86%	-0.85%	
2100	-0.35%	-0.34%	

retirement is so high that the aging effect as described by Breyer, Kifmann and Stolte (1997) dominates and prevents a Pareto improvement.

Looking at the internal rate of return reveals that supplements are below their actuarial levels at least for the first years and in the medium term (see Table 6.1). Otherwise the rate of return would be equivalent to its benchmark counterparts. In the short term it is higher.

6.4.3 Macroeconomic Changes

According to panels (a) and (c) of Figure 6.3 unemployment and employment increase in response to the reform. On account of the relatively high rate of unemployment of elder working cohorts, the rise in the average retirement age implies a higher aggregate rate of unemployment. Though this induces a higher rate of contribution to unemployment insurance, the average rate of implicit tax of unemployment insurance falls. The reason is that older individuals have a lower implicit tax rate since it is more likely that they receive unemployment benefits (see panel (b) of Figure 6.3). A longer working life raises overall employment and thus implies a lower wage (see panel (c) and (d) of Figure 6.3). The effects on the aggregate rate of contribution and implicit tax are smaller than on the rates of the pension system as shown by Figure 6.2(d). The first reason for this outcome is the upward shift of the rate of contribution and implicit tax of unemployment insurance. The second is the reduction in the rate of contribution to health

Figure 6.3: Supplements only: labor market

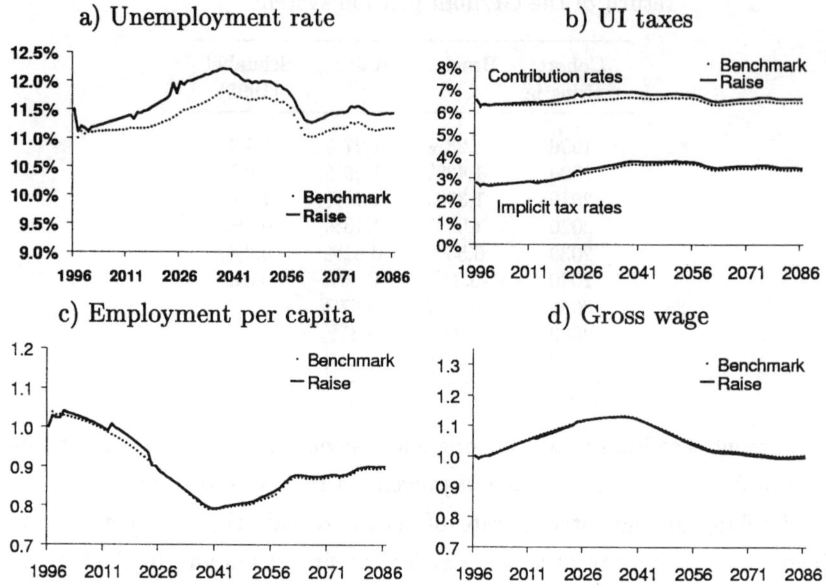

insurance, made possible by growing employment.

The capital stock per capita is slightly lower than the benchmark level, since supplements raise income when old and thus substitute asset income (see panel (a) of Figure 6.4). Individuals can therefore rearrange their saving decisions so that they consume a large part of their assets in the extension of their working life. Hence the reduction of assets is relatively faster, leading to the small reduction in capital accumulation per capita. Therefore the interest rate is above the benchmark level as shown in Figure 6.4(b). By and large, employment increases and the capital stock decreases. Obviously the employment effect dominates, since consumption per capita is also marginally above its benchmark level. Figure 6.4(d) shows the consumption tax rate. Since there are only small changes in all the other variables, this is also hardly changed.

Figure 6.4: Supplements only: capital stock and consumption

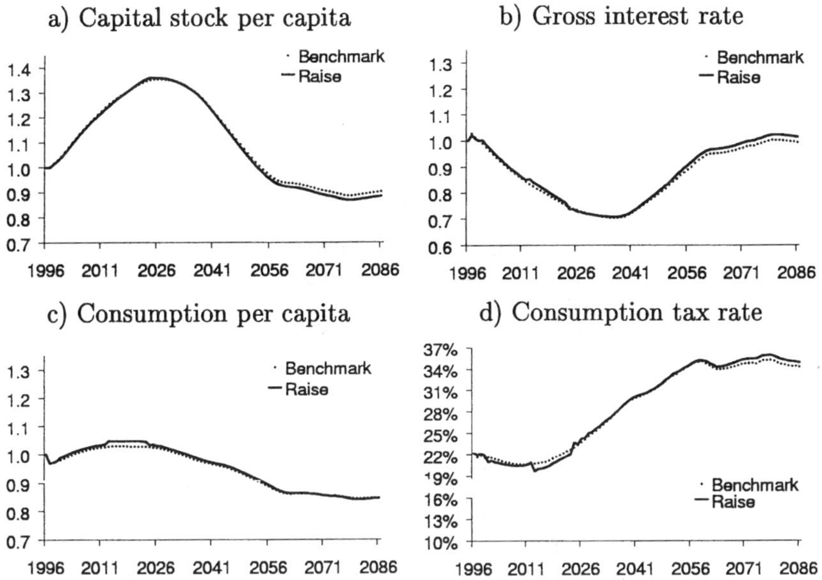

6.4.4 Welfare Effects

In Table 6.2 changes in utility are given and broken down. All values are given as percentages of the remaining lifetime income.

The second column ('ΔU') shows the changes in utility of some cohorts as a percentage of all remaining lifetime resources compared to the case without reform. The reform makes all initially living cohorts except the eldest cohort better off. The gains of the cohorts who work initially (cohort 1946 to 1996) are mainly caused by efficiency gains. These are shown in the last column as inverse changes of excess burden ('ΔEB'). Since the rates of implicit tax and consumption tax are below their benchmark levels during the transition, efficiency gains occur. For future cohorts rates of implicit tax and consumption tax exceed the benchmark levels. This generates additional excess burden, which creates welfare losses for all future cohorts.

Changes in net pension benefits are shown in the third column ('ΔP'). They are negative for the middle-aged, the elderly, and future cohorts. These cohorts receive supplements which are less than actuarially fair.

Table 6.2: Supplements only: decomposition of changes in utility

Year of birth	ΔU^a	ΔP^b	$-\Delta T^c$	ΔEB^d
1921	-0.18	-0.10	-0.08	0.00
1936	0.17	-0.05	0.07	0.02
1946	0.43	-0.18	-0.06	1.11
1956	0.36	-0.13	-0.02	0.71
1966	0.47	0.16	-0.02	0.56
1976	0.64	0.29	0.03	0.59
1986	0.45	0.22	0.06	0.38
1996	0.02	0.01	0.12	0.00
2006	-0.62	-0.34	0.21	-0.30
2016	-0.51	-0.28	0.25	-0.37
∞	-0.60	-0.34	0.21	-0.07
$\sum$	0.36	-0.12		0.56

In per cent of all remaining lifetime resources.
[a]Change in utility.
[b]Change in net pension benefits.
[c]Change in net tax liabilities.
[d]Change in efficiency.

On the other hand the younger cohorts receive supplements which are higher than actuarially fair supplements. The instantaneous increase in the retirement age, caused by the supplements, reduces the pension benefits of all subsequent cohorts. This creates negative income effects. However, the simultaneous decrease of the rate of contribution generates positive income effects. As these accumulate during the working life, the cohorts who are middle-aged at the year of reform gain considerably less than the younger or future cohorts. For this reason the cohort 1946 suffers a loss in net pension benefits of 0.18% of their lifetime resources, which are 0.3 percentage points below the benchmark level. However, for all subsequent cohorts the reduction in the rate of contribution induces an opposite effect. This effect accumulates over the remaining working life of each cohort. It is therefore higher, the longer the remaining working life. Hence this effect increases from cohort to cohort, and exceeds the loss in pension benefits beginning after cohort 1956. As a result the loss in net pension benefits falls below the initial level for the cohorts 1966 and later.

But in the medium term the rate of contribution exceeds the benchmark level. Therefore future generations lose net pension benefits, which again become negative. These effects are hardly altered by changes in net tax liabilities because the latter are very small.

This reform implies a redistribution from the eldest and future cohorts to the middle-aged and younger cohorts. The value shown in the middle of the last row is a measure of the negative redistribution caused by this reform. It is the present value of all negative distribution effects as a percentage of all remaining lifetime resources. This value is -0.12 which is not very large. Welfare increases by 0.36% of the aggregate remaining lifetime resources (see the last number of the second column in Table 6.2). Since there is no source of overall income effects the present value of all individual income effects must add up to zero. Overall excess burden is also positive but higher than welfare effects (see the last number of the fifth column). However, since efficiency gains are the single source of welfare gains, aggregate excess burden ought to equal changes in utility. But they do not. This must be caused by applying utility decomposition to discrete changes in the simulation. As discrete changes are larger in the case of reform, where individuals change their retirement age, the aggregation is not accurate. Overall these deviations are not very large and do not conceal the main result: differences in individual changes in utility are caused by intergenerational redistribution on account of changes in net pension benefits as well as by changes in excess burden, both with equal significance.

6.4.5 Sensitivity Analysis

To evaluate the significance of the modeling of unemployment, health insurance and the decision about retirement, we have performed three further simulations. In the first experiment the reform is examined in a model without unemployment and without unemployment insurance. In the second experiment health insurance is omitted. The last experiment is the simulation of the case of a lower increase in the strength of the preference for leisure. This implies a stronger response of the age of retirement to policy reforms. The results are presented in Table 6.3 and 6.4.

Table 6.3: Supplements only: sensitivity analysis – macroeconomic effects

Year	Base Case	No UI[a]	No HI[b]	Low α[c]	Base Case	No UI	No HI	Low α
	Old age dependency ratio				Unemployment rate: x			
1996	0.37	0.37	0.37	0.37	11.5	–	11.5	11.5
1997	0.37	0.37	0.37	0.34	11.1	–	11.2	11.0
2001	0.36	0.36	0.36	0.33	11.2	–	11.3	11.1
2041	0.74	0.79	0.74	0.74	12.1	–	11.6	11.9
∞	0.56	0.56	0.56	0.60	11.5	–	10.4	11.1
	Consumption tax rate: τ^c				Pension contr. rate: θ^P			
1996	22.2	21.7	17.3	22.2	19.2	19.2	19.2	19.2
1997	22.0	21.8	17.4	20.6	18.8	18.8	18.9	17.4
2001	21.1	21.0	17.2	19.5	18.6	18.6	18.6	17.7
2041	30.1	27.6	21.4	29.0	35.5	37.5	36.2	34.1
∞	31.8	30.7	22.6	29.4	29.1	29.0	28.9	28.5
	Implicit pension tax: τ^P				Aggregate contr. rate: θ^{SI}			
1996	13.9	14.7	13.2	14.0	39.9	34.2	25.7	40.0
1997	13.1	13.7	11.9	11.3	38.9	33.6	25.1	37.3
2001	12.9	13.4	11.5	11.6	38.9	33.2	24.9	37.7
2041	30.0	32.9	29.1	28.4	62.6	58.3	43.0	60.9
∞	23.1	23.9	21.6	22.5	54.3	48.6	35.5	53.6
	Aggregate implicit tax: τ^{SI}				Employment per capita			
1996	30.9	29.7	15.4	31.1	1.00	1.00	1.00	1.00
1997	29.7	28.5	14.0	27.7	1.03	1.03	1.02	1.06
2001	29.5	28.1	13.6	27.9	1.04	1.03	1.03	1.06
2041	53.9	53.7	32.2	52.1	0.79	0.77	0.81	0.81
∞	45.3	43.5	24.3	44.5	0.90	0.90	0.90	0.90
	Capital stock per capita				Consumption per capita			
1996	1.00	1.00	1.00	1.00	1.00	1.00	1.00	1.00
1997	1.00	1.00	1.03	1.00	0.97	0.97	0.97	0.99
2001	1.06	1.05	1.06	1.07	0.99	0.99	0.99	1.01
2041	1.22	1.22	1.21	1.24	0.97	1.00	1.02	0.98
∞	0.96	0.97	1.03	1.01	0.89	0.90	0.97	0.90

[a]No unemployment and no unemployment insurance.
[b]No health insurance.
[c]Slower increase in the strength of the preference for leisure.

What are the effects if there is *no unemployment*? The columns 'No UI' of Table 6.3 give the changes in the macroeconomic variables. Since each modification of the model requires the adjustment of the data base there might be some deviations between the benchmark data base and the data base of each experiment. These deviations can be derived from the rows "1996". A bar means no data. For example, the consumption tax rate in 1996 is 21.7% if there is no unemployment insurance compared to 22.2% in the benchmark case.

Let us discuss only some differences to the base case. The retirement age in 2041 is reduced if there is no unemployment insurance. This is represented by a higher old age dependency ratio which raises the rate of contribution to the pension system, θ^P, by 2 percentage points. A similar effect can be seen with regard to the overall rate of contribution, θ^{SI}. Since this rate is 5.7 points lower in 1996 but only 4.3 points lower in 2041, the rate of contribution is actually raised by about 1.4 percentage points compared to the base case. Similar changes are found for implicit pension taxes, τ^P, and implicit social insurance taxes, τ^{SI}. The results shown in Table 6.3 are puzzling with respect to one point. Why do individuals retire earlier in 2041? The reason is as follows: since the cohorts near retirement have high rates of unemployment, net income gains from working are relatively smaller when unemployment is considered than in the case without unemployment. Therefore working becomes more attractive if there is no unemployment. On the other hand the implicit tax rate of the pension system increases if there is no unemployment, because unemployment insurance pays a part of the contributions. This raises the incentive to retire earlier. Obviously the latter effect dominates during the time of the highest rate of contribution and implicit tax.

If there is no *health insurance* ('No HI') net pension benefits increase and thus the implicit tax rate of the pension system decreases because pensioners do not pay contributions to health insurance. In addition grants to pension and unemployment insurance can be lower. This leads to a lower consumption tax rate. Also, the aggregate rate of contribution and implicit tax are considerably lower than in the case with health insurance. These are the changes in the base data, given in rows 1996 in the columns 'no HI' of Table 6.3. These changes also occur to a greater extent during the demographic transition. The lower increase in the implicit tax rate implies higher income and, therefore, demand for consumption. Moreover, savings are raised to finance higher consumption during retirement. As a result the aggregate capital stock increases both in the short and long term. Since higher savings during the working life also mean that assets are reduced during retirement, the capital stock decreases in the medium term, where the latter effect dominates. Employment per capita (L/N) increases on account of a lower implicit tax rate. However, there is an opposite effect on employment. As health insurance no longer consumes resources, less employment is required to produce all goods. Obviously this effect is stronger in the short term, and weaker in the medium term.

The third sensitivity analysis considers a slower increase in the *strength of the preference for leisure* (see columns 'Low α' in Table 6.3). It is assumed that this variable increases from 1.5 to 2 from age 64 instead of 60. This change raises the variability of the retirement age. In addition supplements are reduced by 1.5 percentage points on average, since lower supplement rates are sufficient to achieve a higher average retirement age. Introducing these supplements leads to a higher retirement age and, thus, to a lower old age dependency ratio during the transition. According to Table 6.3 this change occurs only in 1997 and in 2001. But in 2041 there is no change in the retirement age compared to the base case, and in the new steady state the retirement age is one year lower. The short term response is due to a more elastic retirement age. Introducing supplements promotes longer working life which implies a lower old age dependency ratio. However, in the medium term this incentive is no longer high enough to cause a deviation from the retirement age compared to the case of introducing supplements with a lower strength of the preference for leisure. The long term supplement rate of 5% instead of 7% is not high enough to ensure a postponement of retirement. Therefore the old age dependency ratio exceeds the level of the base case. Nonetheless the rate of contribution and implicit tax can be lower. The gains from lower supplement rates exceed the losses from a shorter working life.

Table 6.4 shows the changes in utility and excess burden between the

Table 6.4: Supplements only: sensitivity analysis – changes in utility

Year of birth	Base Case	No UI[a]	No HI[b]	Low α[c]		Base Case	No UI	No HI	Low α
ΔU					ΔEB				
1921	-0.18	-0.12	-0.18	0.85	1921	0	0.01	0.01	0
1936	0.17	0.13	0.16	0.31	1936	0.01	0.01	0.01	0.01
1946	0.43	0.23	0.42	0.48	1946	1.11	0.86	0.80	1.45
1966	0.47	0.30	0.39	0.86	1966	0.56	0.35	0.32	0.63
1976	0.64	0.36	0.51	1.06	1976	0.59	0.36	0.33	0.69
1996	0.02	-0.14	-0.52	0.27	1996	1.50	-0.12	-0.15	0.25
∞	-0.60	0.10	-0.77	-0.01	∞	0.01	0.10	-0.11	0.00
$\sum$	0.36	0.23	0.28	0.65	$\sum$	-0.07	0.10	0.36	0.77

In per cent of all remaining lifetime resources.
[a]No unemployment insurance.
[b]No health insurance.
[c]Slower increase in the strength of the preference for leisure.

base case, the case without unemployment ('No UI'), without health insurance ('No HI'), and a higher strength of the preference for leisure compared to the benchmark path, measured in percentage points of remaining lifetime resources. The results show that modeling *unemployment* considerably affects utility and efficiency. The changes in utility and efficiency are so high that for the cohorts 1996 and younger even the sign changes. Changes in excess burden are lower and for the youngest cohort in 1996 even negative. Similar results are obtained by omitting *health insurance.*

A slower increase in the *strength of the preference for leisure* raises welfare compared to the base case (see column 'Low α' of Table 6.4). The initially eldest cohort gains due to lower consumption taxes and higher pension benefits. Owing to the adjustment to net wages, pension benefits grow since the rate of contribution to the social insurance system falls. These two effects raise net tax liabilities and net pension benefits. In addition all other cohorts are also better off compared to the base case on account of lower rates of implicit and consumption tax. This also produces efficiency gains ('ΔEB'), which are higher for all middle-aged and younger cohorts. The elderly hardly experience efficiency gains since they are not able to change their decisions very much. Therefore, changes in utility of the elderly are mainly determined by income effects.

Let us summarize the findings: actuarial supplements granted to compensate for a rise in the retirement age are too high and enlarge the PAYGO system more than necessary. At least for a specific overlapping generations model with zero economic growth but a moderately declining population and endogenous retirement decisions, a rise in the average retirement age can be achieved in a Pareto improving way (Hirte, 1999a). However, if the population decline is very large, as is expected in Germany, these results seem no longer to be true. Nonetheless our earlier study (Hirte, 1999a) and the current study emphasize the main point of our reasoning: if one wants to discuss whether a rise in the retirement age could be carried out in a Pareto improving way and reduce the financial problems of a PAYGO public pension system facing a population decline one has to consider utility but not actuarial compensation. For this reason the results of Breyer, Kifmann and Stolte are not appropriate, since their conclusion depends on actuarial supplements whereas utility compensation is the correct method. Hence a discussion of pension reforms might be misleading if it focuses only on actuarial compensation.

Other outcomes of this section are less encouraging. The results of these and further simulations suggest that a Pareto improving supplement scheme cannot be found in the German case if the aging trend is fully implemented. Therefore one can conclude that, though not generally proven, such a policy reform is not a useful proposal for ameliorating the pension crisis.

In the next section the proposal for raising the retirement age which is stipulated in the German Pension Act of 1992 is examined.

6.5 Raising the Statutory Retirement Age

Since a pure rise in the statutory retirement age does not cause any effects if early retirement is permitted, individuals should be induced by additional measures to voluntarily increase their retirement age. Such a measure is, for instance, a deduction rate levied on pension benefits if individuals choose early retirement. This is exactly the way the German Pension Act of 1992 (Rentenreformgesetz 1992) operates. Therefore we also assume that the rise in the statutory retirement age is accompanied by deductions.

These are introduced to discourage individuals from retiring early.

The welfare implications are as follows: since individuals receive the benefit level they would receive without reform if and only if they retire later, i. e. at the statutory retirement age, all individuals are worse off. However for the currently young and the future cohorts these losses are overcompensated by efficiency gains due to lower implicit taxation.

6.5.1 *Partial Equilibrium Effects*

Income Effects

Assume there are three generations. The old is already retired and is not subject to supplements or deductions. Then, looking at the income effects which can be derived by using equations (4.9) on page 76 and (4.21) and (4.20) on page 81, one sees that this policy reform does not affect the initially old generation. It is already retired and the reform does not alter its pension benefits.

The effects on the initially middle-aged generation, m, which is on the threshold of retirement, depends on the response of this generation. Assume that a deduction from pension benefits is imposed on the middle-aged generation if it retires, while there is no deduction if retirement is postponed. In addition assume this generation prefers retiring to working before the reform is carried out. Then define net pension benefits as

$$P_{ms} = b_s^P + \frac{p_s}{1+r_{s+1}} b_{s+1}^P, \tag{6.3}$$

which is a slightly modified version of equation (4.23) on page 81. One can derive the changes in net pension liabilities due to the introduction of deductions. If the representative member of the middle-aged generation retires these are

$$\Delta P_{ms} = -\left[b_s^P + \frac{p_s}{1+r_{s+1}} b_{s+1}^P\right] \Delta\theta_s^{z,i}, \tag{6.4}$$

where θ^z is the rate of deduction from pension benefits. Each rate of deduction, however high, reduces net pension taxes and thus imposes negative income effects on the individual, provided he or she retires. This shows that pension benefits decrease if the retirement decision is unchanged. Therefore levying deductions on pension benefits reduces expenditure by the pension system even if the average retirement age does not respond to the policy reform.

If individuals alter their decision and shift to working instead of retiring, their change in net pension benefits amounts to the additional pensions they will receive in the future due to a longer working life minus contributions to the pension system and implicit taxes on unemployment and health insurance and current pensions corrected by deductions which are not applied since they work. Since the discrete time prevents the differentiation of equation (4.23), one cannot derive this change exactly. But one can write it simply as the difference between net pensions when working and when retired, which is

$$\Delta P_{ms} = \frac{p_s}{1 + r_{s+1}} \Delta b^P_{s+1} - \left(\theta^P_s + \overline{\tau}^X_s + \tau^H_s\right) w_s l_s - \left(1 - \theta^z\right) b^P_s . \tag{6.5}$$

Suppose the pension benefits of an individual are reduced due to deductions if he or she retires in period s, while there are no deductions if retirement takes place in period $s+1$. If deductions are introduced current pension benefits, i. e. the last term in equation (6.5), are reduced. In addition deductions are not levied when working so that Δb^P_{s+1} also increases. This effect is included in the first term of equation (6.5), which expresses all changes in future pension benefits caused by working now. Hence net pension benefits are raised by introducing deductions. If time were continuous this would certainly raise the retirement age. However, in our case where time is discrete such an increase occurs only if the incentive is high enough (see Figure 2.4).

The generation young at the year of reform as well as all future generations experience positive income effects if deductions are less than actuarially fair and the middle-aged generation chooses to work. This case constitutes a redistribution from this middle-aged generation to the young and future generations. In the case of actuarially fair deductions no income effects occur, ceteris paribus. If deductions are above this actuarially fair level, redistribution takes place from the young and future generations to the generation which is middle-aged at the year of reform.

Excess Burden

Efficiency effects arise, ceteris paribus, due to changes in the marginal rate of implicit tax. This is equivalent to a change in the payroll tax. If the individual retires in the period in which deductions are levied, his or her marginal rate of implicit tax increases and efficiency losses occur. On the other hand lower pension benefits allow the rate of contribution of the working generations to be reduced. This lowers their marginal rate of implicit tax. If these cohorts are also subject to deductions the net effect on the marginal rate of implicit tax is theoretically unambiguous, as are efficiency effects.

If however the deduction leads to a higher retirement age the rate of contribution falls faster and the marginal rate of implicit tax decreases unambiguously. Then efficiency gains arise for these generations.

6.5.2 Evaluating Part II of the German Pension Act of 1992

As a device to achieve an increase in the average retirement age the German Pension Act of 1992 provided some new regulations. The regulations concerning this aim become effective in 2001. In the following these specific regulations are called 'Part II' of the German Pension Act of 1992. The main points are:

- A gradual rise in the statutory retirement age for normal pensions of men from 63 to 65, and of women and unemployed persons from 60 to 65 from the year 2001[4].
- Reductions of the pension benefits amounting to 0.3% of the pension level for each month individuals retire before the statutory retirement age, and supplements of 0.5% for each month retirement is postponed beyond the statutory retirement age. Accordingly, an age factor $a_s^{M,i}$, which is the aggregate deduction or supplement rate, is added to the pension formula (2.31) on page 42

$$b_s^{P,i} = a_s^{M,i} \times e_t^{P,M} \times a_s^R.$$

[4]To be correct the rise in the statutory retirement age is introduced gradually within 10 years. We consider an immediate implementation in the following

Table 6.5: Pension Act of 1992: internal rate of return of the pension system

Cohort retiring in	Benchmark	Act 92	Schnabel (1998)
1996	1.28%	1.30%	3.5%
2000	1.43%	1.35%	2.0 %
2010	1.39%	0.90%	1.1%
2020	1.09%	0.72%	0.8%
2030	0.55%	0.35%	0.2%
2040	-0.34%	-0.40%	0%
2050	-0.72%	-0.77%	
2060	-0.86%	-0.92%	
2100	-0.35%	-0.38%	

Internal Rate of Return of the Public Pension System

Table 6.5 compares the internal real rate of return provided by Schnabel (1998) with the internal rate of return obtained by the simulations. Introducing a rise in the statutory retirement age together with deductions causes an increase in the average retirement age from 61 to 62. This response causes a strong reduction in the internal rate of return. Owing to the countervailing effect of a reduced implicit tax rate the internal rate of return passes its benchmark level after some time. This shows that the reform mitigates the adverse effects of the population decline. Currently middle-aged cohorts are worse off, at least with respect to the internal rate of return achieved, while future cohorts are better off.

Though the computed rate of return is lower than the benchmark value until 2020 it is considerably higher than the value found in Hirte (1999b). One reason for this deviation is that only Part II of the Pension Act is considered as policy reform and Part I is included in the benchmark, while in Hirte (1999b) the whole act is taken into account. A second reason is that the population decline is delayed by about 10 years in this simulation study. A third reason is that the increase in the rate of contribution in Hirte (1999b) is overestimated, since no general equilibrium effects have been taken into account. Nonetheless the tendency is the same, though the rate decreases faster in Hirte (1999b).

Figure 6.5: Pension Act of 1992: social insurance variables

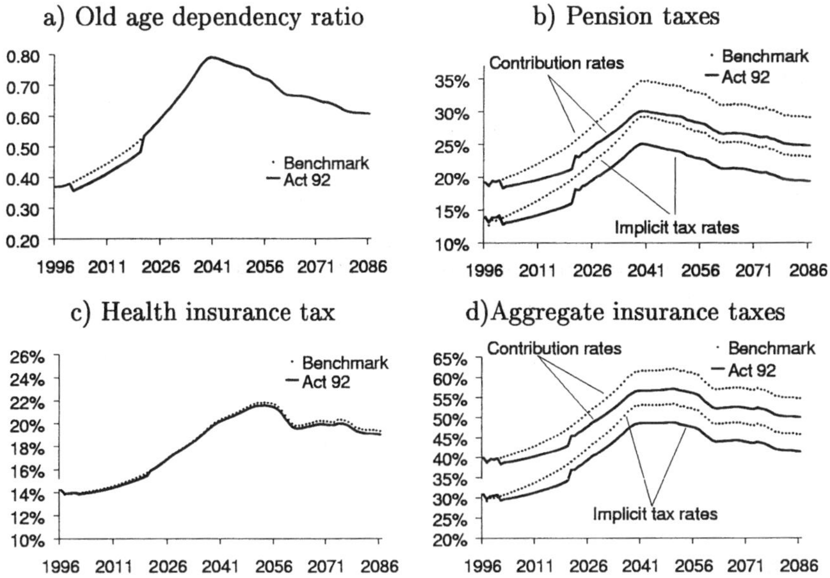

Social Insurance and Macroeconomic Effects

Since the increase in the statutory retirement age and the introduction of deductions have already been announced, the responses of individuals are smoothed. This means that individuals already retired are not affected, and the other cohorts increase labor supply and savings to offset the loss in future pension benefits while they simultaneously reduce their consumption. These responses are very small in aggregate. Consequently neither taxes nor the rate of contribution are changed during the first five years. Thereafter, however, the pension level decreases due to the deductions from 65.5% to about 57% of the net income of a fully employed person.

As the old age dependency ratio shown in panel (a) of Figure 6.5 implies, this reduction is sufficient to cause a rise of the retirement age by one year in the medium term but insufficient to cause a permanent rise in the retirement age. The first result is in line with estimates of Siddiqui (1995, 1997a, b, and c) who forecast that the average retirement age of men will rise by about 1.2 years due to the Pension Act of 1992. Despite

Figure 6.6: Pension Act of 1992: labor market

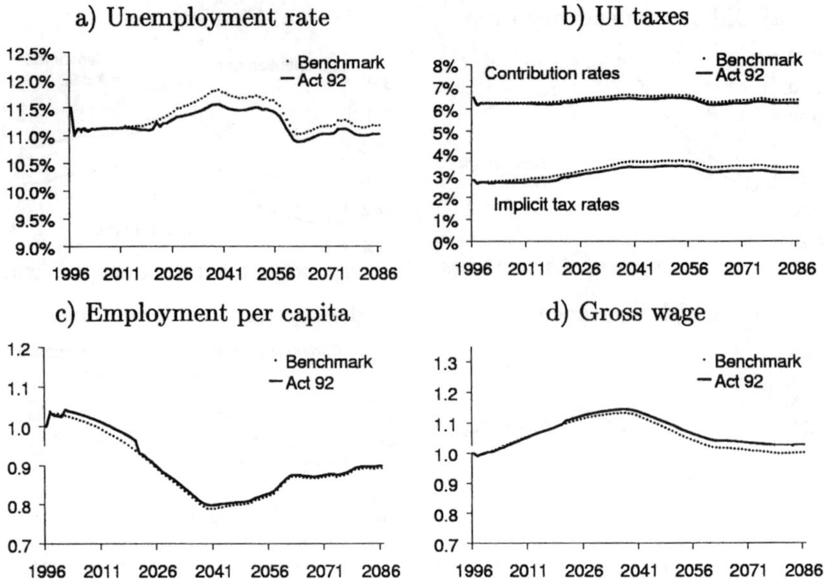

the lack of response in the permanent retirement age, the reduction in pensions implies a decrease in the rate of contribution. This is enhanced by each new cohort entering retirement (see panel (b) of Figure 6.5). Even when all pensioners receive lower benefits, which is the case after 27 years, contributions fall as long as the newly retiring cohorts are larger than the dying cohorts. Hence the difference in the rate of contribution between this reform and the benchmark case reaches its maximum when the old age dependency ratio peaks in 2040. Then the rate of contribution falls by 3.7 percentage points to 30.9%. This is almost entirely a reduction in the marginal rate of implicit tax and should therefore induce efficiency gains.

All other effects are caused by the changes in the pension system. Individuals rearrange their lifetime resources to compensate for lower pension benefits. This implies a small increase in employment and a large increase in the capital stock per capita compared to the benchmark case shown by panels (a) of Figure 6.6 and Figure 6.7.

When considering unemployment, it is convenient to look at the individual decisions in more detail. The middle-aged working generations face a rise in the implicit tax rate, since they receive lower pension benefits, while the decline in the rate of contribution takes place after retirement. Therefore their net wage decreases and leisure increases. On the other hand lower pension benefits reduce their remaining lifetime resources implying a higher labor supply. This income change dominates and labor supply increases.

In contrast, the younger cohorts gain from the future decline in the rate of contribution, which offsets the reduction in pension benefits. Their implicit tax rate falls and the net wage decreases. However, higher net pension benefits raise their income. Again, the latter dominates and labor supply decreases. This dominant income change does not, however, affect unemployment. It depends almost entirely on the average and marginal net wage, which are above their benchmark levels for the young cohorts. For this reason the young are willing to work more and the rate of unemployment specific to the cohort increases in comparison with the benchmark case – in period one to 9.66% compared to 9.53%. The same argument applies to the middle-aged cohorts.

The difference between labor supply with and without rationing depends only on the change in average and marginal net wages. These are relatively lower for the middle-aged cohorts. Consequently their excess of labor supply over employment falls and their rate of unemployment is relatively lower than in the benchmark case – 15.98% instead of 16.28%, again in period one. In general this change in the distribution of unemployment leads to a lower overall rate of unemployment (see panel (d) of Figure 6.5). Consequently, the rate of contribution and the implicit tax rate of unemployment insurance fall. This is shown in Figure 6.6(b).

In spite of the reduction in the marginal productivity of labor and capital, labor and interest income and thus wage and interest tax receipts increase compared to the benchmark level. In addition public expenditure can be lowered because the grants to the pension system and unemployment insurance decrease. Furthermore consumption per capita increases due to higher factor input above the benchmark level (see panel (c) of Figure 6.7). For these reasons the consumption tax rate declines relative to its benchmark level (see panel (d) of Figure 6.7).

Figure 6.7: Pension Act of 1992: capital and consumption

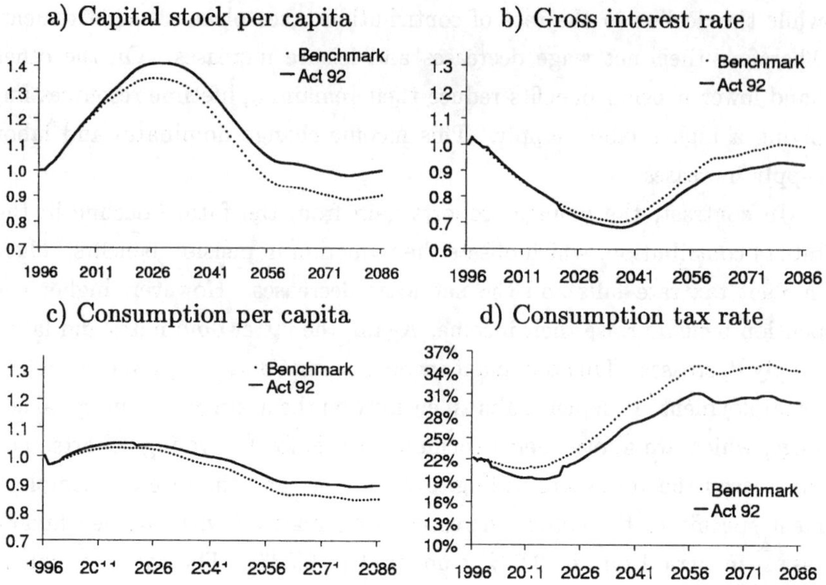

Though lower pension benefits and unemployment reduce the contributions of pensioners to health insurance relative to the benchmark case, the increase in employment and wages causes a relative decrease of the rate of contribution to health insurance (see panel (c) Figure 6.5).

The result of aggregating all rates of contribution and implicit tax is shown in Figure 6.5(d). These aggregate rates increase with a smaller rate than in the benchmark case until the 2050s. Then the aggregate rate of contribution is about 58.2%, while it is 62.2% in the benchmark case. The reform also reduces the marginal aggregate rate of implicit tax from 53.4% to 59.7%. In the long term the difference is about 3.5 percentage points.

The long term levels of almost all variables are better after reform than in the benchmark case. For instance, the capital stock per capita reaches again its initial level with reform, while it remains about 4.8 percentage points below the initial level without reform. (see panel (a) of Figure 6.7). Figure 6.7(c) shows that consumption per capita reaches 90.2% of the initial level in the case of reform compared to 86.4% without reform.

Welfare and Distribution

Let us now turn to welfare and distribution effects[5]. Table 6.6 presents the changes in utility equivalents, 'ΔU', in efficiency effects, 'ΔEB', in net social insurance benefits, 'ΔP', and in net tax liabilities, 'ΔT', each in per cent of discounted remaining lifetime income for the representative member of the cohorts born in year t, given relative to the base year 1996[6]. Changes in factor income are omitted, since they approximately add up to the difference between overall utility change and the other variables. The Pension Act of 1992 is depicted on the left-hand side of this table. The bottom line gives the aggregate changes in the variables of all current and future cohorts discounted to the year of reform. On account of the previous announcement generations born in 1923 or earlier do not suffer utility losses. The cohort which enters retirement in 1996, i. e. cohort 1936, is better off, while the initially middle-aged cohorts 1946 and 1956 are worse off. Beginning with the initially younger cohorts – for example generation 1966 – all younger and future cohorts are better off.

The third and fifth column show that changes in net social insurance transfers and excess burden determine the gains of the young and future cohorts. This reflects the relative reduction of the rate of implicit and consumption tax. The former implies lower absolute implicit tax liabilities and, thus, higher net transfers. Net pension benefits are negative only in the short term, and this explains the loss in utility of the initially middle-aged cohorts, because benefits decline while the implicit tax rate is hardly reduced. Moreover efficiency gains occur due to the reduced rate of consumption and implicit tax. Despite lower consumption tax liabilities, revenues from the capital income tax and the wage tax increase while interest payments on public debt decrease. This implies higher net tax liabilities. However, efficiency effects and changes in net pension benefits are dominant. This constitutes an intergenerational redistribution from the initially middle-aged to all young and future cohorts, and to a much smaller extent to cohorts just retired. Aggregate negative distribution effects amount to -0.44% of the remaining lifetime resources, which is con-

[5] This decomposition of changes in utility is based on FEHR (1999b).

[6] Note that the cohort 1976 enters working life at year 1996.

Table 6.6: Pension Act of 1992: welfare and efficiency effects

Year of birth	Pension Act of 1992 ΔU^a	ΔP^b	$-\Delta T^c$	ΔEB^d
1921	-0.11	-0.03	-0.01	0
1936	0.59	0.17	0.26	0.02
1946	-1.32	-2.02	0.23	0.46
1956	-0.28	-0.71	0.06	0.37
1966	0.70	0.33	0.04	0.45
1976	1.58	0.92	0.03	0.80
1986	2.37	1.50	-0.11	1.21
1996	2.99	1.78	-0.34	1.50
2006	3.58	2.01	-0.56	1.72
2016	4.25	2.30	-0.73	2.04
∞	4.53	1.84	-0.60	1.83
$\sum$	0.50	-0.44		0.53

In per cent of remaining lifetime resources.
[a]Change in utility.
[b]Change in net pension benefits.
[c]Change in net tax liabilities.
[d]Change in efficiency.

siderably higher than in the case of the reform considered above. Overall utility gains amount to 0.5% of the present value of all remaining lifetime income, which is induced by efficiency gains.

Sensitivity analysis

Changing the model gives additional information about the significance of different features of the model. Therefore we modify the model and simulate the above reform. Table 6.7 and Table 6.8 show the effects of three modifications: omitting unemployment, omitting health insurance, and a slower rise in the strength of the preference for leisure.

First, consider the results of the case *without unemployment.* According to the upper part of the first column 'No UI' in Table 6.7, the old age dependency ratio is higher in 2001 and lower in 2041 and later compared to the base case. This reflects changes in the retirement decision. The reason for these changes is that unemployment makes working less attractive during the last year of period of employment[7]. Hence individuals prefer a shorter working life. Therefore the average retirement age is reduced in the medium term and long term. Consequently the old age dependency ratio is lower in the case without unemployment in the medium and long term. In the short term individuals postpone retirement longer if there is unemployment, since they have to offset the loss in pension benefits. This requires them to work longer due to lower income in each working year. If unemployment is not considered individuals earn enough money to offset the loss in pension benefits without changing their retirement age. Hence the old age dependency ratio is higher in the case without unemployment. This effect drives the changes in tax rates of social insurance. The rate of contribution to the pension system is raised in the short term and lowered in the medium term. Surprisingly, there is no long term reduction in θ^P although the old age dependency ratio decreases.

The implicit tax rate of the pension system is higher in the initial year since individuals pay all contributions, while in the case with unemployment part of the contributions is paid by unemployment insurance. Subtracting the latter from the figures given in column τ^P reveals that the changes in implicit pension taxes are similar to the changes in the rate of contribution. Again, the long term effect is very small. Since there is no unemployment insurance in this simulation the rate of contribution and implicit tax are lower in 1996 compared to the base case. Since unemployment insurance provides a positive tax benefit linkage, the difference in the aggregate rate of contribution, θ^{SI}, is higher than with the aggregate rate of implicit tax, τ^{SI}. The positive effect on the pension system leads to higher employment, capital stock, and consumption per capita in the long term.

[7]Note that SIDDIQUI (1995, 1997a, b, and c) found no evidence for a positive influence of unemployment on the retirement decision in Germany. However, SIDDIQUI (1995, p. 163) doubts the results of the estimates since a large part of unemployment of the elder labor force is hidden, which distorts the data base used in the studies. The estimates of SCHMIDT (1995) and RIPHAHN and SCHMIDT (1997) provide evidence for a highly significant influence of unemployment in the last year of the working life on the retirement age. But they also question their result.

Table 6.7: Pension Act of 1992: sensitivity analysis – macro effects

	Pension Act of 1992				High	Pension Act of 1992				High
Year of birth	Base Case	No UI[b]	No HI[c]	Low α[d]	D.[a]	Base Case	No UI	No HI	Low α	D.
	Old age dependency ratio					Unemployment rate: x				
1996	0.37	0.37	0.37	0.37	0.37	11.5	–	11.5	11.5	11.5
1997	0.37	0.37	0.37	0.37	0.37	11.0	–	11.1	11.0	11.0
2001	0.36	0.38	0.36	0.38	0.36	11.1	–	11.2	11.0	11.2
2041	0.79	0.74	0.79	0.74	0.69	11.5	–	11.2	11.4	12.3
∞	0.60	0.56	0.60	0.60	0.56	11.1	–	10.9	11.0	11.2
	Consumption tax rate: τ^c					Pension contr. rate θ^P				
1996	22.2	21.7	17.3	22.2	22.2	19.2	19.2	19.2	19.2	19.2
1997	21.8	21.6	17.3	21.7	22.2	18.7	18.7	18.8	18.7	18.8
2001	20.8	21.3	16.9	20.3	21.3	18.2	19.4	18.3	18.2	18.3
2041	27.3	23.9	18.8	26.3	26.3	30.0	28.6	30.6	28.4	29.5
∞	27.3	25.6	18.5	26.1	24.2	24.3	24.3	24.1	24.3	21.2
	Implicit pension tax: τ^P					Aggregate contr. rate: θ^{SI}				
1996	13.9	14.7	13.2	14.0	13.9	39.9	34.2	25.7	40.0	39.9
1997	13.1	13.8	11.8	13.1	13.8	38.7	33.4	24.9	38.8	39.0
2001	12.8	14.7	11.4	12.8	13.4	38.3	39.7	24.5	38.4	38.6
2041	25.0	24.3	24.2	23.3	24.6	56.7	48.9	36.9	54.8	56.3
∞	19.0	19.7	17.4	18.9	16.3	49.1	43.3	30.2	49.1	45.6
	Aggregate implicit tax: τ^{SI}					Employment per capita				
1996	30.9	29.7	15.4	31.1	31.0	1.00	1.00	1.00	1.00	1.00
1997	29.6	28.4	13.9	29.8	30.4	1.04	1.03	1.03	1.03	1.02
2001	29.3	35.0	13.5	29.3	30.1	1.04	1.02	1.04	1.04	1.03
2041	48.6	44.7	26.9	46.6	47.9	0.80	0.81	0.81	0.82	0.80
∞	40.6	38.7	19.8	40.5	37.3	0.90	0.91	0.90	0.90	0.91
	Capital stock per capita					Consumption per capita				
1996	1.00	1.00	1.00	1.00	1.00	1.00	1.00	1.00	1.00	1.00
1997	1.00	1.00	1.00	1.00	1.00	0.97	0.97	0.97	0.97	0.97
2001	1.06	1.06	1.06	1.06	1.05	0.99	0.99	0.99	1.00	0.99
2041	1.30	1.32	1.31	1.30	1.35	1.00	1.04	1.05	1.01	1.03
∞	1.08	1.09	1.17	1.11	1.17	0.94	0.97	1.01	0.95	0.98

[a]Higher deductions on pension benefits.
[b]No unemployment and no unemployment insurance.
[c]No health insurance.
[d]Slower increase in the strength of the preference for leisure.

Omitting *health insurance* changes the marginal aggregate rate of implicit tax considerably (see column 'No HI' and τ^{SI} in Table 6.7). This also affects retirement decisions. A lower implicit tax rate raises the net wage and make working more attractive compared to retiring. As a consequence the number of cohorts postponing retirement is raised. To show the effects in more detail it is useful to consider the old age dependency ratio during the whole time horizon. Figure 6.8 shows that the old age dependency ratio is relatively lower in the case without health insurance for a longer time, though there is no deviation in the long term. Additionally, there is a high increase in the long term level of the capital stock and consumption per capita. Some reasons are: a lower implicit tax rate raises net income; zero contributions to health insurance imply higher net pension benefits; higher income lead to higher consumption and savings.

The third modification, i. e. a *slower increase in the strength of the preference for leisure* (columns '*Low* α' in Table 6.7), leads to a stronger response in the retirement age. As shown in Figure 6.8 more cohorts postpone retirement during the transition. Therefore the old age dependency ratio is lower during some periods of the transition. In addition at the peak and shortly afterwards the old age dependency ratio is also lower, since individuals retire one year later on average. The ratio decreases to 0.74 in 2041. Owing to this change the rate of contribution and implicit tax are also lower in 2041. The rate of contribution to the pension system is by 1.6 percentage points lower and reaches 28.4% in 2041 compared to 30.0% in the base case. The rise in the average retirement age causes an increase in employment per capita.

There are also significantly high welfare effects as shown in Table 6.8. *Omitting unemployment* ('No UI') reduces the welfare gains of the initially younger pensioners, raises welfare losses of the middle-aged cohorts, and raises welfare gains of the future cohorts. The younger cohorts 1966 and 1976 are worse off compared to the case with unemployment (base case). Welfare gains amount to only 78% of the welfare improvement occurring in the base case.

If the model is modified by *omitting health insurance* ('No HI') the signs are also unchanged. Again, the difference in welfare and excess burden

Table 6.8: Pension Act of 1992: sensitivity analysis – differences in utility to base case

	Pension Act of 1992				High
Year of birth	Base Case	No UI[b]	No HI[c]	Low α^d	D[a] ΔU
ΔU					
1921	-0.11	-0.01	-0.08	-0.23	-0.41
1936	0.59	0.26	0.51	0.64	0.90
1946	-1.32	-1.33	-1.53	-1.21	-1.72
1966	0.70	0.35	0.44	0.89	1.55
1976	1.58	1.11	1.33	1.92	3.10
1996	2.99	3.09	2.81	3.19	4.84
∞	4.78	5.20	3.85	4.16	7.06
$\sum$	0.50	0.39	0.37	0.69	1.11
ΔEB					
1921	0	0.01	0.01	-0.01	0
1936	0.02	0.02	0.02	0.04	0.06
1946	0.46	0.28	0.33	0.61	0.92
1966	0.45	0.28	0.26	0.58	1.10
1976	0.80	0.56	0.49	0.84	1.64
1996	1.50	1.34	0.99	1.57	2.65
∞	2.03	2.21	1.23	1.91	3.20
$\sum$	0.53	0.35	0.36	0.61	1.08

In percentage points of remaining lifetime resources
[a]Higher deductions from pension benefits.
[b]No unemployment insurance.
[c]No health insurance.
[d]Slower increase in the strength of the preference for leisure.

Figure 6.8: Act 1992: sensitivity analysis – old-age dependency ratio

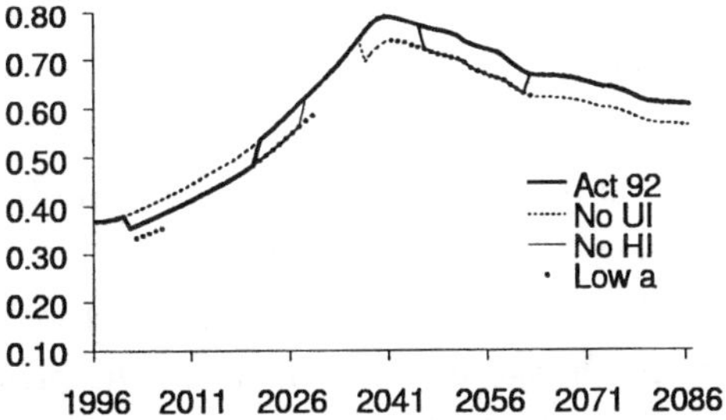

is relatively large. But, in this case, differences in welfare are mainly caused by changes in excess burden. Remember that the implicit tax rate is considerably lower while the retirement age is changed only in some periods. A lower implicit tax rate generates efficiency gains which are lower than in the base case. Also, each cohort facing lower efficiency gains is worse off in terms of utility.

Finally, let us discuss the case of the *slower increase in the strength of the preference for leisure*. The welfare effects are shown in the column 'Low α' in Table 6.8. Because of a stronger reduction in the rate of implicit and consumption tax, welfare and efficiency effects increase. Most cohorts gain while the initially eldest and future cohorts lose compared to the base case. The losses of future cohorts are caused by a higher marginal rate of wage tax, which increases since employment increases. The resulting excess burden obviously exceeds the lower excess burden induced by a falling consumption tax rate. The changes in welfare and efficiency effects are given in the last row of Table 6.8. Though they must be equal, they in fact differ. This demonstrates that the decomposition is again not very good since changes in retirement age differ between the main simulation and the simulation of the substitution effects. Welfare is 38% higher than in the base case. These results show, that the pattern of the strength of the preference for leisure affects the pension system. The reason is that this variable determines the strength of the response of the retirement age to policy changes.

6.5.3 Higher Deductions

One aim of the Pension Act of 1992 was to raise the average retirement age. For this reason the mandatory retirement age was raised and deductions were introduced. Since the first draft of the Pension Act has been published a number of authors have argued that deductions are too low since they are not actuarially fair (for instance Schmähl, 1990, Genosko, 1993 and Breyer, Kifmann and Stolte, 1997). In Hirte (1999a) we raised objections to this view since the change in utility and not the present value of net pension benefits is the really significant variable. We also suggested higher deductions as incentives for postponing retirement. This discussion is in line with the findings presented above. The 3.6% deduction rate on pension benefits is not a sufficient incentive to postpone retirement. We describe below an additional experiment, where the deduction rate is raised to 7% for each year in which retirement is postponed beyond the mandatory retirement age.

The high deduction forces individuals to delay retirement and the average retirement age increases initially to 64 and then reduces to 63 and later to 62. Therefore the old age dependency ratio falls in the medium term to 0.69 instead of 0.79 and in the long term to 0.56 compared to 0.60 (see column 'High D.' in Table 6.7). This implies a relatively lower rate of contribution to the pension system. According to Table 6.7 the rate is 0.5 percentage points lower after forty five years and 3.1 percentage points lower in the long term. It is more than surprising that the reduction in the rate of contribution to the pension system is so low in 2041, considering that the average retirement age is raised by 2 years for the newly retiring cohorts during this year compared to the base case. One can explain this puzzling information by looking at employment. Despite the relative rise in the length of the working life of two years, employment per capita is lower with high deductions in the short term. Therefore employment of the middle-aged and younger cohorts has to be lower than in the base case, since additional employment of the elderly due to a longer working life requires a reduction in employment of the younger cohorts for employment to fall. Since the wages of the elderly are below average a higher rate of contribution is necessary if pension expenditures are not to fall very strongly. While the length of retirement is less in the case of higher deductions in the medium term, the level of pension benefits per retiree is higher. The implicit tax rate of the pension system, τ^p, and the implicit tax rate of social insurance, τ^{SI}, are lower after forty five years by about 0.4 and 0.7 percentage points. However, in the long term the implicit tax rate of the pension system is considerably lower than in the case of the Pension Act of 1992.

The merits of this proposal seem to be mainly in the long term. But, especially at the peak of the problems of social insurance, it might cause only a small reduction in the rate of contribution to the public pension system. As shown in Table 6.8 welfare effects tend to differ between cohorts. The cohorts entering retirement during the first years of the reform cannot sufficiently adjust to the reform in advance. They are therefore worse off while young and future cohorts gain. Overall efficiency and welfare gains increase compared to the base case by 0.6 percentage points of remaining lifetime resources.

This simulation provides another result. The old age dependency ratio is not always a good indicator of the effects on the pension system. While in the 2040s it is considerably lower than in the case of the Pension Act of 1992, the rate of contribution is almost the same during these years. Hence, the old age dependency ratio might be misleading when considered as the only indicator for the problems of the pension system.

6.6 Conclusions

The two ways discussed in the literature to achieve an increase in the average retirement age are to increase the minimum retirement age, and to increase the statutory retirement age and simultaneously introduce deductions for early retirement (see Holzman, 1993). The latter is, for example, chosen by the U.S., and discussed in Japan and Italy. In the U.S. the 1983 reform enacted an increase in the standard retirement age from 65 to 66 by 2009, and further to 67 by 2027. Germany uses a mix of both reform schemes. However in Germany individuals can evade the higher minimum retirement age by choosing disability or invalidity retirement. For this reason we have only discussed the rise in the statutory retirement age. If the deductions are actuarially fair, the pension system becomes actuarially fair in the marginal case.

Though the deductions stipulated in the German Pension Act of 1992 are not actuarially fair, the simulations described above produced an increase in the average retirement age by one year during the first 25 years of the transition. This reform, though very successful in mitigating financial problems of the pension system, reduces the welfare of the currently middle-aged generations. The reason is that individuals are not compensated for a longer working life. Hence the reform is not Pareto improving but redistributes from currently middle-aged to young and future cohorts who gain by the decrease in the rates of contribution. We have found evidence in another study (Hirte, 1999a) that there might be an alternative reform scheme which is Pareto improving. This scheme aims at raising the average retirement age by granting supplements to the pension benefits if individuals postpone retiring beyond the age of 60. Unfortunately, we have simulated only a small population decrease in that study. If one considers the strong aging trend Germany is facing, the result is no longer true. As has been demonstrated in this chapter, granting supplements does not provide a Pareto improving easing of the financial problems of the social insurance system in the German case. A reduction of the financial strain on the public pension system is much easier achieved by implementing the German Pension Act of 1992 than by only introducing incentives. Hence from the perspective of the stability of the pension system, the German Pension Act is not a bad policy. But this reform is at the expense of the cohorts currently of middle age.

Chapter 7

Changing the Tax Base

7.1 Introduction

In the following we examine the effects of a switch from payroll to consumption taxation. According to Auerbach and Kotlikoff (1987a) consumption taxation provides efficiency gains compared to payroll or income taxation. Fehr (1999a) has recently replicated this result for Germany. The reason for the efficiency gains is that consumption taxes, provided they do not differ too strongly between periods, have a lump sum tax component and therefore cause lower intertemporal substitution effects. Since a consumption tax is the most efficient of the major types of taxes, switching from payroll to consumption taxation as a source of revenue of the pension system should provide considerable efficiency gains. As the simulations of Hirte and Weber (1997a and b) and Kotlikoff (1996) show, the size of these gains depend on the tax benefit linkage built into the pension formula and, thus, on the implicit tax rate of the pension system. If the former is zero the implicit tax rate equals the rate of contribution. Then the reform, provided it is revenue neutral, yields very large efficiency gains as shown by Auerbach and Kotlikoff (1987a). If the tax benefit linkage is not zero, which is the case in Germany, efficiency gains caused by the abolishment of the implicit tax rate are lower. As a consequence a switch to consumption taxation does not unambiguously enhance efficiency (Hirte and Weber, 1997b). Moreover, the effects depend on revenues required if the tax base is changed and the relative size of the tax base. Since in the German pension system the size of pension benefits depends on net wages, the pension benefits and, thus, the expenditure by the pension system increase when consumption taxes replace payroll taxes. If this interrelationship is not altered the tax reform no longer yields the same revenue. Consequently consumption taxes have to be raised further and efficiency gains can be expected to be lower (see Hirte and Weber, 1997b).

Furthermore, as a consumption tax disadvantages the pensioners such a reform induces intergenerational redistribution effects in favor of the middle-aged, young and future cohorts. These effects could be expected to be very large if there is a full switch to financing by consumption tax. On the other hand, higher pension benefits occurring due to the net wage adjustment rule compensate the elderly for a higher consumption tax rate and should therefore reduce intergenerational redistribution effects. This is another indication that there is a trade-off between efficiency and redistribution effects.

Although a full switch to consumption taxation promises to generate a 'wonderland of efficiency' compared with the status quo, it is not considered a feasible policy reform scheme in the debate in Germany. The reason is that this implies an extremely strong increase in the consumption tax rate to a level which would presumably not be accepted by the majority of the voters. Nonetheless the message of the efficiency of consumption taxation has reached the politicians. The former as well as the current German government have raised consumption taxes in order to lower the rate of contribution to the pension system. In 1998 the value-added tax rate has been raised from 15% to 16%, while in 1999, 2000, and 2001 energy taxes have been raised. A large part of the additional tax revenue has been used to increase grants to the pension system and lower the rate of contribution. Of course, these are very small steps compared to a full switch in the tax base but they show the direction in which future pension reforms might go.

In addition the German government has suspended the net wage adjustment in pension benefits in 2000 and 2001. Instead pension benefits are adjusted according to the inflation rate. Since income tax reforms and the rise in governmental grants to the pension system reduce the aggregate taxation of wages, tying pension benefits to net wages raises the size of pension benefits and, thus, pension outlays and the rate of contribution.

In order to enhance the positive effects of policy reforms on labor income it would therefore be useful to suspend the net wage adjustment if taxation is reduced. This, however, would produce stronger redistribution effects.

While the policy reforms of 1999 and 2000 do not further change the pension formula, another question arises. How should pension benefits be calculated when a growing part of the budget of the pension system is collected by consumption taxation? Should benefits be linked to income or contributions, or should they be flat benefits? Regardless of other effects it is clear that switching to flat benefits raises the implicit tax rate and thus creates efficiency losses compared to the case of benefits depending on income.

Nonetheless, almost all proposals recommending a switch to consumption taxation also promote flat benefits. We postpone the problem of flat benefits until section 9.3.1 and focus in this chapter on the following issue: what are the effects and problems of a full or partial switch to consumption taxation? First, a full switch, either implemented at once or gradually, is examined. While this experiment is not very realistic, it shows the maximum amount of welfare gains which can be achieved by using the more efficient consumption tax. This general information can be used to assess the direction of the effects of other reform schemes which propose a partial switch to consumption taxation. We consider two proposals for such a partial switch: these are the actual German pension reform of 1999 and the same reform but with a stronger rise in the consumption tax rate spread over ten years.

7.2 Switching Taxation

7.2.1 Effects of Consumption Taxation

As discussed above the German pension system establishes a positive tax benefit linkage and a positive implicit tax rate of the pension system. This implicit tax rate is equivalent to a payroll tax. As long as it is not equal to zero it distorts the intratemporal leisure/consumption decision. Provided this implicit tax rate is the same in all periods no intertemporal substitution effects arise during the working life. However due to retirement some intertemporal substitution effects occur between the working and retirement life. Moreover, as the implicit tax rate of the pension system depends on age, some intertemporal substitution effects occur during the working life. Since the implicit tax rate decreases with age, the price of leisure increases and leisure now is substituted for leisure later on.

If a constant *implicit* payroll tax is replaced by a lump sum tax all distortions of the payroll tax vanish (Breyer and Straub, 1993). If it is replaced by an *explicit* payroll tax no gains in efficiency occur (Fenge, 1995). In our experiments, however, the rate of contribution is replaced by a consumption tax which is also distortionary. Moreover, abolishing the rate of contribution but not the tax benefit linkage implies a negative implicit tax rate of the pension system. Thus this reform is equivalent to lowering the implicit tax rate by exactly the size of the rate of contribution.

A consumption tax distorts the intratemporal leisure/consumption decision during working life and the intertemporal leisure/consumption choice between working life and retirement. Hence the consumption tax also has a payroll tax component. On the other hand, imposing the consumption tax on the elderly is like imposing a non-distortionary wealth tax, provided individuals are not permitted to work or are not willing to work during retirement, and the tax rate does not change across time. Hence consumption taxation has also a wealth tax component which is neutral with respect to efficiency.

Of course, the consumption tax induces additional distortions if the tax rate varies with time — a case relevant during the transition. Then the intertemporal consumption decisions as well as the leisure/consumption decision are distorted. Moreover as Sandmo (1985, p.278) has shown, the net effect of the leisure/consumption distortion on the path of consumption and wealth accumulation cannot be derived unequivocally. Due to these different interactions simulations are needed to determine the overall efficiency effects of this structural tax reform. In addition in a general equilibrium model the effects described above lead to many other effects not considered up to now.

Auerbach and Kotlikoff (1987a) have carried out the first comprehensive study of the efficiency and welfare effects of a switch to consumption taxation[1]. However, in their simulations the tax reform yields the same revenue whereas in our case the revenue of the consumption tax differs from the revenue from the original payroll or implicit tax rate. The reasons for this are that revenue from consumption tax has to replace revenue collected via contributions, not implicit pension taxes, and, that pension benefits differ according to the net wage adjustment rule. The enlargement of the tax base is particularly high in the year of the reform since a consumption tax is levied on consumption of all cohorts, while a payroll tax only taxes labor income of the working cohorts. Hence there are two opposite effects. The enlargement of the tax base allows the consumption tax rate to be raised by only a smaller amount than the payroll tax is reduced, but the higher revenue requirement leads to a higher consumption tax rate. It is generally known that in the case where a consumption tax has to yield higher tax revenue than the former payroll tax, the distortions caused by the consumption tax can more than offset the gains from reducing the implicit pension tax. However, as Hirte and Weber (1997b) have shown, the difference in tax revenue ought to be relatively large to neutralize the efficiency gains of the consumption tax.

[1] Of course, since AUERBACH and KOTLIKOFF (1987a) have presented their seminal study many other simulations have been carried out which examine the effects of a switch from other taxes to different kind of consumption taxes. A comprehensive survey of the literature on this switch is provided by FEHR (1999a, pp. 122–130). Among the CGE studies examining the transformation from a corporate to a cash-flow based consumption tax are KEUSCHNIGG (1991), HUTTON and KENC (1996), and FEHR (1999a). In his study FREDERIKSEN (1997) replaces the Danish income tax by a combination of a cash-flow and a proportional wage tax. A similar experiment has been carried out for Germany by FEHR (1999a). AUERBACH (1996) and ALTIG et. al. (1997) study the effects of performing four different types of consumption tax proposals, while KOTLIKOFF (1996) simulates a switch from the U.S. income tax system to retail sales taxes. Further studies are collected by AARON and GALE (1996), and also İMROHOROĞLU (1998). The results of different studies are compared by ENGEN, GRAVELLE and SMETTERS (1997). Despite considerable differences in the approach chosen all studies report efficiency gains from a switch to a tax system based on consumption taxes.

Figure 7.1: Full tax switch: social insurance variables

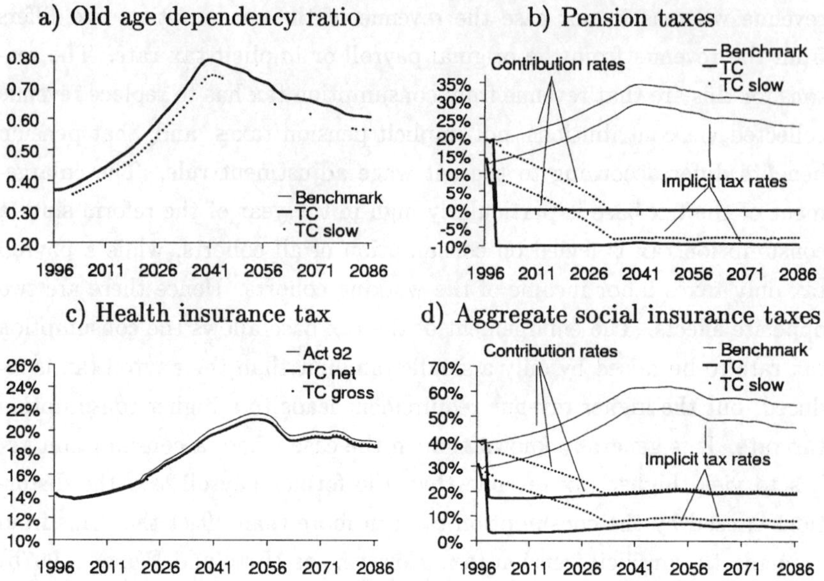

7.2.2 Consumption Tax Financing

The first experiment carried out is an immediate switch to full consumption tax financing without changing the current German pension formula. Accordingly, pension benefits grow with net wages. The second experiment is also a full switch to consumption taxation. But here the transition lasts forty years. This second reform scheme is regarded as a more realistic alternative. It is therefore accompanied by the regulations enacted in the Pension Act of 1992 and the reform scheme of 1999. The latter states that the size of pensions is adjusted only to the inflation rate in 2000 and 2001. Since inflation is not modeled this regulation is replaced by fixing the current pension value.

Macroeconomic Effects

Let us discuss first the *immediate full switch.* As discussed above, welfare effects depend on the relative change in tax rates and, therefore, on tax revenue required to finance pension benefits and the implicit tax rate. In

Figure 7.2: Full tax switch: social insurance variables

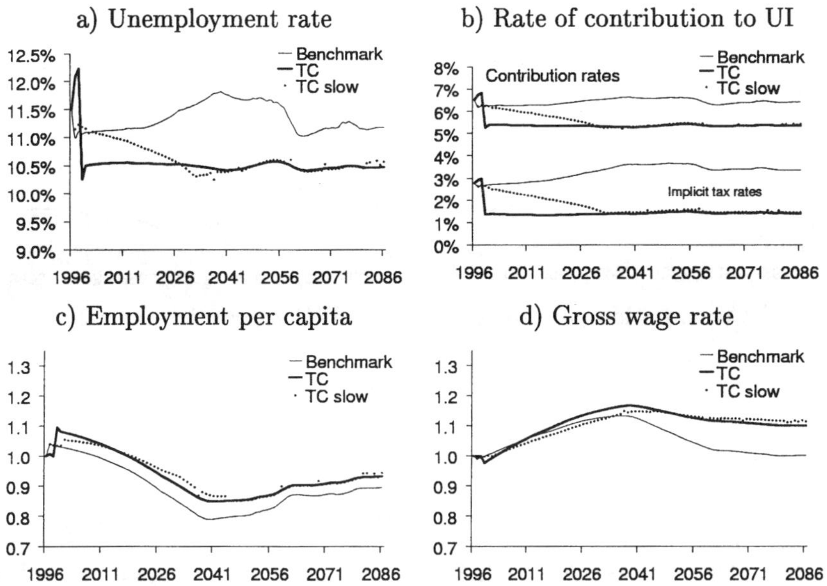

the case of the net wage adjustment, pension benefits increase initially because the reduction in the implicit tax rate raises net wages and thus pension benefits. This leads to a rise in pension benefits so that they reach about 131% of the size of pension benefits in the benchmark case. This is equivalent to a replacement rate of 70.2%, approximately the same level as computed in the benchmark case. Obviously the growth in pension benefits is quite close to the growth in net wages. This is a result of the German formula for the current pension value (see 2.32).

The change in the rate of contribution to the pension system implies a very substantial reduction in the aggregate rate of implicit tax, as shown by Figure 7.1(d). This effect is enhanced by the reduction in the rate of contribution to health insurance which is a result of the rise in employment.

The old age dependency ratio is not affected by this reform (see Figure 7.1(a)). Assume individuals prefer retiring one year later to retiring now. Owing to the longer working life they lose the pension benefits of a year but are entitled to receive higher pensions in the future. After all benefits depend on relative income and the length of the working life which increases

Figure 7.3: Full tax switch: macro variables 2

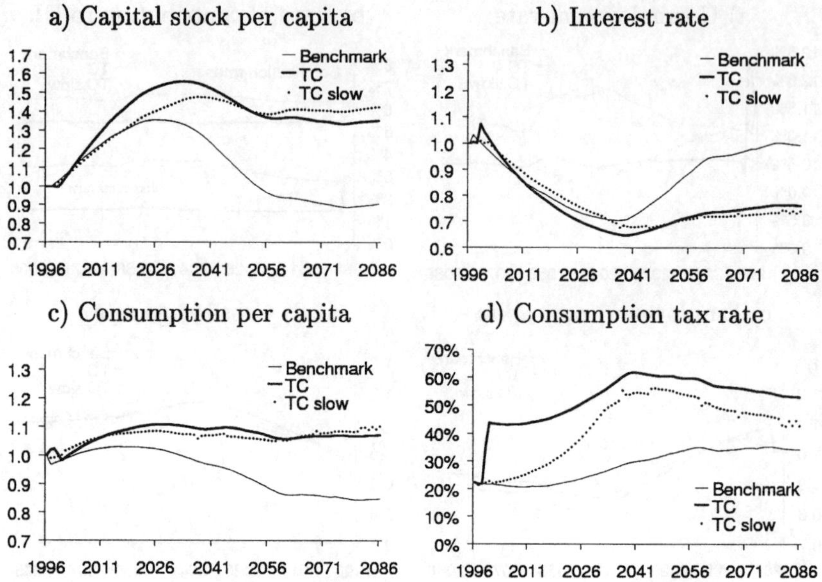

in this case. But it appears that this positive change in the present value of additional pension benefits is not high enough to compensate the individual for changes in utility caused by a postponement of his retirement age. Consequently the retirement age stays at its benchmark level.

Figure 7.2 shows that employment and unemployment are strongly affected even though the average retirement age does not change. The relatively lower rise in the consumption tax rate in comparison with the reduction in the rate of contribution leads to a relatively lower payroll tax component. As a result the relative price of leisure increases and individuals substitute consumption for leisure and labor supply increases. The rise in the supply of labor puts a downward pressure on gross wages and, thus, enhances demand for labor and employment. Since the implicit tax rate is higher the younger the individual, the younger cohorts increase their labor supply more than the older working cohorts. As the younger have a lower rate of unemployment the aggregate rate of unemployment decreases. These results and the reduction in the contributions to the pension system paid by unemployment insurance lower the rate of contribution to unemployment insurance. However, in the short term, the elder individuals increase their labor supply to compensate for higher consumption tax liability in the future. Hence aggregate labor supply becomes 'older' in the years after the announcement. It follows that unemployment increases immediately after the announcement.

The change in the dynamic behavior of taxation reduces intertemporal substitution effects since taxation is more smoothed over the whole life of the individual. This increases tax liabilities of the old and reduces tax liabilities of the young. To compensate for lower income in the future, individuals accumulate more assets. This explains why in panel (a) of Figure 7.3 the capital stock is relatively higher than in the benchmark case after some years. The production sector employs more capital and labor and raises production. As a consequence income and consumption increase. The former implies higher revenue from income tax and the latter a broadening of the consumption tax base. Both allow the consumption tax rate to be lowered so that the deviation from the benchmark rate is reduced (see panel (c) and (d) of Figure 7.3).

The *second reform scheme* is supposed to produce smaller effects during the transition since the consumption tax rate is phased in while the rate of contribution is phased out. The impact on the social insurance system, shown by the graphs 'TC slow' in Figure 7.1, shows that the effects are still large. The gradual rise in the consumption tax rate to over 54% in 2041, which is documented in Figure 7.3(d), allows the rate of contribution to the pension system and, thus, the implicit tax rate to be lowered. Since pensions are tied to former income, the implicit tax rate of the pension system becomes negative after 2028. In 2033 it reaches its minimum value of -8%. Therefore the true wage increases and working becomes more attractive than retiring. Consequently retirement is postponed in some years compared to the Pension Act of 1992. Panel (a) of Figure 7.1 shows the impact on the old age dependency ratio. It is close to the ratio computed until 2021 for the Pension Act of 1992. Then the old age dependency ratio returns to the benchmark case for the Pension Act of 1992, i. e. the average retirement age falls from 61 to 60. However, under the current scheme for reform this ratio stays below the benchmark level until 2044, except in one year. In comparison with the immediate switch to consumption taxation the incentives to retire later increase due to the Pension Act of 1992, which is included in the second scheme.

There are two major reasons why labor supply is also affected: first, the reduction in the implicit tax rate, and, second, the postponement of retirement both increase labor supply. However, the first is of minor significance in the year of reform. But it becomes more important with time since implicit taxes are phased out. For these reasons the aggregate labor supply is older in the year of reform and the average rate of unemployment is higher than in the case of the instantaneous switch to consumption taxation. But with time younger cohorts supply more labor and the average age of the supply decreases. This explains the decline in the rate of unemployment during the transition period, as shown in panel (a) of Figure 7.2. Though the rate of unemployment is still higher than in the 'TC' scenario after some years, employment per capita is raised (see panel (c) of Figure 7.2). Figure 7.1 shows that this lowers the rate of contribution to health insurance, which in turn increases the reduction in the aggregate rate of implicit tax. Furthermore, the switch to the more efficient tax stimulates consumption per capita. Altogether, the aggregate rate of contribution falls from about 40% in 1996 to 19% in 2032, a reduction of 21 percentage points. Thereafter it stays between 21.5% and 19%. The implicit tax rate decreases from 31% to 7.5–9.5%.

Welfare Effects

As the initially old cohorts cannot change labor supply, raising the consumption tax rate reduces their possibilities for consumption. The longer the remaining retirement life the larger is this effect. In contrast, net wages and thus the money value of the personal earning points increase. This raises pension benefits with a time lag of one year compared to the change in net wages. In the case of the instantaneous switch in taxation the latter effect is too small to offset the higher net tax liabilities. Therefore the utility of the cohort retiring in 1996, i. e. cohort 1936, decreases. Due to the slow speed of adjustment both effects cancel out in the second experiment so that the initial retirees do not lose (see Table 7.1).

Table 7.1: Full tax switch: decomposition of changes in utility

Year of birth	$T^{C\,a}$				T^C gradual[b]			
	ΔU^c	ΔP^d	$-\Delta T^e$	ΔEB^f	ΔU	ΔP	$-\Delta T$	ΔEB
1921	-0.07	-0.05	0.04	0.01	0.01	0.05	-0.06	0
1936	-2.67	4.26	-6.89	-0.20	0.07	0.79	-1.21	-0.03
1946	-1.51	6.87	-9.21	0.83	-2.07	-0.71	-2.59	0.48
1956	0.51	9.72	-10.81	1.74	-0.58	1.82	-3.91	0.72
1966	3.17	12.59	-11.40	2.39	1.32	4.23	-4.42	1.20
1976	6.48	17.15	-13.30	3.37	3.75	7.55	-5.27	1.92
1986	9.73	20.60	-15.90	5.33	6.78	13.27	-8.25	3.61
1996	12.62	24.78	-18.81	6.88	10.70	20.52	-12.90	5.87
2006	15.80	29.06	-21.91	8.77	14.97	27.36	-17.92	8.43
2016	18.55	31.28	-23.95	10.30	18.51	30.12	-20.87	10.47
∞	16.61	24.52	-19.73	7.91	17.88	23.36	-16.84	8.15
$\sum$	1.99	-1.32		2.12	1.48	-0.89		1.33

All changes in per cent of all remaining lifetime resources.
[a]Full consumption tax financing of pensions.
[b]Gradual transition to a pension system fully financed by a consumption tax. This transition is introduced at the same time as the Pension Act of 1992 and the pension reform of 1999.
[c]Change in utility.
[d]Change in net pension benefits.
[e]Change in net tax liabilities.
[f]Change in efficiency.

Similar effects occur for all younger cohorts. They face higher tax liabilities due to a higher consumption tax rate, but benefit from the reduction in the rate of contribution and the rise in pensions. Since their savings in expenses for contributions accumulate over their remaining working life, changes in net pension benefits are greater the younger they are. An analogous reasoning applies to efficiency effects. As the implicit tax rate is higher for the younger cohorts while the consumption tax rate is the same, they experience efficiency gains which are higher than those of the elder working cohorts. Adding up these effects produces changes in utility which grow from cohort to cohort but with a decreasing rate until 2040. Then all initially working generations are retired and some of these effects vanish.

Equally, changes in income and efficiency effects as well as in utility are higher the younger the cohort in the case of a gradual switch to consumption taxation. However the rate of growth of all effects increases. The reason is that the consumption tax rate increases until the 2040s while the implicit tax rate decreases. In this case the initially eldest working cohorts lose. But the reduction in the implicit tax rate is low in their last working years. Accordingly, the first experiment causes an intergenerational redistribution from the cohorts born between 1921 and 1946 to the younger cohorts. The second reform scheme redistributes from the middle-aged to all others but most to the younger cohorts.

Welfare and efficiency gains add up to 2% of the present value of all remaining lifetime resources in the instantaneous tax switch scenario and to 1.5% in the gradual scheme. These gains are achieved at the expense of redistribution. The index of the amount of redistribution is -1.32% in the first and -0.89% in the second case. This is further evidence that there is a trade-off between efficiency and distribution.

These experiments are not at all realistic policy choices. The consumption tax rate exceeds 55%, a level which would presumably not be accepted by the voters and is hardly feasible in an open economy. Nonetheless these experiments provide something like an upper ceiling for efficiency gains which can be achieved by using consumption taxes to finance the pension system. For this reason we will not further discuss these experiments, leave out the sensitivity analysis, and consider other reform schemes. In the next section we examine a partial switch to consumption taxation which is a more realistic proposal.

7.3 A Partial Switch in Taxation

The former German government has enacted a partial switch to financing by consumption tax. In 1998 the value-added tax rate was raised from 15% to 16% to finance higher grants to the pension system. The present government has continued in this direction by raising energy taxes in 1999, 2000, and 2001. The additional tax revenue is used to finance higher grants to the pension system.

In the late nineties a new debate was initiated focusing on the link between the growth of pension benefits and net wages. The income tax and pension reform schemes, either enacted or intended, narrow the gap between gross and net wages. Though the net wage adjustment maintains the relative standard of living of pensioners it burdens the pension system in a situation where wage taxes decrease. The reason is that a reduction in the wage tax raises net wages and, thus, implies higher pension benefits in the subsequent periods. This, in turn, causes an increase in the rate of contribution to the pension system, and, finally, puts pressure on the government budget since grants to the pension system have to be raised. The latter effect occurs since the grants from the government to the pension system are linked to the rate of contribution. This is stipulated in the Pension Act of 1992. For this reason each income tax reform imposes a 'double burden' on the federal budget.

These are some of the reasons why the government decided in 1999 to suspend the net wage adjustment for at least two years. Instead, pension benefits are regulated to grow only at the inflation rate in 2000 and 2001. This policy marks a first departure from the net wage adjustment rule. It raises the question whether a fixed rule is better than a discretionary adjustment or a mixture of both. The answer depends on the purpose. If the intention is to maintain the relative standard of living of retirees, the net wage adjustment rule should be applied. If, however, the purpose is to reduce the financial pressure on the pension system, pension benefits should be tied to net wages in times of rising taxes and contributions but to gross wages or the inflation rate if the tax burden on wages is lowered. Since some experiments not reported in this study have shown that a permanent return to a gross wage adjustment rule is out of the question – it would initially reduce the replacement rate but after some years it would easily exceed 70% – we refrain from examining these rules in this study. Instead we focus on the rise in consumption taxes and government grants. Additionally, the two year postponement of the net wage adjustment in pension benefits is included. But as there is no inflation in the model we assume pension benefits to be constant during these two years. In a second step the same reform is simulated except that grants and the consumption tax rate are now raised over a period of ten years. In other words, we assume that the switch to financing by consumption tax started is carried on in the future.

7.3.1 Proposal 1: Reform of 1999

Although the activities of the new German government also include other changes affecting the pension system, our investigation is confined to the partial switch to financing by consumption tax and the way the size of pensions is tied to wages. Another reform which strongly affects the pension system is the introduction of a liability to social insurance for the so-called 630 German Marks jobs and self-employed who are actually not independent. These regulations cannot be examined in the model used in this study, since we consider only one representative individual per cohort. Instead we could examine the effects of raising contributions to the social insurance system from pensioners who have a 630 Marks job. Due to the new regulations these pensioners have to pay contributions but do not obtain additional claims against the social insurance system. On account of health contributions which they pay from their pensions they already have health insurance. And, since the size of pension benefits depends only on income earned before retirement they cannot raise their pensions by working after retiring. Therefore this reform is equivalent to levying a tax on wages earned after retiring. Since in the model pensioners are allowed to work up to an upper time limit, which mirrors the income ceiling of 630 Marks, this extension of the contribution tax base could be simulated in this model. Nonetheless we refrain from implementing this in this study in order to focus on changes in the type of tax or pension benefits.[2]

Let us now turn to the regulations governing the partial switch to financing by consumption tax and the wage adjustment of pension benefits. We model this policy change by raising the rate of grant to the pension system by 2.5% in 1998, 1999, and 2000. Since the government budget is balanced by adjusting consumption taxes, raising the rate of grant implies, ceteris paribus, an increase in the consumption tax rate. In addition pension benefits are kept constant in 2000 and 2001. Here our implementation differs from the reform of the German government. Since a change in consumption taxation accelerates inflation an accurate modeling of this reform scheme could be implemented by adjusting pension benefits accord-

[2] In Hirte (2000a) this specific feature of the reform of 1999 has been taken into account. This changes the results for some years.

ing to the growth of the consumption tax rate. However, due to the lack of economic growth such a scheme would cause an almost constant replacement rate. In contrast, the reform of 1999 was expected to decrease the replacement rate to about 67%. For this reason we decided to fix the size of net pension benefits. Moreover, in order to evaluate the policy reform of the German government we also consider the rise in the mandatory retirement age and the introduction of deductions to pension benefits in the case of early retirement. These are the regulations of the Pension Act of 1992 which become effective in the year 2001. It is therefore appropriate to use the results of the simulation of the Pension Act of 1992 as the base case.

Social Insurance and Macroeconomic Effects

The effects on the social insurance sector and other macroeconomic changes are shown in Figure 7.4, Figure 7.5, and Figure 7.6. The reform of 1999 is shown as the curves called 'R99', while the base case is represented by the curves called 'Act 92'.

Figure 7.4 shows that the average retirement age behaves exactly as computed for the Pension Act of 1992, except in 2022. Obviously, the decrease in the replacement rate from 70.1% to 68.5%, which is caused by fixing the size of pension benefits in 2000 and 2001, as well as the reduction in the rate of contribution, which is the result of the lower pension level, have only a small effect on the retirement decision. The changes in these variables cause the true wage, the decisive variable for the retirement decision, to change in the opposite direction. Remember that the true wage is defined as the changes in the value of time endowment plus unemployment benefits plus the change in the present value of pension benefits when working instead of retiring minus pensions not received when working (see equation (2.29) on page 35). A lower rate of contribution as well as lower pension benefits raise the true wage. An opposite effect is caused by the decrease in future pension benefits and, thus, in the present value of future benefits accruing when working now. Since the German system is less than actuarially fair, postponing retirement reduces the present value of pension benefits net of contribution payments. For this reason lower-

Figure 7.4: Reform of 1999: social insurance variables

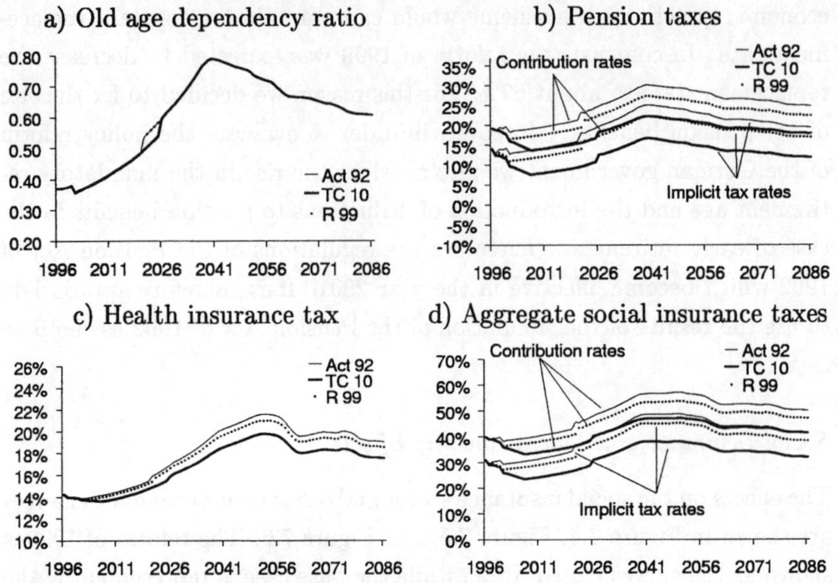

ing pension benefits also decreases the extent of this reduction and, thus, provides an incentive to retire later.

As shown in panel (a) of Figure 7.4 this effect only matters in one year. Again, the use of discrete time provides an explanation for this result. After all individuals can only retire once a year which is the chosen length of a unit of time in the simulations. Therefore, changes in the retirement age occurring in a continuous time framework only carry over into a change of the retirement age in the simulation if they are large enough. This explains why the old age dependency ratio is the same as that obtained by the simulation of the Pension Act of 1992, except for year 2022.

Panel (d) of Figure 7.6 shows that the consumption tax rate is above the level it had under the Pension Act of 1992, an outcome consistent with the reform scheme chosen in this simulation. In 2041 the consumption tax rate reaches 28.3% compared to 27.3%, the rate achieved without the reform of 1999. This difference is approximately constant thereafter. This rise in the consumption tax rate as well as the fixing of the size of pension benefits allows the rate of contribution to the pension system to be lowered

Figure 7.5: Reform of 1999: labor market

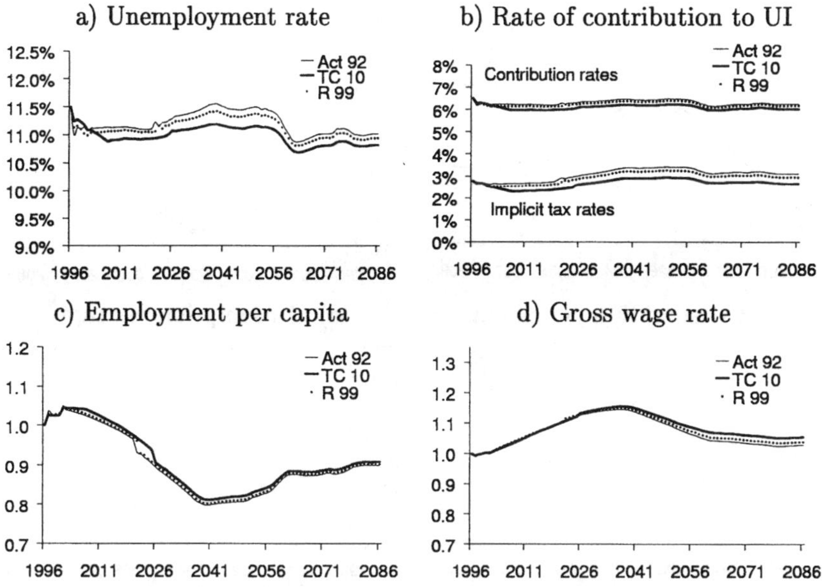

by 1.6 percentage points in 2001 (see Figure 7.4(d)). This also reduces the implicit tax rate of the pension system. The rate of contribution is 27.3% in 2041 instead of 30% without this reform, the implicit tax rate is 22% instead of 25%. This entails a decrease in the aggregate rate of contribution from 56.7% to 53.4% and a decrease in the marginal aggregate rate of implicit tax from 48.7% to 45.1% in the year 2041. Hence the reform of 1999 eases the financial problems of the pension system. Nonetheless the aggregate rate of contribution remains too high to ensure the sustainability of the social insurance system. However, in the short term considerable gains occur with respect to the aggregate contribution burden. It is not until 2021 that the contribution and implicit pension tax exceed their 1996 levels.

Since the increase in the consumption tax rate counteracts the decrease in the implicit tax rate, the sign of the change in the relative price of leisure is ambiguous. In any case, either the reduction in pension benefits which implies a negative income effect or the decrease in unemployment is the main cause of the small increase in labor supply. This is reflected by a

Figure 7.6: Reform of 1999: macro variables

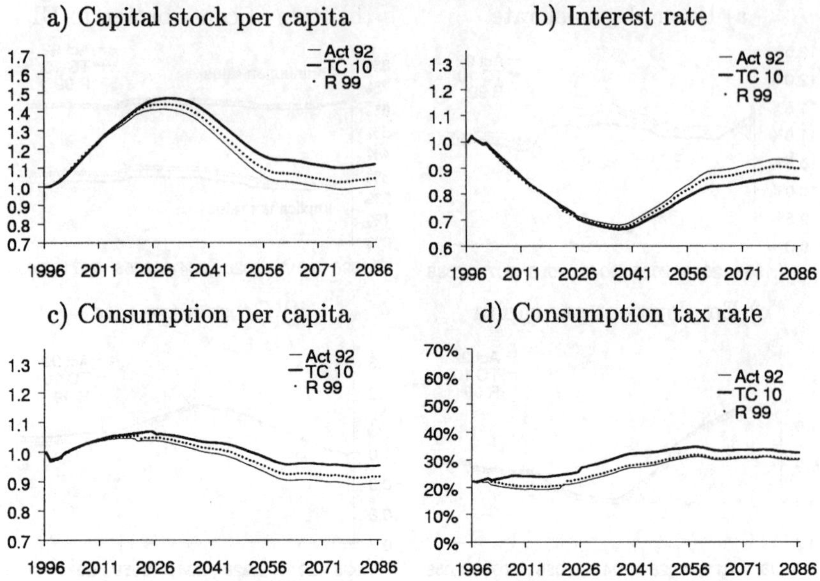

slightly higher employment rate per capita (see panel (c) of Figure 7.5). As the younger employees face the highest marginal rate of implicit tax, the reduction in this rate and, thus, a stronger increase in the marginal net wage stimulates their supply of labor more than that of the elder working cohorts. This augments the proportion of younger labor in the effective labor force. Since these cohorts are also the least unemployed the aggregate rate of unemployment decreases as shown in Figure 7.5(a).

This reform accelerates capital accumulation since individuals accumulate more assets to offset the loss of income they experience due to the reduction in the relative size and the purchasing power of their pension benefits. However, the middle-aged cohorts change the amount they save less than the younger cohorts. The former can only adjust their decisions on labor supply, consumption, and savings during the last part of their life, but the latter can do so during their whole life. This explains why panel (a) of Figure 7.6 shows that capital accumulation grows faster until all cohorts alive were born in the year of reform or later. Equally, efficiency gains induced by the switch to consumption taxation increase from cohort

Table 7.2: Reform of 1999: decomposition of changes in utility

Year of	Reform of 1999				Ten years tax rise			
birth	ΔU^a	ΔP^b	$-\Delta T^c$	ΔEB^d	ΔU	ΔP	$-\Delta T$	ΔEB
1921	-0.37	-0.03	-0.38	0.00	-0.12	-0.02	-0.10	0.01
1936	0.23	0.20	-0.12	0.02	-0.10	0.60	-0.92	-0.10
1946	-1.55	-1.78	-0.29	0.56	-1.75	-1.17	-1.31	0.59
1956	-0.20	-0.15	-0.59	0.59	-0.18	0.79	-1.78	0.75
1966	1.13	1.17	-0.63	0.76	1.47	2.53	-1.87	1.03
1976	2.43	2.15	-0.74	1.25	3.26	4.16	-2.18	1.67
1986	3.45	2.94	-0.99	1.77	5.00	6.03	-3.11	2.65
1996	4.32	3.45	-1.36	2.20	6.35	7.08	-3.81	3.32
2006	5.16	3.85	-1.73	2.59	7.56	7.79	-4.57	4.06
2016	6.04	4.26	-1.99	3.02	8.85	8.48	-5.50	4.69
∞	6.12	3.40	-1.70	2.56	8.71	6.84	-4.34	3.85
Σ	0.72	-0.56		0.78	1.01	-0.69		1.04

All changes in per cent of all remaining lifetime resources.
[a]Change in utility.
[b]Change in net pension benefits.
[c]Change in net tax liabilities.
[d]Change in efficiency effects.

to cohort. Both effects and the rise in employment per capita augment consumption per capita (see panel (c) of Figure 7.6).

Welfare Effects

All these effects determine the changes in utility, income and efficiency effects which are shown in Table 7.2.

Since changes in pension taxes are subsumed under net pension liabilities and consumption taxes under tax liabilities, a switch from contributions to consumption tax causes positive income effects due to higher net pension benefits, ΔP, and negative income effects due to a rise in net tax liabilities. This transfer of tax burden reflects the shift from implicit to explicit taxation. These effects increase with the level of the implicit tax rate and the remaining length of life. Therefore net tax liabilities increase from the elderly to the young and future generations. They are higher than in the case of the Pension Act of 1992 due to the rise in the con-

Table 7.3: Reform of 1999 - net wage adjustment: sensitivity analysis – macro effects

	Reform of 1999[a]				Reform of 1999			
Year of birth	Base Case	No UI[b]	No HI[c]	Low α[d]	Base Case	No UI	No HI	Low α
	Old age dependency ratio				Unemployment rate: x			
1996	0.37	0.37	0.37	0.37	11.5	–	11.5	11.5
1997	0.37	0.37	0.37	0.37	11.1	–	11.2	11.1
2001	0.36	0.36	0.36	0.36	11.0	–	11.2	10.9
2041	0.79	0.74	0.79	0.74	11.4	–	11.1	11.5
∞	0.60	0.56	0.60	0.60	11.0	–	10.9	10.9
	Consumption tax rate: τ^c				Pension contr. rate: θ^P			
1996	22.2	21.7	17.3	22.2	19.2	19.2	19.2	19.2
1997	22.0	21.8	17.4	21.9	18.7	18.8	18.8	18.8
2001	22.1	21.8	18.0	21.6	16.5	16.5	16.6	16.5
2041	28.3	24.7	19.7	27.9	27.3	26.1	27.9	26.6
∞	28.2	26.2	19.3	27.3	22.4	22.4	22.2	22.4
	Implicit pension tax: τ^P				Aggregate contr. rate: θ^{SI}			
1996	13.9	14.7	13.2	14.0	39.9	34.2	25.6	40.0
1997	13.0	13.8	11.7	13.1	38.9	33.6	25.0	39.1
2001	10.9	11.6	9.6	11.0	36.3	31.0	22.7	36.4
2041	22.2	21.8	21.5	21.3	53.4	46.0	34.1	52.6
∞	16.9	17.7	15.4	16.8	46.8	41.1	28.3	46.7
	Aggregate implicit tax: τ^{SI}				Employment per capita			
1996	30.9	29.7	15.4	31.1	1.00	1.00	1.00	1.00
1997	29.6	28.5	13.8	29.8	1.03	1.03	1.03	1.03
2001	27.1	26.1	11.6	27.2	1.05	1.04	1.04	1.05
2041	45.1	41.6	24.0	44.1	0.80	0.82	0.81	0.82
∞	38.0	36.3	17.6	37.9	0.90	0.91	0.91	0.90
	Capital stock per capita				Consumption per capita			
1996	1.00	1.00	1.00	1.00	1.00	1.00	1.00	1.00
1997	1.00	1.00	1.00	1.00	0.97	0.97	0.97	0.97
2001	1.06	1.06	1.06	1.05	0.99	0.99	0.99	1.00
2041	1.33	1.35	1.35	1.33	1.01	1.05	1.06	1.02
∞	1.11	1.12	1.20	1.13	0.96	0.98	1.02	0.96

[a]Three year rise in consumption tax financing with net wage adjustment.
[b]No unemployment and no unemployment insurance.
[c]No health insurance.
[d]Slower increase in the strength of the preference for leisure.

sumption tax rate (see Table 6.7 on page 134). On the other hand income gains caused by reduced implicit taxation grow from the elderly to the young and future cohorts for the same reason. Table 7.2 also shows that all cohorts experience efficiency gains. These grow inversely to age since a longer remaining lifetime allows for the exploitation of the more efficient tax by changing individual decisions. Welfare is improved by 0.72% of the present value of all remaining lifetime resources. Hence, the reform of 1999 enhances the welfare gain caused by the Pension Act of 1992, which is 0.50% (see Table 6.6 on page 132) by about 50%. All differences in utility between the reform of 1999 and the Pension Act of 1992 are mainly due to differences in efficiency effects. Looking at these tables we see that the reform of 1999 generates a redistribution in favor of the young and future cohorts compared to the Pension Act of 1992. This is caused by the partial switch from a tax levied on the working population to a tax collected from all cohorts but relatively more from elder cohorts. This intergenerational redistribution is reflected by aggregate negative income effects which add up to -0.56% of all remaining lifetime resources, compared to only -0.44% in the case of the Pension Act of 1992 (see Table 6.7). On account of the additional redistribution effects which occur due to a higher consumption tax rate, this value is absolutely higher than without the reform of 1999.

Sensitivity Analysis

The results of the simulation without unemployment and unemployment insurance, called 'No UI', without health insurance, 'No HI', and with a higher elasticity of retiring, 'Low α', are shown in Table 7.3 and Table 7.4.

Remember that the reform of 1999 is carried out together with the second stage of the Pension Act of 1992. Therefore differences in the old age dependency ratio can be expected to occur between the three modifications. The reasons for a change in the average retirement age are the same as outlined in the previous chapter (see p. 135). In the following we compare Table 7.3 with Table 6.7 to give an idea of the effects of the reform of 1999 in the different versions of the model.

Let us start with the case of *full employment* ('No UI'). A lower implicit tax rate – lower by 8.9 percentage points in 2001 and 3.1 percentage points

Table 7.4: Reform of 1999: sensitivity analysis – differences in utility to base case

	Reform of 1999				Ten years tax rise			
Year of birth	Base Case	No UI[a]	No HI[b]	Low α^c	Base Case	No UI	No HI	Low α
ΔU								
1921	-0.37	-0.30	-0.32	-0.53	-0.40	-0.36	-0.32	-0.50
1936	0.23	0.07	0.09	0.38	-0.10	-0.17	-0.22	0.22
1946	-1.55	-1.56	-1.82	-1.53	-1.75	-1.66	-2.11	-1.64
1966	1.13	0.91	0.73	1.39	1.47	1.26	0.93	1.62
1976	2.43	2.05	1.94	2.77	3.26	2.85	2.44	3.38
1996	4.32	4.22	3.79	4.41	6.35	5.87	5.15	5.89
∞	6.12	6.03	5.07	5.72	8.71	8.85	6.85	7.84
Σ	0.72	0.62	0.50	0.95	1.01	0.93	0.64	1.20
ΔEB								
1921	0	0	0	0.06	0	0.01	0	0.09
1936	0.02	0.01	0.02	-0.22	-0.01	-0.03	-0.01	-0.55
1946	0.56	0.35	0.38	0.38	0.59	-0.08	0.38	0.66
1966	0.76	0.50	0.41	0.68	1.03	0.66	0.57	0.85
1976	1.25	0.88	0.73	1.16	1.67	1.15	0.94	1.54
1996	2.20	1.96	1.35	2.27	3.32	2.90	1.92	3.29
∞	2.56	2.61	1.53	2.53	3.85	3.72	2.19	3.79
Σ	0.78	0.52	0.50	0.65	1.04	0.66	0.64	0.83

As percentage points of all remaining lifetime resources.
[a]No unemployment insurance.
[b]No health insurance.
[c]Slower increase in the strength of the preference for leisure.

in 2041 compared to the corresponding simulation for the Pension Act of 1992 – constitutes an incentive to supply more labor and retire later. This postponement effect is stronger in this sensitivity analysis than the effect of not considering unemployment. Nonetheless there is no change in the retirement age during the first part of the transition though retirement is postponed later on. The latter also occurs in the sensitivity analysis of the Pension Act of 1992, where the average retirement age decreases during the first years of the transition since individuals can compensate losses in pension benefits without raising their retirement age (see p. 135). This effect is too weak in the simulation of the reform of 1999, so that there is no change in the retirement age compared to the base case. This relatively higher retirement age implies a lower rate of contribution and implicit tax, compared to the corresponding simulation of the Pension Act of 1992. The differences to the base case, however, have the same causes as in the sensitivity analyses of the Pension Act of 1992 (see p. 132). On the other hand, most differences between the sensitivity analysis of the reform of 1999 and the Pension Act of 1992 are due to the same causes which determine the differences between both base case simulations.

When considering the case without *health insurance* ('No HI') one cannot find any noticeable differences to the interpretations given for the Pension Act of 1992. This means that the main differences between the base case simulation and the simulation of the modified model without health insurance are not affected by the reform of 1999.

A *slower rise in the strength of the preference for leisure* ('Low α') leads to a relatively higher retirement age but only in the medium term (year 2041). Therefore all deviations from the base case are only transitory. For instance, the higher average retirement age implies a reduction in both the rate of contribution to and the implicit tax rate of the pension system. Consequently aggregate rates also decrease. These changes raise employment and consumption per capita in 2041. However these effects are not as large as in the case without unemployment insurance.

Differences between the three model specifications examined are more emphasized with respect to changes in utility. Table 7.4 shows that all cohorts are worse off if *unemployment is omitted* ('No UI'). Welfare is lowered by 0.1 percentage points, almost exactly the same amount as occurs in the case of the Pension Act of 1992 (see Table 6.7 on page 134). But in that simulation individuals choose to retire earlier during the first years of the transition. This generates a higher rate of contribution and entails welfare losses for the middle-aged, younger, and future cohorts, while the elderly receive higher net pension benefits and are better off. In the case of the reform of 1999, however, there is no change in the retirement age and, thus, this intergenerational redistribution effect vanishes. Therefore redistribution in favor of the young and future cohorts is stronger. There are lower efficiency gains compared to the case with unemployment on account of a lower implicit tax rate. As efficiency gains increase approximately with the square of the tax rate, lowering the tax rate in an environment with a generally lower tax rate causes relatively lower efficiency gains. But these are higher then under the Pension Act of 1992 and future cohorts are better off due to a lower marginal rate of implicit tax.

This effect is even more pronounced in the case *without health insurance* ('No HI'). Efficiency gains for all younger and future cohorts are lower than in the case without unemployment and lower than in the base case. Therefore these welfare gains are also smaller for these cohorts. The relatively lower efficiency gains are the main reason for the reduction in the utility occurring in the case without health insurance.

Finally, consider the case of a *slower increase in the strength of the preference for leisure* ('Low α'). This implies a steeper consumption profile at the end of life. Therefore a switch to consumption tax financing disadvantages the eldest cohort but favors the initially youngest cohort in comparison to the base case. Since for almost all cohorts consumption in the future is relatively higher, efficiency losses are higher for all cohorts alive in 1996, except the youngest and the eldest. The initially eldest cohort does not experience an increase in the consumption tax rate during its remaining lifetime. For this and future cohorts there are hardly any changes, whereas all other elder cohorts experience a reduction in efficiency compared to the base case. However, changes in income effects dominate, so that almost all initially living cohorts are relatively better off than in the base case.

From these results the following conclusion can be drawn: modifications of the implementation of the social insurance system can cause considerable welfare differences. But these differences depend to a large extent on effects on the retirement decision. Consequently, the modeling of endogenous retirement is very important. But if one considers endogenous retirement it is also appropriate to model at least unemployment and unemployment insurance.

7.3.2 Proposal 2: A Ten Years Tax Rise

Since the regulations enacted in 1998 and 1999 mark a change in the financing of the pension system, one can expect that this is also the direction in which future schemes for reform will go. For this reason we perform an experiment in which the same yearly rise in financing by consumption tax takes place over ten years. We perform this by assuming that the rate of the grant is raised by 2.5% per year over ten years starting in 1998 and ending in 2007. Thereafter there is no change. Hence, the part of the pension budget financed by grants increases from about 14% in 1996 to about 39% in 2007 and beyond. In addition the regulations for the adjustment of pension benefits are the same as in the case of the reform of 1999. In 2000 and 2001 the adjustment of pension benefits to net wages is suspended. But from 2002 on benefits grow again with net wages.

Base Case

This reform is supposed to intensify all the positive effects of a tax switch. This includes raising the per capita levels of employment, the capital stock, and consumption, and lowering the interest rate and rate of unemployment. At least in the medium or long term these effects are exactly shown by Figures 7.4, 7.6, and 7.6. The rise in grants from the government lowers the rate of contribution to the pension system until 2007, when it reaches its minimum of 13.4%. This is 5.8 percentage points lower than the level reached under the Pension Act of 1992 (see panel (b) of Figure 7.4). In the course of time this difference grows to about 10 percentage points. Approximately the same reduction in the implicit tax rate of the pension system occurs, while the reduction is even higher for the aggregate rate of contribution and implicit tax (see panel (b) and (d) of Figure 7.4).

This decline in the implicit tax rate, which is stronger than in the case of the reform of 1999, raises the true wage and, thus, the incentive to lengthen the working life. However this does not entail a longer working life for most years on account of the discrete character of time and the unit of time chosen. Nevertheless the return to the benchmark path of the old age dependency ratio is postponed from 2020 to 2025. This effect is more pronounced than under the reform of 1999.

Table 7.5: Ten year tax rise: sensitivity analysis – macro effects

Year of birth	Ten year tax rise[a] Base Case	No UI[b]	No HI[c]	Low α^d	Ten year tax rise Base Case	No UI	No HI	Low α
	Old age dependency ratio				Unemployment rate: x			
1996	0.37	0.37	0.37	0.37	11.5	–	11.5	11.5
1997	0.37	0.37	0.37	0.37	11.2	–	11.2	11.2
2001	0.36	0.36	0.36	0.36	11.1	–	11.3	11.1
2041	0.79	0.79	0.79	0.79	11.2	–	10.4	11.3
∞	0.60	0.56	0.60	0.60	10.9	–	10.4	10.8
	Consumption tax rate: τ^c				Pension contr. rate: θ^P			
1996	22.2	21.7	17.3	22.2	19.2	19.2	19.2	19.2
1997	22.0	21.8	17.5	21.9	18.8	18.9	19.0	18.8
2001	22.5	22.3	18.7	21.6	15.9	16.0	16.1	16.3
2041	32.4	28.4	24.1	32.5	22.2	22.2	22.2	23.3
∞	30.7	27.8	24.0	30.4	17.8	18.1	17.9	17.8
	Implicit pension tax: τ^P				Aggregate contr. rate: θ^{SI}			
1996	13.9	14.7	13.2	14.0	39.9	34.2	25.7	39.9
1997	12.4	13.3	12.1	12.6	39.1	33.7	25.4	39.2
2001	9.7	10.6	9.2	10.3	35.8	30.6	22.3	36.4
2041	16.6	17.7	16.1	19.8	47.0	41.3	27.8	48.6
∞	11.8	12.9	11.5	11.8	41.2	35.7	23.5	41.1
	Aggregate implicit tax: τ^{SI}				Employment per capita			
1996	31.0	29.7	15.4	31.1	1.00	1.00	1.00	1.00
1997	29.1	28.1	14.2	29.4	1.03	1.02	1.03	1.02
2001	25.9	25.2	11.2	26.7	1.05	1.04	1.04	1.11
2041	38.1	36.7	18.7	17.8	0.81	0.81	0.82	0.81
∞	31.7	30.6	13.7	11.8	0.91	0.92	0.91	0.91
	Capital stock per capita				Consumption per capita			
1996	1.00	1.00	1.00	1.00	1.00	1.00	1.00	1.00
1997	1.00	1.00	1.00	1.00	0.97	0.97	0.97	0.97
2001	1.05	1.05	1.06	1.04	1.00	1.00	0.99	1.00
2041	1.38	1.40	1.40	1.38	1.03	1.07	1.07	1.03
∞	1.19	1.20	1.26	1.20	0.99	1.02	1.05	1.00

[a]Ten year rise in financing by consumption tax.
[b]No unemployment and no unemployment insurance.
[c]No health insurance.
[d]Slower increase in the strength of the preference for leisure.

The general results for welfare and distribution effects are consistent with expectations. Table 7.2 shows the relevant changes. Welfare gains amount to 1.01% of the present value of all remaining wealth. They are about a quarter higher than under the reform of 1999. This is mainly due to the efficiency property of consumption taxes. It is for the same reason that the partial switch to consumption taxation raises the efficiency gains of all cohorts not retired in 1996 compared to the reform of 1999 (see columns ΔEB in Table 7.2).

In addition higher financing by consumption tax transforms implicit taxation into explicit taxation. Therefore net pension benefits and net tax liabilities increase, except for cohort 1921. Since this proposal is identical to the reform of 1999 during the first years there are only small changes in the taxation of the initially elderly. All other cohorts suffer losses in net tax liabilities more than twice as high as in the case of the reform of 1999.

Nonetheless gains in net pension benefits and efficiency are high enough to improve utility of the cohorts born in 1956 and later compared to the reform of 1999. The cohorts 1936 and 1946 are worse off compared to the Pension Act of 1992 and the reform of 1999. Since they have to pay high consumption taxes but are restricted in adjusting their labor supply to at most some periods, their gains from lower implicit taxation are too low to compensate for additional losses caused by higher consumption taxation.

Since consumption taxation imposes additional burdens on the retirees, it creates intergenerational redistribution in favor of the young and future cohorts. This redistribution is higher in this case than with the reform of 1999. The index of the extent of redistribution is -0.69%, a value higher than in the case of the reform of 1999 and the Pension Act of 1992.

Sensitivity Analysis

The sensitivity analysis of the proposal for a ten year partial switch of taxation confirms the results qualitatively and quantitatively. The figures shown in Table 7.5 and Table 7.4 show the effects of the ten years tax rise in the base case, the model without unemployment ('No UI'), the model without health insurance ('No HI'), and the model with a higher elasticity of the retirement age ('Low α').

The retirement age is almost uniform across the different modifications. If unemployment is not modeled only the retirement age is higher in the long term and, thus, the old age dependency ratio lower. Of course there are differences in the retirement age in some years, which are not reflected in the data shown in Table 7.5. However, they are smaller than in the case of the reform of 1999. Since there is a stronger switch to consumption taxation, gains from net pension benefits are higher and individuals are more willing to postpone retiring.

The right hand side of Table 7.4 shows that all changes in utility, except of cohort 1936, have the same sign and similar size across all cohorts. The cohort 1936 is worse off in the fully specified model but is better off if the retirement age is more elastic. The reason is that the consumption demand of this cohort is lower compared to the base case due to a lower value of α. Since the consumption profile is steeper at the end of life, the switch to consumption taxation disadvantages the initially eldest cohorts more than the other variants of the model. Omitting unemployment or health insurance reduces the utility of most cohorts on account of a lower implicit tax rate. It is for the same reason that this effect is more pronounced if health insurance is not considered.

7.4 Conclusions

A switch from payroll to consumption tax financing of pension benefits is the policy recommendation which can be derived from the literature on the efficiency of different tax bases. Since the consumption tax is more efficient than a payroll tax (see Auerbach and Kotlikoff, 1987a), a full switch to consumption taxation is thought to produce very strong efficiency gains and, thus, a large improvement in welfare. The results of the simulations presented in this chapter confirm this conclusion. A full tax switch could produce an improvement in welfare and efficiency amounting to about 2% of all remaining lifetime resources. However, there is a strong trade-off between efficiency and redistribution, since consumption taxation is levied on the consumption of all cohorts while a payroll tax only burdens the working cohorts. Hence, there is a strong redistribution from the elder to the younger and future cohorts and the index of aggregate redistribution effects becomes extremely high. But it is not only due to these negative redistribution effects that such a complete switch, even if carried out gradually, is considered to be infeasible. The main reason is that the consumption tax rate would exceed 50%. Therefore the subsequent experiments focus on partial financing by consumption taxation[3].

The first of these experiments is the reform of 1999. This policy of the German government introduced a partial switch to financing by consumption tax. Though this reform includes a gradual rise in consumption taxes over a period as short as three years, the effects on the social insurance system and employment are surprisingly large. Reinforced by a two years suspension of the net wage adjustment, the rate of contribution to the pension system is lowered by 2.7 percentage points in 2041, compared to the Pension Act of 1992. The aggregate rate of contribution is reduced even more and decreases by 3.3 percentage points. The rate of contribution to the pension system does not exceed its 1996 level until 2021. This shows that the reform of 1999 is primarily a short term policy. This is in line with the intentions of the government, which has announced a more fundamental reform to be enacted in 2001. In addition there is a strong effect on employment per capita. It jumps from 105% of the initial level right after the start of the reform to about 110%.

Due to efficiency gains mainly induced by the partial switch to consumption taxation this reform improves welfare by about 50% more than the Pension Act of 1992. But due to lower pension benefits and the adverse redistribution effects of consumption taxation, negative redistribution is raised by roughly a quarter compared to the Pension Act of 1992. This additional redistribution disadvantages the cohorts aged 50 and older but favors all other cohorts. Due to this effect it is not surprising that the new government came under strong pressure after announcing the reform of 1999. Carrying on this policy by raising grants from the government for a further seven years would strengthen most of these effects. Welfare is even more improved but redistribution is reduced. Both reform schemes alleviate the financial stress which aging puts on the pension system. But

[3]A switch to a pension system financed by mixed consumption and income tax is considered in the next chapter.

the reform of 1999 does not ensure the sustainability of the social insurance system, because the mitigation of the financial problems is too low.

What can be concluded from these results? Financing pension benefits by consumption tax is a device to create large efficiency gains. But the gains are obtained only at the expense of the middle-aged and elder cohorts. It is not certain whether such a tax switch could be carried out in a Pareto improving way by changing, for instance, the time pattern of taxation. Only this could make the trade-off between distribution and efficiency vanish. The literature gives the impression that there is at least one way to reduce the adverse intergenerational redistribution. The findings of Hirte and Weber (1997b) show that in a world with fixed population a switch to a mix of debt and consumption taxation could achieve a Pareto improving transition from a PAYGO to a fully funded system. One can infer from this result that it is likely that there is also a Pareto improving transition from financing by payroll tax to financing by a mix of debt and consumption tax if the PAYGO system is not changed. However, the result of Hirte and Weber (1997b) is not very reliable since it is only true for very small changes in parameters. Additionally, considering intragenerational redistribution makes it less likely that a Pareto improving transition can be achieved (Brunner, 1994 and 1996, and Fenge and Schwager, 1995). Moreover, Fehr (1999a) argues that a compensation scheme is hardly a pure lump sum transfer system but would consist of changes in the redistribution pattern of an existing transfer system. Applying this argument, there remains a trade-off between efficiency and redistribution in the case of a switch to financing of pension benefits by a consumption tax. The existence of such a trade-off is also emphasized by the simulations of a switch from a tax system based on income taxation to a tax system based on consumption taxation in Germany (see Fehr, 1999a).

Chapter 8

Smoothing Pension Taxes

8.1 Introduction

Since Barro presented his seminal paper tax smoothing is considered an appropriate method to minimize intertemporal substitution effects (Barro, 1974). According to Barro tax rates should be set so that they equalize the intertemporal marginal costs of taxation. In a world without permanent shocks and economic growth this requires tax rates to be smoothed over time (Barro, 1979). The main reason for this outcome is that tax collection costs and distortions are minimized if tax rates are constant. Provided financing of public expenditure by issuing of debt does not cause other effects, e. g. the costs of issuing debt which are higher than excess burden caused by distinct taxes, then tax smoothing is optimal. Barro (1979) has also proved that public debt should be used to absorb temporal economic shocks. Hence, it ought to fluctuate according to the extent of economic shocks (Barro 1979, Lucas and Stockey 1983)[1]. Many other researchers have investigated this outcome by means of econometric studies, mainly

[1]LUCAS and STOCKEY (1983) proved that the result of BARRO (1979) is also true if a government with a short planning horizon is considered. They also discuss the issue of time inconsistency as do TURNOVSKY and BROCK (1980). Time inconsistency arises if the government has a short planning horizon but is not committed in advance to redeem the debt of its predecessor. Then it is optimal to tax all income accruing from the existing capital stock with a rate of 100%. The reason is that this capital stock is inelastically supplied. Therefore the tax rate should be extremely high, a result of the inverse elasticity rule of optimal taxation (see LUCAS and STOCKEY, 1983). If government debt issues are characterized by a particular maturity pattern, time inconsistency can be overcome and tax smoothing is optimal (see LUCAS and STOCKEY, 1983). Otherwise tax smoothing is inferior (TURNOVSKY and BROCK, 1980). There

looking for evidence that the tax rate follows a random walk, a hypothesis resulting from the tax smoothing result (e.g. Barro, 1984, Kingston and Layton, 1986, Trehan and Walsh, 1990, Gardner and Kimbrough, 1992, Huang and Lin, 1993, Gosh, 1995, Evans and Amey, 1996, and Strazicich, 1996). But the findings are ambiguous. For example Gosh (1995) finds evidence for an increase in tax rates over time in Canada and the U.S., which can be explained by a discount rate of government higher than the rate of time preference. Strazicich (1996) examines tax smoothing for the U.S. states and Canadian provinces and finds evidence for tax smoothing only for the latter. In general one can follow van der Ploeg (1993, p.161) who states in essence that marginal distortions from current and future sources of raising public revenue should be equalized. From this it follows that borrowing should be used only for financing transitory increases in public spending.

However, if one considers a more sophisticated model in which individual actions are explicitly implemented, one can show that the tax smoothing hypothesis is not always valid. Such a model is, for instance, a dynamic model of optimal taxation. Using such an approach Swaroop (1989) confirms the tax smoothing result for a wage tax in an optimal tax model, where government maximizes the indirect utility of its representative consumer given a time path of public expenditure. He uses a model with an additive production function. One condition not found in the Barro model is that the compensated elasticities of labor supply with respect to net wages must be constant over time, a result of a modified inverse elasticity rule derived by Swaroop (1989). As he shows, this result also holds if a synthetic income tax is considered.

It is tempting to deduce from the results of Barro (1974) and Swaroop (1989) that smoothing the implicit tax rate of the pension system could reduce efficiency losses and thus provide additional funds to mitigate the financial problem aging imposes on the pension system. This means in the

are some other extensions to the base case of BARRO (1979). Barro himself considers economic growth and deduces that the tax rate should grow with the rate of economic growth if growth is permanent (BARRO, 1979). Other extensions are price and interest expectations (BARRO, 1979). See also RAZIN and SVENSSON (1983), KIMBROUGH (1986), and ASCHAUER (1988).

context of a pension system with a non-zero tax benefit linkage such as the German, that the marginal rate of implicit tax of the pension system should be smoothed. However, seeking to smooth the implicit tax rate requires that the pension system is allowed to issue debt or accumulate assets. This is immediately clear when considering the pure effects of aging on the implicit tax rate in section 5.2. This ranges from 14% to 28% depending on aging.

However due to political risks one cannot expect that the savings of the public pension system accumulated during periods of low dependency ratios are not 'touched' by politicians. In addition the Barro model does not consider the interrelationship between pension benefits and the retirement decision, the capital market, and the rate of interest (see Marchand and Pestieau, 1991). Of course it is generally possible to include capital in Barro's model. Then tax rates should adjust to changes in the interest rate (Swaroop, 1995). But the direction and extent of the influence of public debt on the interest rate is controversial and the numerous empirical studies quoted by Seater (1993) present ambiguous results.

The significance of tax smoothing for aging is questioned by Cutler et al. (1990), who find very low efficiency gains from smoothing tax rates. But as Marchand and Pestieau (1991) state, distortions would be higher if taxes used to finance public pensions increase excessively, which is or would be the case in most OECD countries if no other adjustments of the public pension system were made. Consequently the idea of tax smoothing has also been adopted to pension policies. For instance, Chauveau and Loufir (1997), Hirte and Weber (1997b), Broer (1999a and b), and Wrede (1999) refer to tax smoothing.

Although the source of distortions caused by the pension system is the marginal rate of implicit tax, many CGE studies on pension policies neglect the tax benefit linkage and instead focus on smoothing the rate of contribution. Some examine whether changing the time pattern of the rate of contribution matters. For instance Chauveau and Loufir (1997) compare the case of a constant rate of contribution with the case of a constant rate of benefits. Different welfare criteria produce different results for the seven major OECD economies. These are modeled as small open economies. According to their results a constant rate of contribution implies a redistribution in favor of young and future cohorts, and long term gains in welfare. However we have an objection to these results. They neglect the tax benefit linkage which is non-zero in some of these countries. But if there is a non-zero tax benefit linkage, smoothing tax rates means smoothing the implicit tax rate instead of the rate of contribution. However, their scheme of a constant rate of contribution and a variation in pension benefits implies large alterations of the implicit tax rate.

Another CGE study which examines the effects of smoothing the rate of contribution to the pension system has been carried out by Broer (1999a and b). He simulates the imperfect smoothing policy of the Netherlands. This reform scheme includes an immediate upward shift of the rate of contribution used in the initial years to accumulate assets which are used later to finance the rise of the expenditure on pensions. This proposal achieves efficiency gains but disadvantages the currently elderly more than a policy which reduces pension benefits. Broer (1999a) concludes that the majority of voters would vote against this reform, so that it is not sustainable.

In the following we examine the macroeconomic and welfare effects of different smoothing arrangements. Knowing that the marginal rate of implicit tax should be smoothed, we examine reform schemes where the rate of contribution to the pension system is fixed and pension benefits adjust to balance the budget of the pension system. As it turns out this also constitutes an approximate smoothing of the implicit tax rate. Thereafter we examine a policy similar to the policy of the Netherlands (Broer, 1999a and b). The rate of contribution is raised so that the pension system can build up reserves. These are used in the 2030s and 2040s to finance additional pension outlays. The size of the initial rise in the rate of contribution is chosen so that the rate can be maintained at this level, which is 24%, for at least 40 years. In the last experiment we examine the Pension Act of 1999 which has been suspended by the new government. In this act a demographic factor is introduced which is intended to neutralize the impact of the increase in longevity on the pension system. Thus it constitutes a partial smoothing of the rate of contribution.

Of course, not the marginal rate of implicit tax of the pension system but the marginal aggregate rate of implicit tax should be smoothed. This, for instance, suggests that health and long term care insurance also accumulate high reserves to ease the strain which aging is expected to impose on health and long term care insurance, mainly in the 2030s to 2050s. But since this study deals with pension policies it concentrates on the implicit tax of the pension system in the subsequent sections.

What does such a policy mean for pension benefits? Suppose there is a consensus that the pension system should sustain itself and the subsidies should be constant. Then all changes in the expenditure of the pension system ought to be financed by contributions. Logarithmically differentiating the budget constraint of the pension system

$$b^P N^P = (1+z)\,\theta^P wlN^l,$$

where N^P is the number of retirees, z is the subsidy rate, l is labor supply and N^l is the aggregate number of employees, gives the growth rate of pensions (see also Hirte, 1999a)

$$\widehat{b}^P = \omega + \widehat{l} - \left(n^P - n^l\right).$$

Note that the rates of growth of the rates of contribution and subsidy are assumed to be constant. In a self-sustaining or self-financing pension system, pension benefits can only grow with the aggregate growth rate of wages and labor supply, minus the growth rate of the old age dependency ratio. This shows clearly that, given a constant rate of subsidy, a policy of smoothing contributions implies that pensions fully adjust to changes in the old age dependency ratio, employment and unemployment, and the wage. Hence, a rise in life expectancy raises n^P and, thus, the old age dependency ratio, would entail lower pensions. An equivalent conclusion can be drawn for a decrease in the rate of population growth. In line with this reasoning a demographic factor is like implementing a partial smoothing of contributions to deal with a rise in life expectancy. Furthermore a similar factor should be included in the pension formula which deals with fertility and the change in the retirement age. The latter is considered when introducing deductions from and supplements to pension benefits.

Finally, a wage adjustment rule seems to be the better choice, provided all other corrections are implemented.

In the next section, we examine such a scheme where the rate of contribution is fixed and pension benefits are adjusted to balance the budget of the pension system. This system is equivalent to adjusting pension benefits to fluctuations in labor income and the old age dependency ratio. Accordingly, this proposal also includes a demographic factor to adjust for a longer lifetime and for lower benefits on account of lower fertility of a cohort when young. This is in accordance with the proposal of Sinn (1999) who suggests that individuals without children should be forced to accumulate more wealth than parents. However, in the present study one cannot distinguish between parents and retirees without children but only between cohorts with different fertility rates. Nonetheless the decomposition of the effects of aging into effects caused by a decline in population growth and those imposed by a rise in life expectancy gives an idea of the degree of adjustment necessary to match the former and the latter.

8.2 Switching to a Defined Contribution System

In the first experiment the rate of contribution to the pension system is fixed at its 1996 level, which is 19.2%. Instead of the rate of contribution pension benefits are adjusted in each year so that the budget constraint balances. To maintain the principle of equivalence this policy is modeled by altering the current pension value, α^R, in each iteration while personal earning points are not affected. Thereafter a similar experiment is performed in which the rate of contribution is fixed at 22% forever once it reaches this level. Both policies cause an annual adjustment of the replacement rate which can be expected to decrease dramatically until 2040. These scenarios are similar to the reform scheme suggested by Raffelhüschen (1997) and Besendorfer, Borgmann and Raffelhüschen (1998). They propose that the net wage adjustment of pension benefits is suspended between 1998 and 2004 with the result that the replacement falls to 61% in 2004. This level is maintained in subsequent years, while the rate of contribution balances the budget of the pension system. The rate of contribution does not reach its initial level of 20.3% again until 2017. Starting with this year the rate

Table 8.1: Constant rate of contribution: replacement rate of pension benefits

Cohort retiring in	Bench[a]	CCR 19[b]	CCR 22[c]
1996	70.1%	70.1%	70.1%
2001	70.2%	68.2%	66.7%
2011	70.4%	58.8%	69.7%
2021	70.6%	49.0%	58.2%
2031	70.7%	39.3%	46.6%
2041	70.3%	32.6%	38.8%
2051	70.0%	34.0%	43.3%

[a]Benchmark case.
[b]Constant rate of contribution at the 1996 level (19.2%) with full adjustment of pension benefits.
[c]Constant rate of contribution at 22% with full adjustment of pension benefits.

of contribution is fixed for the future whereas the replacement rate is now the variable used to balance the budget. According to their simulations of the generational accounts the minimum replacement rate is 42% of wage income, which will be reached in 2038.

This policy constitutes a switch from a defined benefit PAYGO system in which the rate of contribution varies to balance the budget, e. g. the current German system[2], to a defined contribution PAYGO system in which the replacement rate is adjusted to balance the budget.

8.2.1 Constancy of the Rate of Contribution at the Level of 1996

Social Insurance and Macroeconomic Effects

Table 8.1 shows the replacement rate or the ratio of gross pension benefits to wage income. While the replacement rate stays at about 70% in the benchmark path it decreases from 70.1% to 32.6% in 2041 in this experiment ('CCR 19').

[2]In Germany the formula by which the replacement rate is calculated is stipulated by law. In contrast, the rate of contribution is fixed annually so that expected revenue matches expected expenditure. For this reason the German system is basically a system in which the rate of contribution varies to balance the budget.

Figure 8.1: Constant rate of contribution: social insurance variables

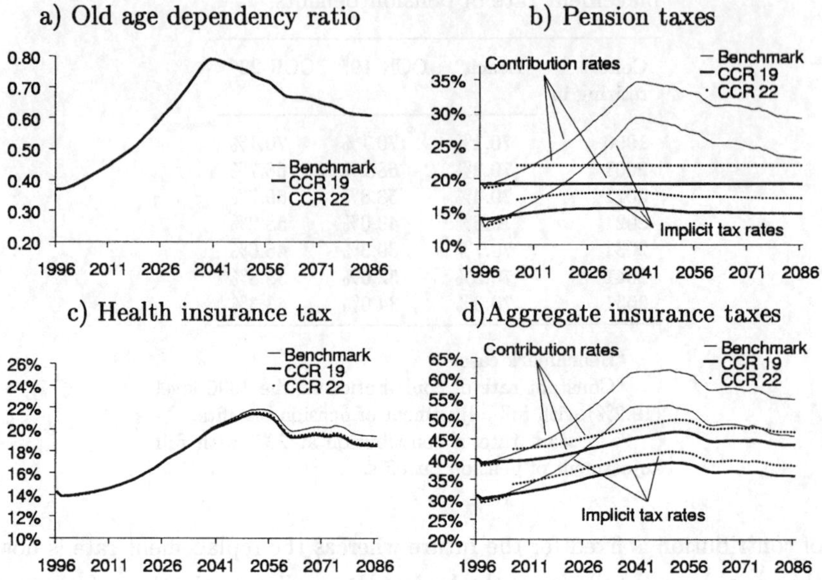

This outcome is more pessimistic than the replacement rate of 42% obtained by Besendofer, Borgmann, and Raffelhüschen (1998) for a rate of contribution fixed at a level of 20.3%. However, while they compute generational accounts where individual behavior is assumed to remain unchanged, in the present study all general equilibrium effects are considered. This accounts for the differences in the results.

The constancy of the rate of contribution is shown in the solid curve 'CCR 19' in panel (b) of Figure 8.1. As the principle of equivalence is not changed, reducing pension benefits and fixing the rate of contribution entail only a small change in the implicit tax rate of the pension system. The latter is in the range of 13.9% to 15.3%. Hence, this policy almost smoothes the implicit tax rate.

Despite the strong reduction in the size of pensions there is no alteration of the retirement age, as shown by panel (a) of Figure 8.1. As this is counterintuitive it is explored more thoroughly. Using the definition of the true wage (see equation 2.29), the relatively lower rate of contribution raises earned income and, thus, creates an incentive to retire later. On the

Figure 8.2: Constant rate of contribution: employment and unemployment

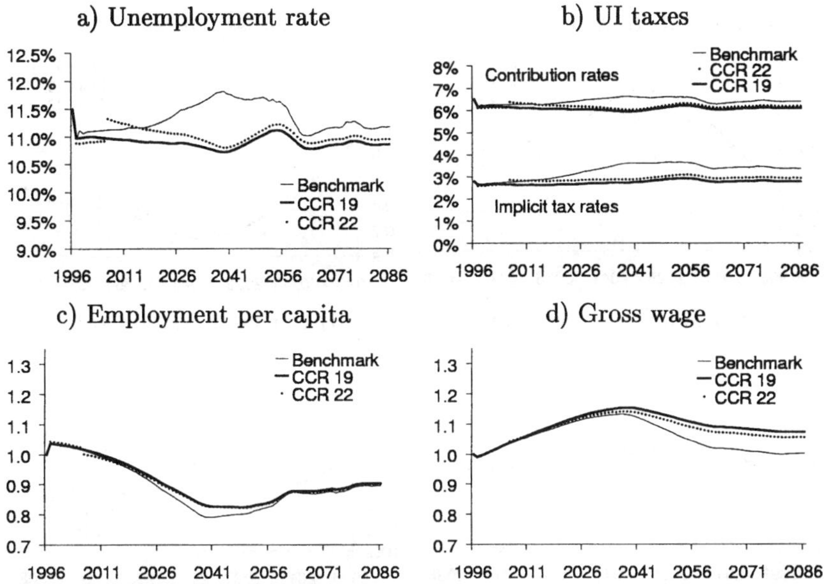

other hand, reducing pension benefits has two opposite effects. First, due to the lower current pension value the increase in future pension benefits caused by working now diminishes. This reduces income and intensifies the preference for retiring earlier. Second, reducing pension benefits unequivocally reduces the loss in current pension benefits, $b_s^{P,i}$, caused by working. This lowers the price of working relative to retiring and encourages retiring later. Hence, there are opposite effects on the true wage and, thus, the incentive to retire. However, as in fact the average rate as well as the marginal rate of the implicit tax decrease, the reduction in the rate of contribution exceeds the reduction in future pension benefits. Consequently, this policy should imply a higher retirement age. But Figure 8.1(a) does not show such a response. From this one can deduce that the incentive is too weak to cause a postponement of retirement in the simulation where the smallest unit of time is one year.

Nonetheless, a lower marginal rate of implicit tax implies a higher net wage and, hence, a larger supply of labor. Moreover, an additional income

Figure 8.3: Constant rate of contribution: capital accumulation and consumption

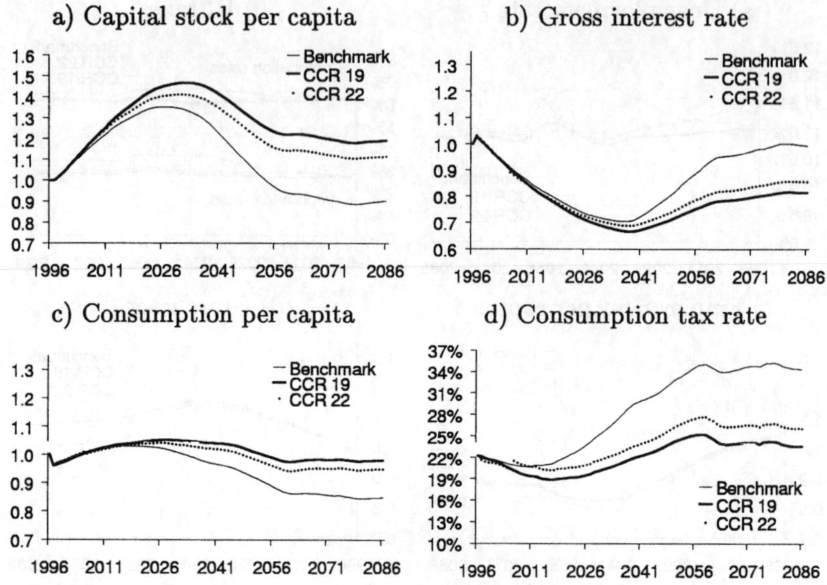

effect occurs. Income is reduced by the reduction in pension benefits based on individual earning points already collected. This effect is stronger the closer individuals are to retirement. This creates an additional incentive to supply more labor. As a result earned income increases and the loss in future pension benefits is partially compensated for. Both effects are very low directly after the reform is launched. Beyond the 2040s the replacement rate rises and the gap between the implicit tax rate in the benchmark case and the case of a fixed rate of contribution narrows. Accordingly, employment per capita comes nearer to its benchmark level in the long term (see panel (c) of Figure 8.2).

Panel (a) of Figure 8.2 shows that the rise in labor supply is accompanied by a decrease in the rate of unemployment. This is due to the fact that younger individuals benefit more from the reduction in the implicit tax rate and raise their labor supply relatively more. This increases the relative share of the younger labor in the effective labor force. Since the younger working cohorts are relatively less unemployed than the elder working cohorts the aggregate rate of unemployment decreases. The lower rate of unemployment and the rise in gross wages occurring in the medium and long term reduces the rate of contribution to unemployment insurance (see panels (b) and (d) of Figure 8.2). This causes a further decrease in the aggregate rate of contribution.

Capital accumulation grows inversely to the reduction in pension benefits because individuals accumulate more assets to offset the loss in pension benefits. This explains the upward shift of the graph shown in panel (a) of Figure 8.3. A higher capital stock reduces the marginal productivity of capital and, thus, the interest rate. This is shown by the solid curve in Figure 8.3(b). All in all, higher savings and higher net income allow consumption per capita to increase and the consumption tax rate to decline (see panel (c) and (d) in Figure 8.3).

Welfare Effects

Tax smoothing is supposed to enhance efficiency, a result confirmed by the figures shown in Table 8.2. The left hand part of this table shows the changes in utility and its components which occur if the rate of contribution to the pension system is fixed at 19.2%. The column ΔEB shows that the efficiency of most cohorts, except cohort 1946 and 1956, improves. These two cohorts are in the second half of their working life during the year of reform. Since the marginal rate of implicit tax is greater than its benchmark counterpart before the year of reform, these cohorts lose. Only the subsequent cohorts benefit from a relatively lower marginal rate of implicit tax. Due to an increasing deviation of the marginal rate of implicit tax from its level in the benchmark case the gains are higher the younger the cohort (see panel (d) of Figure 8.1). It is only after the 2040s that this deviation becomes smaller.

Column $-\Delta T$ shows the changes in net tax liabilities which are relatively low in comparison to changes in net pension benefits (column ΔP). The gains from the reduced rate of contribution grow from about zero for the cohort initially close to retirement to a maximum for those cohorts which work during the years of the most adverse old age dependency ratio, i. e. the cohorts 2006 and 2016. The reason for the lower contribution payments is that the initially young and future cohorts avoid contribution payments over their whole working life. The closer individuals are to retiring the lower their gains from reduced rates of contribution. These gains exceed the negative effects of lower pension benefits for the cohorts born in 1976 and thereafter. The elder cohorts, except cohort 1921, lose because they receive lower benefits but avoid only a small amount of contribution payments. Consequently the changes in net pension benefits grow inversely to the age of the cohorts from negative to considerably high positive values. Only the cohorts which die prior to the start of the reform in 2001 do not lose pension benefits. Aggregating these effects gives the changes in utility. They reflect the changes in net pension benefits in sign and size. The cohorts 1936 to 1966 lose and the younger and future cohorts gain.

Welfare amounts to 0.35% of the present value of all remaining lifetime resources. The index of redistribution is higher, indicating that this reform scheme produces relatively low welfare gains compared to the negative redistribution it induces.

8.2.2 Constancy of the Rate of Contribution at a Higher Level

The German pension reform of 2001 contains many different regulations. It aims at reducing the pension level mainly of individuals retiring in 2002 and thereafter. For this purpose the net wage adjustment rule is changed, so that the growth in gross wages is reduced by contributions to private pension plans. The second aim is to lower the increase in the rate of contribution to the public pension system so that it stays below 22% in the medium term. Moreover individuals are supposed to make private pension plans to compensate for lower public pensions. In the medium term these private pension plans should amount to 4% of gross income. Though the specific arrangements of the Reform of 2001 where not known in detail during the preparation of this study, we have examined a similar experiment which includes two aims of the reform, i. e. the constancy of the rate of contribution at a level of 22% and the implied increase in private savings, or private pension plans. However, these simulations have been performed without taking into account the Pension Act of 1992. Moreover, the reduction in pension benefits is considerably stronger than expected in

Table 8.2: Constant rate of contribution: decomposition of utility changes

	CCR with $\tau^P = 19.2$[a]				CCR with $\tau^P = 22.0$[b]			
Year of birth	ΔU[c]	ΔP[d]	$-\Delta T$[e]	ΔEB[f]	ΔU	ΔP	$-\Delta T$	ΔEB
1921	0.11	0.35	-0.21	0.01	0.01	-0.04	0.04	0.01
1936	-0.69	-0.90	0.39	0.02	-0.26	-0.30	0.19	-0.01
1946	-1.54	-1.67	0.47	-0.15	-0.39	-0.41	0.12	0.01
1956	-1.21	-1.35	0.27	-0.07	-0.84	-0.92	0.18	-0.12
1966	-0.04	-0.44	0.17	0.29	-0.37	-0.61	0.14	0.01
1976	1.71	0.75	0.11	0.92	0.67	0.08	0.12	0.39
1986	4.16	2.59	-0.16	2.04	2.09	1.04	0	1.03
1996	7.00	5.03	-0.70	3.48	5.02	3.51	-0.43	2.55
2006	9.54	7.43	-1.46	4.88	7.64	5.89	-1.09	3.99
2016	11.09	8.41	-2.14	5.68	9.17	6.86	-1.71	4.81
∞	9.11	4.39	-1.30	3.77	6.78	2.98	-0.94	2.80
$\sum$	0.35	-0.69		0.51	0.25	-0.41		0.29

In per cent of all remaining lifetime resources

[a]Constant rate of contribution, which is fixed at 19.2%. Full adjustment of pension benefits.

[b]Constant rate of contribution, which is fixed at 22%. Full adjustment of pension benefits.

[c]Change in utility.

[d]Change in net pension benefits.

[e]Change in net tax liabilities.

[f]Change in efficiency effects.

the German pension reform of 2001.

In our experiment the rate of contribution is fixed at 22% to avoid such a strong reduction in the size of pension benefits as occurs with a 19.2% rate of contribution. Again, pension benefits are fully adjusted to balance the budget of the pension system. This reform is called 'CCR 22' in the following. Like the reform considered in the previous section, this reform scheme is equivalent to a reduction in pension benefits accompanied by expanding private pension plans. Note that the CGE model used can neither distinguish between savings and investing in a private pension plan nor between mandatory and voluntary contributions to a private pension plan.

As a result the replacement rate falls 'only' to 38.8% in 2041. This and the higher rate of contribution generate an average marginal rate of implicit tax of the pension system which is about 3% above the level for the reform 'CCR 19' (see panel (b) of Figure 8.1). Consequently, all other effects are slightly lower including the changes in the capital stock and consumption per capita (see Figure 8.3). Moreover utility changes, and income and efficiency effects are also lower for almost all cohorts. According to Table 8.2 welfare gains amount to only 0.25% instead of 0.35% of the present value of all remaining lifetime resources. The index of redistribution is also reduced. The only cohort which becomes worse off compared to the reform 'CCR 19' is the cohort 1966. While it is almost unaffected by the reform 'CCR 19', it loses about 0.37% of its remaining lifetime wealth. The reason is that the relative increase in contribution payments exceeds the relative gains in pension benefits accruing to this cohort.

8.2.3 Summary

These two simulations are used to obtain an impression of the general effects of tax smoothing. The results shown in Table 8.2 show that tax smoothing achieves welfare effects which are only small compared to a change in the tax base or a transition to a fully funded system. This is in line with the results of Cutler et. al. (1990) who estimate that tax smoothing will generate only small efficiency gains. In the case under consideration the gains are only 0.25% or 0.35% but amount to 1.85% or 1.99% if there is a full switch to consumption taxation as shown in Table 7.1. Hence, tax smoothing provides only small welfare gains. In contrast it can alleviate the financial problems of the pension system. However, the strong reduction in the replacement rate is the reason why we do not examine this specific experiment in more detail[3]. Therefore we are not interested in whether these differences change in the sensitivity analysis.

[3] We wonder why the German government can expect a considerably higher replacement rate when the contribution rate is almost fixed at 22%. Even if the Pension Act of 1992 is taken into account, which we have not done in our experiment, the difference between the replacement rate in our experiment and the rate expected by the government is huge.

Therefore the sensitivity analyses are omitted[4]. Instead some more realistic experiments are carried out.

The results of the two experiments described above suggest that smoothing the rate of contribution is an almost perfect substitute for smoothing the implicit tax rate of the pension system. This is shown in panel (b) of Figure 8.1. It shows that smoothing the rate of contribution implies an almost constant average marginal rate of implicit tax. One should however bear in mind that the rate depicted in the figure is the average marginal rate of implicit tax. Constancy of this rate is not necessarily equivalent to a constant marginal rate of implicit tax either across cohorts or over the working life of each individual. At any rate the latter is not true because the age profile of implicit pension taxes shows a declining rate up to the age of 60. This rate is not smoothed as long as the rate of contribution or personal earning points are not distinguished according to age. Nonetheless we consider the case of the smoothing of contributions to the pension system and, thus, an average marginal rate of implicit tax as a strong and, for this study, final step in the direction of full tax smoothing. This is correct at least from the perspective of aggregate variables.

8.3 A Capital Stock and a Demographic Factor

In the previous section all burdens resulting from trying to rescue the PAYGO financed German public pension system were shifted to the retirees due to the strong reduction in pension benefits. Holding the 1996 rate of contribution constant would require the reduction of pension benefits to a level far lower than the social assistance granted in Germany. Although social assistance is not built into the model one can expect that it actually prevents such a reform being carried out. Therefore we perform a second experiment by raising the rate of contribution of 22%. But, again, all further adjustments in the pension budget are shifted to the retirees. Hence, this experiment also constitutes a full shift to a defined contribution PAYGO system.

In the following we discuss two other reform schemes which do not

[4] Actually, we have performed sensitivity analyses but do not present them in this study. The size of the effects are very similar.

contain a permanent tax smoothing mechanism but can be classified as belonging to the group of schemes referred to as tax smoothing. Since the theory of tax smoothing suggests that tax rates should be smoothed by issuing debt or accumulating savings during times of economic slow-down or growth, smoothing pension taxes should also be accompanied by the issuing of debt or accumulating surpluses in the pension system. This is not exactly what is done in the experiments described above. The reduction in the rate of contribution is equivalent to a reduction in the amount of new implicit debt issued, compared to the benchmark case. This is equalized across periods whereas the rate of implicit tax of the pension system is adjusted to balance the budget by changing the replacement rate. A pure tax smoothing policy requires that the implicit tax rate is fixed and the rate of contribution, and thus implicit debt issues, fluctuate to ensure the constancy of the implicit tax rate. The cases considered above are therefore only an imperfect substitute for a tax smoothing policy. Therefore switching to debt and surplus financed smoothing is in the strict sense more in line with the theory of tax smoothing than the reform schemes considered above.

Furthermore, raising the rate of contribution above the level necessary to balance the current budget of the pension system and setting aside the surplus to accumulate a capital stock is a option for mitigating the problems of aging. Since the generations who work at the beginning do not produce enough future contributors to the pension system, they have to increase their savings to avoid having a large decrease in their standard of living when old. Generating savings (reserves) in the pension system today is also a way to achieve this goal. Since this is also in accordance with the theory of tax smoothing we subsume this policy into the tax smoothing schemes. It could also have been discussed in the next chapter which is about the transition to a fully or partially funded system.

Such a reform scheme for accumulating high reserves now for use in the middle of this century has been enacted in the U.S. (1977 and 1983 Social Security amendments). Such reserves are, for instance, part of the pension system of the Netherlands and the German public pension system between 1957 and 1969. However, history tells that such a fund is subject to heavy policy risk. For instance, large reserves of the German pension system were distributed among employees and retirees after 1972; the reserves of the same system, which are much lower today, were used to finance pension benefits for the inhabitants of the eastern provinces ("Länder") after German unification.

We describe two experiments below. In a first experiment tax smoothing during the next 80 years is achieved by an instantaneous upward shift of the rate of contribution to 24%, a level clearly above the benchmark rate. The surplus created is accumulated and used later to finance part of the pension outlays at the peak of the demographic problems. The level of 24% is chosen since some other experiments have shown that a rate of contribution of 24% succeeds much more in avoiding a strong increase in the rate of contribution after this capital stock will have been used up than a rate of 22% or 23%.

This pension scheme implies that the pure PAYGO system is not used for a period of time. Thereafter the rate of contribution adjusts fully to balance the budget of the pension system. Unfortunately, due to instability occurring in the simulation, we were not able to investigate this proposal together with the Pension Act of 1992. Therefore we assume that the reform is enacted in 2001 and the second stage of the Pension Act of 1992 is suspended. At any rate, implementing the Act of 1992 would require the rate of contribution to be raised only by a lower amount than in this experiment. Since the surplus is used to accumulate a fund for the pension system, this proposal establishes a partially funded system. However, benefits are determined according to the pension formula and usually differ from the compensations paid in a privatized, partially funded system. Hence, this proposal for accumulating a capital stock for the public pension system is not a privatization policy, which we discuss in the next chapter. Furthermore, we define in the following a funded system as a pension plan which is privately held and organized. Accordingly, accumulating a capital stock of the pension system is not considered as a switch to a funded system. Despite this clear distinction we know that this definition is purely artificial since the concepts of implicit debt and taxes make clear that all these funding strategies are independent of whether the organization is private or public[5]. A similar reform scheme has been suggested, for instance, by Jäger (1990).

In the second experiment, i. e. the Pension Act of 1999, the adverse effects of the increase in life expectancy on the pension system are lowered. This reform would generate smooth tax rates if population growth is constant and aging is only caused by a growing life expectancy. For this reason introducing a demographic factor in the calculation of the pension benefits can be considered as a step to tax smoothing. This should generate efficiency gains compared to former simulations. Whether these are sufficiently high to outweigh other adverse repercussion effects remains to be examined.

8.3.1 Transitive Tax Smoothing and a Capital Stock

In the first experiment the PAYGO public pension system is permitted to accumulate assets but not to issue debt. In addition the rate of contribution is shifted to 24% in the year 2001 and stays at this level until the budget can only be balanced by either raising the rate of contribution or issuing debt. Then the rate of contribution is adjusted to finance pension outlays. As long as contribution payments exceed expenditure the pension system accumulates assets. These are used to finance additional pension benefits at the peak of the aging trend. This reform scheme does not include any change in pension benefits other than those caused by the net wage adjustment rule. In a much weaker way the current German system also allows the pension system to accumulate assets but not to issue debt. However these assets or reserves (*Schwankungsreserve*) are restricted to pension outlays of two months at most. They are used to offset short term fluctuations in expenditure and revenue.

Altering the time pattern of contribution taxes but not pension outlays is equivalent to a change of the time pattern of implicit debts and taxes. In this proposal the rate of contribution is raised above the benchmark

[5]This equivalence breaks down if the risks to public and private assets differ. This can be the case, for example, if the political risk of a publicly organized pension fund is much stronger than that of a privately held pension fund (see DIAMOND, 1997a). Another difference might stem from the way investments are placed (see REISEN and WILLIAMSON, 1997, and the case study of Chile by FONTAINE, 1997).

rate in the short term but falls below the benchmark rate in the medium term. Hence, implicit debt is increased in the short term but decreased in the medium term. As a consequence of the equivalence of implicit and explicit debt, the theories of public debt can be applied to this change in implicit indebtedness.

Theory suggests that public debt is neutral (see Barro, 1974). If there is an operative bequest motive and repayment of debt is financed by lump-sum taxes, the timing of public debt is neutral. Though this "Ricardian equivalence" fails theoretically if distorting taxes are employed, the empirical evidence is unambiguous[6]. However, if taxes are distorting, pure Ricardian equivalence no longer holds. Then, public debt policy can be usefully examined in a CGE framework, allowing the calculation of efficiency and redistribution effects. At least intertemporal redistribution effects only occur if there is no bequest motive.

Starting with the study of Auerbach and Kotlikoff (1987a) many CGE studies have been carried out to examine the consequences of public debt policy in a fully specified general equilibrium framework (see the survey provided by Fehr, 1999a, 219-224). According to the results of Auerbach and Kotlikoff (1987a), raising public debt accelerates capital accumulation until taxes have to be raised to finance interest payments. Lowering public debt inverts these effects: raising taxes in the short term disadvantages the cohorts initially alive but makes future cohorts better off. Since interest payments are lower in the future the younger and future cohorts face lower tax liabilities (e. g. Fehr, 1999a, 204-237).

In the reform scheme under consideration the same cohorts which 'lend' money to the public pension system have to accept lower net interest payments due to a higher implicit tax rate. Hence the lending cohorts are subject to higher implicit or payroll taxation and, thus, are expected to be worse off with respect to efficiency. These cohorts will therefore reduce their savings in order to distribute the implicit tax burden across their remaining lifetime. This crowding-out effect reduces the effect of higher savings in the public pension system on capital accumulation. Therefore, even if individuals are selfish in the sense that there is no bequest motive

[6] See the review provided by Seater (1993) and Elmendorf and Mankiw (1999).

there could be effects similar to the Ricardian equivalence. However, in the present case, part of the tax burden is imposed on the individuals initially alive which makes them worse off. If there were a pure Ricardian equivalence future cohorts who benefit from lower implicit taxes make additional transfers to their parents either directly or by higher pension benefits. Since pension benefits are not raised in the reform scheme examined below, debt is not neutral with respect to intergenerational redistribution. Moreover, implicit taxes are distortionary. This implies additional efficiency effects.

Social Insurance and Macroeconomic Effects

Remember that in this experiment the Pension Act of 1992 is suspended. The subsequent figures and tables show the results of this experiment, called 'Capital', together with those of the Pension Act of 1992 and 1999, called 'Act 92' and 'Act 99'. The Pension Act of 1992 is used as the base case because it is the alternative policy option chosen if this experiment is not performed.

Since the replacement rate is not changed the initial rise in the rate of contribution implies an equivalent increase in the marginal rate of implicit tax. In the course of time the base case rates exceed these rates which are held constant. These changes are shown in panel (b) of Figure 8.4. As long as the rate of contribution plus interest earned on funds of the pension system exceed the rate of contribution in the benchmark case, shown in panel (b) of Figure 6.5 on page 127, assets accumulate. Otherwise they decline until all assets are consumed. As shown in Figure 8.4(b) this point is reached in the year 2071 where the rate of contribution jumps from 24% to 30%. Thereafter it converges to the long term level of 28%. Of course, one could avoid this strong jump in the rate of contribution by gradually increasing the rate of contribution prior to the year 2071. Anyway the results for the first 70 years of the transition would presumably be quite similar. Therefore a simpler reform scheme is used. Figure 8.4(b) shows that the average marginal rate of implicit tax of the pension system is almost constant. It only increases from 17.5% in 2001 to 18.5% in 2070. Though individuals do not correct their retirement decision, as shown in

Figure 8.4: Pension Act of 1999: social insurance variables

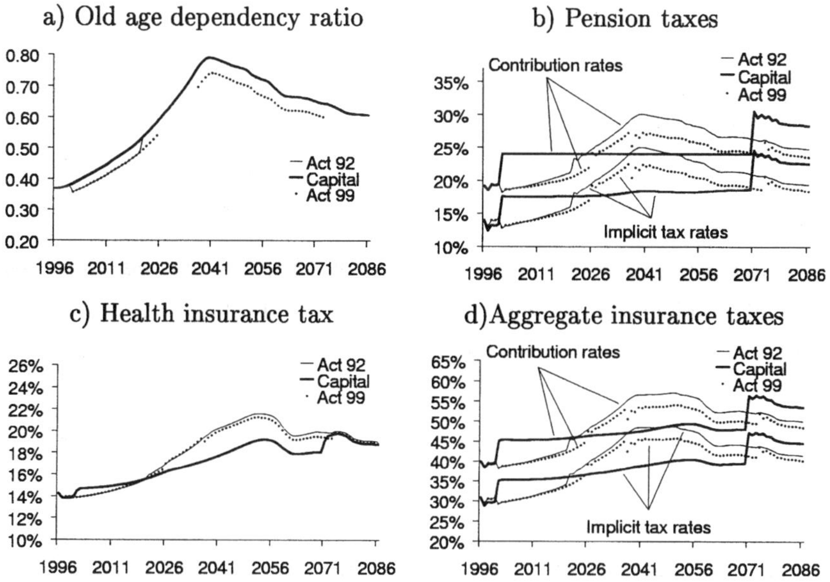

Figure 8.4(a), this reform scheme unambiguously improves the situation of the public pension system. While in 2001 the new rate of contribution is 4 percentage points above the rate of contribution under the Pension Act of 1992, it is by 6 percentage points below the latter rate in 2040. This difference can be expected to be even higher if the reform scheme is implemented together with the Pension Act of 1992.

Let us further examine the retirement decision. A lower implicit tax rate, ceteris paribus, raises the true wage and thus provides an incentive to postpone retiring. Since there are only small changes in pension benefits, the second and third term of the true wage formula (2.29) on page 35, i. e. the terms concerning pension benefits, stay approximately constant. Hence, the true wage increases unequivocally and the retirement age is supposed to increase. The fact that the average retirement age does not change, can again be explained by the choice of the unit of time used in the simulation model. It would have changed if time were continuous, but does not change since time is discrete. The same argument applies to the first part of the transition period. During this time the implicit tax rate

Figure 8.5: Pension Act of 1999: employment and unemployment

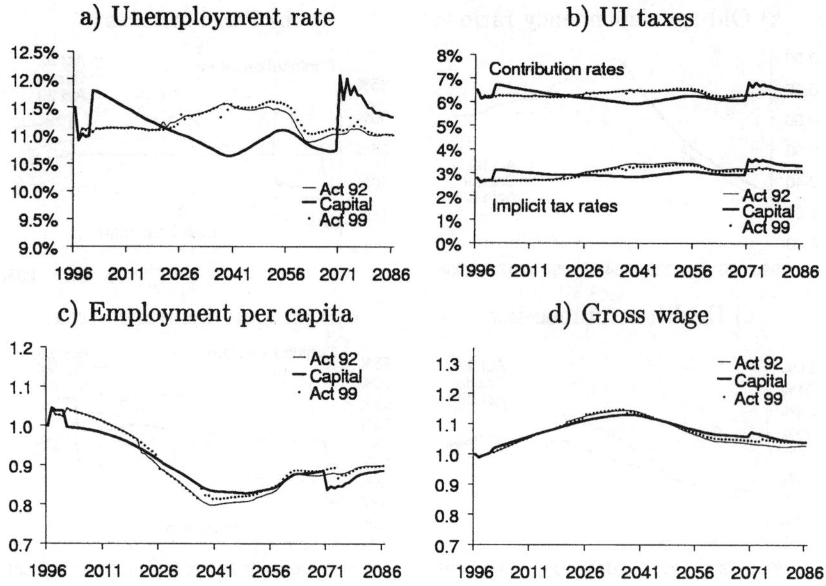

exceeds the benchmark level. Consequently the true wage, ceteris paribus, decreases, and individuals are willing to retire earlier. However nothing really happens. The old age dependency ratio does not change and there is no additional effect on the pension system.

Given the optimal retirement age, changes occur with respect to consumption, leisure, and labor supply. The immediate upward shift in the marginal rate of implicit tax in 2001 lowers the relative price of leisure. Hence there is a substitution of leisure for consumption, and labor supply and consumption decrease. Later, the marginal rate of implicit tax falls below its benchmark level. As a consequence the net wage increases, which changes the sign of the substitution effect. Leisure becomes relatively more expensive and the demands for consumer goods and labor supply are raised. Despite the effects on unemployment, a higher labor supply also increases employment. These effects are very clearly shown in panels (c) in Figure 8.5 and Figure 8.6. The curve reflecting the levels of employment and consumption per capita in the case of asset accumulation – called 'Capital' — is below the level in the case of the Pension Act of

1992 for some time but above it later on.

Unemployment also responds to changes in labor supply. According to the graph shown in panel (a) of Figure 8.5, the rate of unemployment starts with a strong upward shift in the year 2001. Thereafter it declines monotonically until it reaches its lowest level in 2041. Between 2041 and 2071 it is a hump shaped graph. Finally it jumps again and overshoots the long term level and then converges to it. What happens that causes this strange behavior of the rate of unemployment? Remember that the marginal rate of implicit tax of the younger cohorts is higher than that of the elder cohorts. Then the initial increase in the marginal rate of implicit tax lowers the labor supply of the younger employees more than of the elder. This raises the share of elder labor in the effective labor force. Since these are also the cohorts facing relatively higher rates of unemployment the aggregate rate of unemployment jumps instantaneously upward when the reform is implemented.

After the reform is put into effect the difference between the marginal aggregate rate of implicit tax in this case and that computed in the benchmark case declines (see panel (d) of Figure 5.1). Beyond 2016 this rate falls below the benchmark level for the first time and stays below the latter for the whole demographic transition period. The maximum difference between both is reached in 2039 when the rate is 14.1 percentage points below its benchmark level. Compared to the Pension Act of 1992 the implicit tax rate is higher until 2021 and also reaches the maximum difference of 11 points in 2039. As a result younger individuals start to raise their labor supply immediately after the initial downward shift. As this response is stronger than that of the elder employees, the share of younger labor in the effective labor force increases. Therefore the overall rate of unemployment declines. After 2039 the implicit tax rate increases again and the proportion of young labor decreases. This behavior of the rate of unemployment is reflected in changes in the rate of contribution and implicit tax of unemployment insurance, shown in panel (b) of Figure 8.5.

Changes in employment show the inverse pattern. The initial shift in the marginal aggregate rate of implicit tax discourages working and, thus, reduces employment per capita below the level in the base case level. The

Figure 8.6: Pension Act of 1999: macroeconomic variables

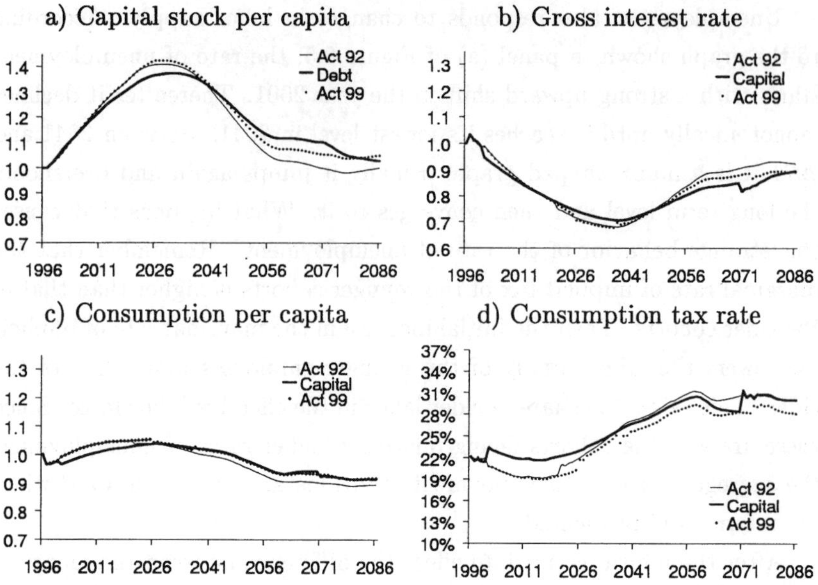

subsequent decrease in employment is reduced compared to the base case on account of the slower rise of the implicit tax rate. These changes in employment inversely affect wages (see panel (d) of Figure 8.5). Both allow the rate of contribution to health insurance, despite being higher in the short term, to be lower in the medium term as shown in panel (c) of Figure 8.4.

The constant rates of the pension system, the relatively slower growing rate of contribution to health insurance, and the inversely changing rates of unemployment insurance together determine the behavior of the aggregate rate of contribution and the marginal rate of implicit tax as shown in Figure 8.4(d). The aggregate rate of contributions increases from 45% in 2001 to 50% in 2056. However, in 2071 it jumps to 55% and then converges to its long term level. If this reform were enacted together with the Pension Act of 1992 the rate of contribution would be lower in the long term. For this reason the main focus is again on the time before 2071. Anyway, this reform alleviates the problems of the pension system in the medium term. It also reduces the rise of the rate of contribution to health insurance. All considered, this reform scheme is a large step in the direction of smoothing the marginal aggregate rate of implicit tax.

Finally, consider the capital stock and interest rate (see panels (a) and (b) of Figure 8.6). Until 2040, the capital stock per capita is almost equal to the capital stock in the benchmark case but lower than for the Pension Act of 1992. Apparently, the savings of the pension system fully crowd out private savings. But after 2040 the capital stock per capita exceeds its benchmark level for the next years. From this time individuals start to raise savings to offset the reduction in earned income caused by the strong upward shift of the implicit tax rate and the reduction in employment which takes place in 2071. In this way the 'shock' of 2071 is 'transferred' back to earlier times. The gross interest rate behaves inversely to the capital stock. It is relatively higher than under the Pension Act of 1992 between 2016 and 2046, the period of time when the capital stock is relatively lower, and is relatively lower thereafter.

Welfare Effects

This reform scheme produces a higher implicit tax rate in the short term but a lower rate in the medium term. In the long term it converges to its benchmark level. In addition the consumption tax rate is higher in the medium term and the marginal rate of wage tax is higher due to higher labor income. Nonetheless, Table 8.3 shows that changes in implicit taxation dominate the other changes in taxation. Changes in excess burden fully reflect the pattern of the changes in the aggregate rate of implicit tax. As the rate is relatively higher in the short term, the middle-aged cohorts, i. e. the cohorts 1946 and 1956, suffer efficiency losses. The younger cohorts entering working life before 2016, the year in which the implicit tax rate falls below its benchmark level for the first time, experience both a time of a relatively higher and a time of a relatively lower implicit tax rate.

If there were an operative bequest motive all intergenerational income effects would be neutralized by adjusting bequests. In this sense the computation of excess burden is equivalent to a model with an operative bequest motive. Hence the column 'ΔEB' shows the deviation from Ricardian equivalence caused by distortionary taxation. It shows that the short

Table 8.3: Decomposition of utility changes

Year of	Capital stock				Act 1999			
birth	ΔU[a]	ΔP[b]	$-\Delta T$[c]	ΔEB[d]	ΔU	ΔP	$-\Delta T$	ΔEB
1921	0.05	0.01	0.04	0.01	-0.05	0	-0.05	0.01
1936	-1.00	-0.50	-0.19	0.04	0.49	0.08	0.28	0.03
1946	-0.81	-0.48	0.06	-0.15	-1.46	-2.25	0.31	0.44
1956	-0.30	-0.35	0.27	-0.10	-0.43	-0.94	0.09	0.35
1966	-0.11	-0.32	0.23	0.04	0.77	0.26	0.07	0.48
1976	-0.06	-0.23	0.15	0.09	1.97	1.04	0.06	0.92
1986	1.57	1.21	-0.08	0.92	3.12	1.87	-0.10	1.50
1996	4.60	4.06	-0.75	2.53	4.33	2.73	-0.39	2.03
2006	7.30	6.78	-1.68	4.06	5.21	3.22	-0.72	2.40
2016	8.82	7.74	-2.45	4.82	6.46	4.20	-0.99	2.85
∞	0.01	-0.02	0	0.03	6.26	2.71	-0.86	2.53
$\sum$	-0.02		-0.45	0.22	0.62		-0.02	0.60

All changes in per cent of all remaining lifetime resources.
[a]Change in utility.
[b]Change in net pension benefits.
[c]Change in net tax liabilities.
[d]Change in efficiency.

term rise in the implicit tax rate disadvantages the initially middle-aged cohorts. Since the additional implicit tax revenue allows the implicit tax rate for the young and future cohorts to be reduced, these cohorts experience efficiency gains.

Changes in net tax liabilities, '$-\Delta T$', are negative for the cohort 1936. The consumption tax liability of this cohort is higher during its whole period of retirement than in the benchmark case. Since consumption per capita increases in the medium term, the relative reduction of the consumption tax rate does not necessarily reduce the tax liabilities of this cohort. On the other hand, the increase in employment and the capital stock in the medium term causes higher wage, capital, and corporate tax liabilities.

The largest changes occur to net pension benefits, shown in column 'ΔP'. The demographic factor reduces pension benefits, which disadvantages the cohorts born in 1936 and thereafter. Since only the younger and future cohorts profit from the reduction in contribution payments, all initially working cohorts lose whereas all future cohorts receive higher net pension benefits.

These effects also determine the sign and magnitude of the changes in utility. All cohorts working or retired in 1996, i. e. the cohorts 1921 to 1976, are worse off while all future cohorts, except those living in the distant future, are better off. The cohort most disadvantaged is the cohort 1936. For younger cohorts the positive effect of lower contribution payments accumulates. The cohort 2016 is the generation who benefits most from this effect and, thus, from this pension scheme.

This policy reform does not change the final steady state since it is only transitory. Hence, the effects on the cohorts living in the final steady state, i. e. cohort ∞, are approximately zero. Nonetheless, the reform causes an intergenerational redistribution in favor of the cohorts starting their working life after the year 1996 but not alive in the final steady state.

According to the figures shown in the last row of Table 8.3 welfare is unaffected by this policy reform. Nonetheless, negative intergenerational income effects amount to 0.45% of the present value of all remaining lifetime resources. This shows that accumulating a capital stock causes relatively low changes in income effects. Efficiency effects are positive. Since they deviate from welfare the computation of efficiency effects is not very accurate. It only provides an idea of the size and sign of the changes in excess burden.

Sensitivity Analysis

Table 8.4 shows the macroeconomic effects of the policy reform under consideration computed for different settings. It shows that there are no differences in the old age dependency ratio. For this reason many other changes are also only moderate. Differences between the base case and the case of a *higher retirement elasticity*, '*Low* α', are the smallest exhibited in this table. A slower rise in the strength of the preference for leisure changes the time pattern of consumption. Consumption increases faster at the end of life but is lower when entering retirement. Since the aging trend raises the share of the eldest cohorts, savings increase. As a consequence the capital stock per capita is higher in 2041 and in the final steady state than in base

Table 8.4: Capital stock: sensitivity analysis – macro effects

	Capital stock				Capital stock			
Year of birth	Base Case	No UI[a]	No HI[b]	Low α^c	Base Case	No UI	No HI	Low α
	Old age dependency ratio				Unemployment rate: x			
1996	0.37	0.37	0.37	0.37	11.5	–	11.5	11.5
1997	0.37	0.37	0.37	0.37	10.9	–	11.1	10.8
2001	0.38	0.38	0.38	0.38	11.8	–	11.8	11.7
2041	0.79	0.79	0.79	0.79	10.6	–	10.5	10.6
∞	0.60	0.60	0.60	0.60	11.2	–	11.1	11.1
	Consumption tax rate: τ^c				Pension contr. rate: θ^P			
1996	22.2	21.7	17.3	22.2	19.2	19.2	19.2	19.2
1997	21.6	21.5	17.2	21.2	18.5	18.6	18.7	18.5
2001	23.5	22.9	18.4	23.2	24.0	24.0	24.0	24.0
2041	26.9	23.2	18.4	26.2	24.0	24.0	24.0	24.0
∞	31.3	30.1	21.9	29.4	28.5	28.5	28.4	28.4
	Implicit pension tax: τ^P				Aggregate contr. rate: θ^{SI}			
1996	13.9	14.7	13.2	13.9	39.9	34.2	25.7	40.0
1997	12.4	13.2	11.0	12.2	38.4	33.2	24.8	38.4
2001	17.5	18.3	15.9	17.4	45.2	39.2	30.8	45.2
2041	18.4	18.8	17.2	18.4	47.6	42.0	29.8	47.6
∞	22.7	23.5	21.1	22.5	53.8	48.2	34.7	53.5
	Aggregate implicit tax: τ^{SI}				Employment per capita			
1996	31.0	29.7	15.4	31.0	1.00	1.00	1.00	1.00
1997	28.8	27.8	13.1	28.7	1.05	1.04	1.04	1.05
2001	35.1	33.6	18.6	35.0	1.00	0.99	1.00	1.00
2041	38.9	36.8	19.3	39.9	0.83	0.84	0.84	0.84
∞	44.8	43.1	23.2	44.6	0.89	0.89	0.90	0.90
	Capital stock per capita				Consumption per capita			
1996	1.00	1.00	1.00	1.00	1.00	1.00	1.00	1.00
1997	1.00	1.00	1.00	1.00	0.97	0.96	0.97	0.97
2001	1.07	1.07	1.07	1.07	0.97	0.97	0.97	0.97
2041	1.31	1.36	1.32	1.32	1.02	1.06	1.06	1.02
∞	0.98	0.99	1.05	1.01	0.89	0.90	0.97	0.90

[a]No unemployment and no unemployment insurance.
[b]No health insurance.
[c]Slower increase in the strength of the preference for leisure.

Table 8.5: Smoothing: sensitivity analysis - changes in utility

	Capital Stock				Pension Act of 1999			
Year of birth	Base Case	No UI[a]	No HI[b]	Low α[c]	Base Case	No UI	No HI	Low α
ΔU								
1921	0.05	0.12	0.08	0.16	-0.05	0	-0.07	-0.20
1936	-1.00	-0.91	-0.85	-0.93	0.49	0.21	0.43	0.52
1946	-0.81	-0.76	-0.62	-0.69	-1.46	-1.50	-1.78	-1.49
1966	-0.11	-0.20	-0.14	-0.13	0.77	0.34	0.40	0.91
1976	-0.06	-0.13	-0.08	-0.06	1.97	1.31	1.49	2.12
1996	4.60	4.13	3.45	4.44	4.33	4.02	3.82	4.42
∞	0.01	0	0.02	0.06	6.26	6.40	5.45	5.92
$\sum$	-0.02	0.02	-0.02	0	0.62	0.36	0.41	0.64
ΔEB								
1921	0.01	0.01	0	0	0.01	0.01	0.01	0
1936	0.04	0.03	0.04	0.04	0.03	0.01	0.02	0.04
1946	-0.15	-0.15	-0.06	-0.17	0.44	-0.21	-0.13	0.06
1966	0.04	0.13	-0.07	0.02	0.48	0.21	0.25	0.61
1976	0.09	0.21	-0.20	0.06	0.92	0.54	0.49	1.00
1996	2.52	2.82	1.09	2.52	2.03	1.83	1.41	2.24
∞	0.03	-0.01	-0.15	-0.17	2.53	2.60	1.72	2.42
$\sum$	0.22	0.33	0.05	0.19	0.66	0.28	0.30	0.60

In percentage points of all remaining lifetime resources
[a]No unemployment insurance.
[b]No health insurance.
[c]Slower increase in the strength of the preference for leisure.

case. It exceeds the initial level by 1% in the final steady state compared to a 2% reduction in the base case. A higher capital stock implies a higher output level. This induces a rise in consumption. Hence, consumption per capita reaches 90% of the starting value in this simulation but only 89% in the base case. Both the effects on the capital stock and consumption raise tax revenue and, thus, reduce the initial upward shift of the consumption tax rate.

The simulation *without unemployment insurance*, 'No UI', shows that the capital stock and consumption per capita are considerably higher in the medium term compared to the base case. The capital stock per capita increases to 136% compared to 131% and the consumption per capita reaches

106% instead of 102% of its initial level. These differences vanish almost completely in the long term. The reason for these effects is that lower implicit pension taxes cause a stronger rise in employment and income if there is no unemployment. Therefore savings and consumption increase when the old age dependency ratio is higher. This effect is stronger in the medium than in the long term.

In the case *without health insurance*, 'No HI', strong differences to the base case occur in the medium and in the long-term. In this scenario the implicit tax rate decreases relatively stronger when the old age dependency ratio increases. This raises income, savings and consumption in the medium and long term. This effect peaks not in 2041 but in the 2050s as outlined in section 5.2.

Finally, let us compare the different settings with respect to welfare and efficiency. The left hand part of Table 8.5 shows these figures. The welfare change is always zero. Of course there are differences in utility changes for the different cohorts between the four simulations. But, except for cohort 1996, these are not very large. The efficiency gains of this cohort in the case without health insurance are less than half as large as in the other cases. This is due to the fact that the aggregate rate of implicit tax is considerably lower without health insurance. Therefore a reduction in this rate generates lower efficiency gains. This difference also appears in utility changes.

8.3.2 The Pension Act of 1999: the Demographic Factor

The Pension Act of 1999 introduces a demographic factor with the aim of reducing the increase in the rate of contribution. Since the new German government has suspended this reform at the end of 1998, an examination of this act allows us to evaluate this action of the new government.

Reform Scheme

The German Pension Act of 1992 is extended in the Act of 1999 (Rentenreformgesetz 1999) by the following regulations:

- The rise in the mandatory retirement age from 60 to 63 is extended to disability pensions.

- Insertion of a demographic factor DF_s in the computation of the current pension value, ensuring that the size of pension benefits decreases if life expectancy increases. Hence (2.32) on page 43 becomes

$$a_s^R = a_{s-1}^R \times \frac{BE_{s-1}}{BE_{s-2}} \times \frac{NQ_{s-1}}{NQ_{s-2}} \times \frac{RQ_{s-2}}{RQ_{s-1}} \times DF_s$$

where

$$DF_s = 1 + \left[\left(\frac{LE_{t-9}}{LE_{t-8}} - 1 \right) \times 0.5 \right] . \tag{8.1}$$

LE_{t-9} is the average life expectancy of an individual aged 65 nine years before, and LE_{t-8} is the average life expectancy eight years before.

The new German government has temporarily suspended the demographic factor and the change in the statutory retirement age for disability pensions in a correction of the Pension Act of 1992 at the end of 1998 (*Rentenkorrekturgesetz*).

Social Insurance and Macroeconomic Effects

The demographic factor reduces the replacement rate of pension benefits with a nine years delay from the period in which the increase in life expectancy takes place. Suppose, as assumed in the simulation, that life expectancy increases for 30 years by 0.1 years per year, then the relative size of pension benefits decreases from the year 2006 to 2036. Hence all effects of the Pension Act of 1992 as described in chapter 6 are intensified.

Individuals increase savings and labor supply more than in the case of the Pension Act of 1992 (see panel (a) of Figure 8.6 and panel (c) of Figure 8.5). In addition individuals postpone retiring between 2022 and 2026 and between 2036 and 2074. This differs from the behavior under the Pension Act of 1992. This is reflected in the old age dependency ratio shown in panel (a) of Figure 8.4. The reason for the stronger effect on the retirement age is the reduction of both the implicit tax rate of the pension system and the pension benefits foregone when working, both raising the true wage. As a consequence working becomes more attractive compared to retiring. In addition the income effect also stimulates working. The loss in future benefits has to be compensated by working more.

These changes in the retirement age strengthen the effect of the demographic factor on the rate of contribution to the pension system. This rate peaks at 27.3% in 2040, 2.8 percentage points below the level it reaches in the simulation of the Pension Act of 1992 (see panel (b) of Figure 8.4). Panel (d) of Figure 8.4 shows the overall contribution and implicit pension taxes. The former reaches its maximum of 54.2% in 2051, compared to 57.2% under the Pension Act of 1992 and 62.2% in the benchmark case. The figures for the latter are 45.8% for this simulation, 48.8% for the Pension Act of 1992, and 53.4% for the benchmark case. Hence the demographic factor reduces the aggregate rate of implicit tax by 3 percentage points in 2050, compared to the Pension Act of 1992. The 'smoothing' effect of this reform is, of course, small since the major problems are generated by the decline in population growth (see section 5.2).

Welfare Effects

The right hand side of Table 8.3 shows the welfare and distribution effects of the Pension Act of 1999. According to column 'ΔU', almost all losses and gains are higher than in the case of the Pension Act of 1992 (see Table 6.6 on page 132).

Since the rate of implicit and consumption tax are relatively lower in the medium term, in comparison to the Pension Act of 1992, excess burdens decrease for the younger and future cohorts (see column 'ΔEB' on the right hand side of Table 8.3). While changes in net tax liabilities are very small – the reduction in the consumption tax rate is partially offset by a higher marginal rate of wage tax which is caused by higher employment –, there are large differences in net pension benefits between the cohorts. For instance cohort 1946 loses 2.25% of the remaining lifetime resources in net pension benefits while it loses 2.02% in the base case, i. e. the Pension Act of 1992. The relative loss of the cohort 1956 is about the same. These are the cohorts most disadvantaged by the demographic factor since they hardly benefit from the relatively lower rate of contribution. The reduction in contribution payments exceeds the loss in pension benefits starting with the cohort 1976. Aggregating all effects shows that these cohorts are also better off if the Pension Act of 1999 is implemented.

Overall utility rises to 0.62% in the long term compared to 0.50% under the Act of 1992 (see Table 6.8), again caused by efficiency effects. Suspending this reform costs about 0.12% of the present value of all remaining lifetime resources, which is 19.8% of the aggregate expenditure of the pension system in 1996. However, the reform scheme of 1999 causes an intergenerational redistribution at the expense of current generations and in favor of future cohorts compared to the Pension Act of 1992. This might be the reason for the suspension of the Act of 1999 (see section 10.1).

Sensitivity Analysis

The sensitivity analysis produces results similar to those of the Pension Act of 1992. Table 8.4 and Table 8.5 show the figures computed in the case of the Pension Act of 1999. Table 6.7 on page 134 and Table 6.8 on page 136 show the results with respect to the Pension Act of 1992.

Omitting unemployment insurance ('No UI') changes the retirement decision in some years. The old age dependency ratio is higher in the short term if this is done but lower in the long term. Reasons are provided in the discussion of the sensitivity analysis of the Pension Act of 1992 on page 132. Since almost all differences between the variables in the three cases are similar to those produced under the Pension Act of 1992 we refer to that case for further explanations.

Let us now discuss utility changes which are shown in Table 8.5. *Omitting unemployment* ('No UI') disadvantages all cohorts initially alive. Only the cohorts living in the final steady state are better off. Consequently overall efficiency and welfare are no longer higher but lower than for the Pension Act of 1992. Since, in the short term, some cohorts retire earlier than in the case with unemployment insurance, the old age dependency ratio and the rate of contribution to and the implicit tax rate of the pension system are higher in 2001. In contrast, in the medium term all rates except the implicit tax rate of the pension system are relatively lower. Since unemployment is not considered, the rate of contribution to and the implicit tax rate of unemployment insurance are zero. This eliminates an-

Table 8.6: Pension Act of 1999: sensitivity analysis – macro effects

	Pension Act of 1999				Pension Act of 1999			
Year of birth	Base Case	No UI[a]	No HI[b]	Low α[c]	Base Case	No UI	No HI	Low α
	Old age dependency ratio				Unemployment rate: x			
1996	0.37	0.37	0.37	0.37	11.5	–	11.5	11.5
1997	0.37	0.37	0.37	0.37	10.9	–	11.1	10.9
2001	0.36	0.38	0.36	0.36	11.1	–	11.2	11.0
2041	0.74	0.74	0.79	0.74	11.1	–	11.2	11.5
∞	0.60	0.56	0.60	0.56	11.0	–	10.9	11.0
	Consumption tax rate: τ^c				Pension contr. rate: θ^P			
1996	22.2	21.7	17.3	22.2	19.2	19.2	19.2	19.2
1997	21.8	21.6	17.2	21.6	18.7	18.7	18.8	18.7
2001	20.8	21.3	16.9	20.3	18.2	19.4	18.3	18.2
2041	25.7	23.0	17.9	25.8	27.0	26.6	28.7	27.6
∞	26.3	23.8	17.0	24.7	23.3	22.4	22.2	22.5
	Implicit pension tax: τ^P				Aggregate contr. rate: θ^{SI}			
1996	13.9	14.7	13.2	14.0	39.9	34.2	25.7	40.0
1997	13.1	13.7	11.9	13.1	38.7	33.3	24.9	38.8
2001	12.8	14.7	11.5	12.8	38.3	34.1	24.5	38.3
2041	22.2	22.5	22.7	22.6	53.4	46.9	24.9	54.1
∞	18.1	18.0	15.9	17.3	48.0	41.3	28.2	47.1
	Aggregate implicit tax: τ^{SI}				Employment per capita			
1996	31.0	29.7	15.4	31.1	1.00	1.00	1.00	1.00
1997	29.6	28.4	14.0	29.7	1.04	1.03	1.02	1.04
2001	29.3	29.4	13.6	29.3	1.04	1.02	1.04	1.04
2041	45.4	42.8	25.3	45.9	0.81	0.82	0.81	0.81
∞	39.6	36.9	18.1	38.7	0.90	0.91	0.91	0.90
	Capital stock per capita				Consumption per capita			
1996	1.00	1.00	1.00	1.00	1.00	1.00	1.00	1.00
1997	1.00	1.00	1.00	1.00	0.97	0.96	0.97	0.97
2001	1.06	1.06	1.07	1.06	0.99	0.98	0.99	1.00
2041	1.32	1.34	1.35	1.34	1.01	1.05	1.06	1.02
∞	1.11	1.15	1.23	1.16	0.95	0.99	1.03	0.97

[a]No unemployment and no unemployment insurance.
[b]No health insurance.
[c]Slower increase in the strength of the preference for leisure.

other reason for the increase in the aggregate rate of implicit tax which occurs in the base case. As a consequence the efficiency and utility gains increase faster, and the cohorts living in the final steady state experience higher utility gains than in the benchmark case. The reason why all other cohorts lose in the case without unemployment insurance is that the level of the aggregate rate of implicit tax and, thus, efficiency gains are lower. Moreover the cohorts who work initially have a relatively higher implicit tax rate for some years to finance the earlier retirement of the elder working cohorts. This also reduces efficiency and, thus, utility gains.

If *health insurance* ('No HI') is not modeled, the level of the marginal aggregate rate of implicit tax is considerably lower. Hence, efficiency and utility gains are also lower. Of course there are other effects working for or against these major effects. For instance, omitting health insurance induces a higher net wage and makes working more attractive than retiring. For this reason the old age dependency ratio is reduced in the 2020s and the mid 2040s. Note that both effects are not shown in Table 8.6.

A *slower increase in the strength of the preference for leisure* is examined in the final sensitivity analysis. This implies a higher elasticity of the retirement age. Column 'Low α' in Table 8.6 shows that the old age dependency ratio is only lower in the long term. Closer inspection of this ratio over the whole time horizon of the simulation shows that it is below the level of the base case in the period 2002-2004 and 2026-2034. As a lower old age dependency ratio is equivalent to a higher average retirement age, the rate of contribution and implicit tax are relatively lower in the long term. This, in turn, increases capital and consumption per capita. In the long term, the former is 116% of its initial level compared to 110% in the base case. The latter is only 3 percentage points below the 1996 level but 5 percentage points below the level in the base case. Nonetheless utility and efficiency effects hardly differ. Welfare gains amount to 0.64% of all lifetime resources. In the base case they add up to 0.62%.

8.4 Conclusions

The results presented in this chapter make clear that smoothing the rate of contribution is not a source of large efficiency gains. Though smoothing the rate of contribution is a not a bad substitute for smoothing the average marginal rate of implicit tax, aggregate efficiency gains are very small compared to other policy changes such as a switch in the tax base. Nonetheless smoothing the rate of contribution generates welfare gains if this is accompanied by an adjustment in pension benefits so that the budget of the pension system is balanced. However, in this case the initially middle-aged cohorts pay for the improvement in welfare and the high utility gains accruing to the younger and future cohorts. If tax smoothing is enabled by allowing a capital stock to be accumulated in the pension system these welfare gains vanish. The initially middle-aged individuals now bear fully the burden of tax smoothing by having higher implicit tax liabilities. Therefore they are not better off than in the tax smoothing scenario. The younger and future cohorts receive higher benefits but pay higher contributions. Consequently their utility gains are approximately the same under both schemes. Although smoothing or fixing the rate of contribution does not promise high welfare gains it appears to be a very good policy to rescue the pension system.

A first step in the direction of smoothing the rate of contribution was the Pension Act of 1999. It smoothes fluctuations in the rate of contribution induced by the growth of life expectancy. The results reported above make clear that the Pension Act of 1999 produces two positive results: first, it raises efficiency and, thus, welfare; second, it improves the financial situation of the pension system. Nonetheless, the new German government promised to suspend this Act in their election campaign and did so in the spring of 1999. This points to the only but nevertheless serious flaw of this reform. It implies an intergenerational redistribution in favor of the young cohorts but at the expense of the middle-aged and elder cohorts compared to the Pension Act of 1992. Hence, suspending the Pension Act can be considered as wrong from a welfare point of view, but from the point of view of political economy it was rational to suspend it (see 10.1).

In chapter 6 we have discussed measures aiming at raising the retirement age, i. e. at changing the old age dependency ratio, which is understood to be one of the major variables in producing problems in the pension system. In this and the previous chapter a switch to financing pension benefits by consumption tax and a smoothed rate of contribution have been explored, both aiming at exploiting efficiency gains as a means of rescuing the pension system. Furthermore switching to financing by consumption tax induces an increase in the grant rate, while tax smoothing implies a reduction in the replacement rate. There remains the need to examine the effects of either a fully or partially funded pension system, or a policy of privatizing public pensions. The next chapter is devoted to this task.

Chapter 9

A Fully or Partially Privatizing Policy

There appears to be a consensus among a large group of economists that a fully funded pension scheme is the best alternative to the unsustainable current PAYGO pension system. The proposals for specific transition schemes are legion. Among them are the contributions of the World Bank (1995), the BIS (1998), Diamond (1997b), Feldstein (1996), Feldstein and Samwick (1998), Glisman and Horn (1997), Holzmann (1997), Neumann (1997), Kotlikoff (1996a and c, 1998), Mitchell and Zeldes (1996) and the papers collected in Feldstein (1998). Boldrin et. al. (1999) summarize the thinking behind these proposals: "*Total earnings ... have been growing slowly during the last two decades (2% a year in the EU, since the mid-1970s) and are likely to grow at a similar pace in the foreseeable future. In contrast, the growth rate of the market value of private investments, as measured by the growth rate of stock market indexes, has been much higher (10% a year in real terms in the EU, since the early 1980s) and is not expected to drop in the future. Consequently working people are putting their retirement eggs in the wrong basket.*" There are however a lot of objections to this reasoning, summarized, for instance, by Boldrin et. al. (1999).

On account of different risks arising in a fully funded system and a PAYGO financed system and the problems of the transition, another proposal is that the future pension system should be a hybrid system consisting of a PAYGO component and a partially funded system (see for instance Boldrin et. al., 1999, Sinn, 1999, Miegel and Wahl, 1985 and 1999, Neumann, 1998, Wissenschaftlicher Beirat, 1998).

The debate on whether a pension system should be a fully funded or a PAYGO system is very old. While it originally focused on the efficiency of both systems (see e.g. Samuelson, 1975), the issue of the transition from an existing PAYGO to a fully funded system is now the main subject (see e.g. Homburg, 1990a, or Fenge, 1995). Almost all theoretical papers deal with the question of whether a Pareto improving transition is feasible. But the magnitude of the gains and losses of different privatization plans could not be assessed in a general equilibrium framework until dynamic CGE models were available (e.g. Raffelhüschen, 1993, Kotlikoff, 1996, and Hirte and Weber, 1997b). The outcomes of these studies made clear that at least the size of the effects depends on the specific transition scheme implemented in the reform, especially on the schedule of the introduction and the timing of the announcement. Hence, each modification of the model can change the magnitude of the effects occurring when the PAYGO system is replaced by a fully funded system. Therefore different scenarios should be examined. However, since the main effects occur in all scenarios, we confine to one proposal. It is examined in the first simulation which computes the consequences of a full transition in the current setting.

As a partially funded system is considered as an alternative to a full transition, the second group of simulations deal with the transition to a partially funded system. Again, different schemes have been proposed. The first is the introduction of a flat pension benefit system with a lower pension level financed by taxes, proposed for instance by Miegel and Wahl (1985 or 1999). Such a system marks a departure from the principle of equivalence which is the basis of the current German public pension system. Another scheme is a reduction in the relative size of pension benefits without abolishing the tax benefit linkage which is accompanied by a voluntary or mandatory private pension plan. This is similar to the German pension reform of 2001. Both reform schemes are considered below, the former by carrying out new simulations, and the latter by referring to the outcomes of simulations presented in the previous chapter. A third way of establishing a partially funded system is the accumulation of a fund integrated in the public pension system. This can be achieved by raising current contributions and accumulating the surpluses generated as reserves in the pension system. We have already considered this proposal in the previous chapter since it is also a strategy for tax smoothing. In the present chapter only funding strategies are examined which are equivalent to a substitutional or additional private pension plan.

These are the issues discussed below. But first we summarize the literature on the transition to a fully funded system.

9.1 Transition to a Fully Funded System

9.1.1 Discussion

The seminal papers on the efficiency of PAYGO social security systems are those of Samuelson (1958) and Aaron (1966), who show that a PAYGO system produces a higher internal rate of return if the aggregate growth rate of wages and population exceeds the interest rate of investments, the so-called Aaron condition. Then and only then the introduction of a PAYGO transfer system from young to old generations improves steady state welfare. This result is confirmed by Hu (1979) and Spreman (1984). These papers examine a small open economy, i. e. constant wages and interest rates. Other papers by Diamond (1965) and Samuelson (1975) proved the Aaron condition for a closed economy in which factor prices are endogenously determined and a life cycle approach is adopted.

The new debate on the efficiency of the PAYGO system splits into two branches. The first deals with the question whether introducing a PAYGO system can improve efficiency. According to the vast majority of papers the answer is 'no' (see for instance, Enders and Lapan 1982, Smith, 1982, Merton, 1983, Gordon and Varian, 1988, Huber, 1990, Homburg, 1990b and 1992, Richter, 1993). The second examines whether abolishing a PAYGO system can enhance efficiency. In addition all papers consider the case where the Aaron condition is violated, i. e. the interest rate is permanently higher than the aggregate rate of growth of wage and population. But even in this case a PAYGO pension system, once implemented, is efficient if labor supply is exogenous and a Pareto improving transition to a fully funded system is not feasible (Breyer, 1989, Verbon, 1989, Peters, 1991). The reason for this outcome is that the presumably higher rate of return of the fully funded system is completely consumed in paying the interest on the amount of public debt that has been taken up to finance the compensations paid to the elder cohorts. The gains of the generation which receives benefits during the introduction of a PAYGO system are the source of intergenerational redistribution in favor of this first cohort of retirees (Breyer 1989, Sinn 1999). Consequently, abolishing the PAYGO system disadvantages at least one cohort (Breyer, 1989). Moreover, since labor supply is exogenous, the rate of contribution is equivalent to a lump sum tax, and the policy reform does not generate any efficiency gains.

Homburg (1990a) introduced endogenous labor supply and showed that a Pareto improving transition is feasible in a small open economy if and only if efficiency gains emerge. In his model these efficiency gains are caused by the abolition of the payroll tax used to finance contributions. Though Homburg and Richter (1990) have calculated the deadweight loss caused by contributions, they have not examined whether there are efficiency gains which allow a Pareto improving transition to a fully funded system to be carried out. Breyer and Straub (1993) confirm this result for a small open economy. Breyer and Wildasin (1993) show that this result cannot necessarily be transferred to a large open economy. This depends on whether the country is a net lender or a net borrower. Moreover, Brunner (1994 and 1996) and Fenge and Schwager (1995) have shown that in an economy with heterogeneous individuals it is not always possible to offset intragenerational redistribution by efficiency gains.

According to Homburg (1997) all these results refer to a pension system where benefits are independent of contributions. But it can be deduced that these results can be transferred to an economy with benefits based on contribution, but where individuals wrongly anticipate the implicit link between utility compensations, benefits, and the tax used to finance benefits and utility compensations. If benefits are linked to contributions no efficiency gains occur if the compensation of the loser of a transition to a fully funded system is financed by the same payroll tax as contributions to the PAYGO system. Consequently a Pareto improving transition to a fully funded system is not feasible without an additional change in taxation (Fenge, 1995, see also Fenge, 1997). From this one can infer that the debate on pension reforms should focus on the design of tax reform rather than on whether the system should be a PAYGO or a fully funded system. After all, each tax reform can also be carried out within the PAYGO system.

Regardless of this theoretical reasoning the issue of a switch to a fully funded system is not out of fashion in the public debate on pension reforms, but it has changed the focus of the analysis. The new question is how should a reform package consisting of a switch to a fully funded system *and* a change in taxation be designed so that a transition to a fully funded system is politically feasible (Hirte and Weber, 1997b), i. e. is accepted either by all members of a society or the majority of voters. Each transition to a fully funded system requires compensation of the losers if these can prevent a reform, for instance, by voting. For this reason any reform scheme should generate efficiency gains which can be used for compensation. Consequently a reform scheme has to be a package containing a reform of the PAYGO system *and* a tax reform. In addition each change in the PAYGO system which alleviates the financial problems of this system almost certainly causes a change in the implicit tax rate and is therefore a tax reform. The first papers which explicitly examined whether a Pareto improving transition is possible in a second best environment if it is accompanied by tax reform, are the CGE analysis of Broer, Westerhout and Bovenberg (1994), Kotlikoff (1996a), and Hirte and Weber (1997b).

Broer, Westerhout and Bovenberg (1994) found that a transition to a fully funded system can be carried out in a Pareto improving way in the Netherlands. This is due to the specific pension system in the Netherlands. A capital stock which already exists can be used to finance the transition. This solution is not available for other countries. However, Kotlikoff (1996) also found a way to achieve a Pareto improving transition provided the current pension system does not tie contributions to benefits. In this case contributions are pure taxes and a change from payroll to consumption taxes produces efficiency gains so that a Pareto improving transition can be achieved. In contrast, Hirte and Weber (1997b) introduced an incomplete tax benefit linkage in their model. Nonetheless they found at least one compensation scheme which allows the compensation payments to be financed by efficiency gains. The scheme they propose consists of financing by debt and consumption tax. The efficiency gains of the switch from payroll to consumption tax, together with the gains from tax smoothing, are high enough to finance lump sum compensation payments. However the compensations they consider are pure lump sum transfers which exactly offset utility losses. It is, however, hardly possible to implement such a scheme for reform in reality. Instead other schemes for compensation should be considered. But each deviation from a pure utility compensation raises the costs of the transition since at least some cohorts are likely to be overcompensated if other compensation schemes are applied. Hence it is less likely that a Pareto improving transition is feasible. It is therefore not surprising that other papers which examine a switch from a PAYGO to a funded system in a CGE model only compute the pure effects of this reform (Raffelhüschen and Kitterer, 1990, Raffelhüschen, 1993, Raffelhüschen and Risa, 1995, and Fehr, 1999a and b).

Despite these discussion the theoretical debate is not yet finished. Recently Wrede (1999) published a paper which shows that in a second best environment a Pareto improving reform of the PAYGO system might be possible. He argues that a PAYGO system causes intertemporal substitution effects if it has an implicit tax rate which is not constant during the working life. According to Hirte and Weber (1997b) the German marginal rate of implicit tax possesses this feature because it decreases with age. Hence an individual is more taxed at the beginning of his working life and less taxed at the end of his working life.[1] This causes intertemporal substitution effects and makes efficiency gains possible by introducing contributions and, thus, an implicit tax rate depending on age. However, the results on tax smoothing obtained in the present study or, for instance, by Cutler et. al. (1990) are pessimistic about the size of these gains. At any rate, such a reform is also a mixed proposal for a tax reform and a transition to a fully funded system. Hence all efficiency gains occurring are caused by the tax reform. Therefore, the argument of Fenge (1995) remains valid.

Another branch of the literature examines other gains from switching

---

[1]According to Hirte (2000c), this is in the German case only true for constant productivity growth.

to a fully funded system. For instance, the transition might improve the efficiency of the capital market. If these gains are high enough, a Pareto-improving transition might be possible (Börsch-Supan, 1998a). Furthermore if one considers human capital or fertility decisions a transition to a fully funded system could strengthen endogenous growth. Endogenous growth and endogenous fertility decisions are, for instance, examined by Zhang (1995). In models with endogenous fertility but exogenous growth, unfunded pension benefits reduce fertility and thus increase growth (Becker and Barro, 1988, Lapan and Enders, 1990, and Wildasin, 1990). In models with endogenous growth an opposite *savings effect* occurs[2]. The overall effect of a PAYGO system on economic growth is nonetheless positive. The reason is that an unfunded social security program reduces fertility but raises investment in human capital per capita (Zhang, 1995). However, a PAYGO system might be Pareto inferior to a fully funded system if fertility is not considered. The reason is that the unfunded system depresses economic growth, as shown by Saint-Paul (1992). But this result is not undisputed. There are models of endogenous growth in which a Pareto improving transition from a PAYGO to a fully funded system is possible in a model with full employment (Belan, Michel, and Pestieau, 1996) as well as in a model with unemployment (Corneo and Marquardt, 1999). If one considers human capital, a transition to a fully funded system could raise investment in human capital and, thus, foster endogenous growth (Wigger, 2000).

All these studies neglect issues of risk, which can worsen the case for a fully funded system as demonstrated by Miles and Timmermann (1999) (see also Miles and Iben, 1998). They provide evidence that the income risk is much higher than expected in the case of a fully funded system. The reason is that a long term average cannot be used to assess the risk of investments in equities or bonds since the timing of accumulating savings is fixed. Consequently, the rate of return near retirement is much more important for the overall rate of return than its long term average. Miles and Timmermann simulate the transition to a fully funded system in a

[2]FELDSTEIN (1974 and 1995) provided evidence that a PAYGO financed pension system actually reduces personal savings by roughly 40% in the U.S..

partial equilibrium setting. One outcome of these simulations is that there are individuals whose compound rate of return in a private pension scheme is negative even if the long-term average rate of return is 6.25%.

Another result in the literature is that pushing the transition path nearer to a Pareto improving transition path reduces welfare and efficiency gains. The reason is that these gains which occur in the future have to be transferred across time to the initially middle-aged cohorts. This transfer is not free of cost even if carried out by raising debt, since it requires a change in the time pattern of taxes at the expense of future cohorts. Taxes have to be raised in the future to finance either repayment of debt or additional interest payments. If the implementation of such a reform also takes into account the political costs of enacting the reform, managing the implementation, etc., a Pareto improving transition appears to be less and less feasible, even if accompanied by partial debt financing and a tax reform as proposed by Hirte and Weber (1997b). For these reasons it is not at all surprising that the current German policy debate focuses on a mixed funded and PAYGO system. In addition, a fully privatizing policy seems not to be politically feasible (Hirte, 2000b). Nonetheless, there are some authors (e. g. Glisman and Horn, 1997, Feldstein, 1995, 1996, and 1998, and Börsch-Supan, 1998c) and institutes which promote a transition to a fully privatized pension system (Deutsches Institut für Altersversicherung, 1998).

In Germany the introduction of a partially privatized system appears to be most likely, and is actually implemented in the pension reform of 2001. Though there is a discussion about the level of the private system or whether such a system should be mandatory, there seems to be a consensus that such a system is necessary. In 1999 the Minister of Labor presented the proposal that employees should pay up to 3% of their income into a private pension plan, which would be mandatory. There was a short and intense debate on this proposal. Then the proposal was changed to make the private pension plan no longer mandatory. Further discussion led to many changes of the proposal. Nonetheless, the introduction of a partially funded system is the most innovative part of the German pension reform of 2001. A similar scheme has been suggested by the Advisory Board of the

Ministry of Economics (Wissenschaftlicher Beirat, 1998). The Advisory Board proposes a hybrid system consisting of a public and a private pension scheme where contributions to both the private and public system should add up to about 24.5% in the first years of the transition and to at most 27% at the peak of the pension crisis. In the long term 50% of the whole pension system should be private. In this way the burden on the employees would be reduced during the most difficult years since they can expect a higher rate of return in their private pension scheme.

The third reform scheme publicly discussed involves flat basic pension benefits. The original proposal is that of Miegel and Wahl (1985) who redesigned their proposal in a recently published study (Miegel and Wahl, 1999). They suggest that uniform pension benefits which are based on a lower replacement rate should be financed by consumption taxes. A similar proposal is part of the program of the "Grünen", the German green party (Bueb, Schreyer, Opielka, 1984), another was recently suggested by the Institut für Wirtschaft and Gesellschaft (1997), and further financing schemes, for instance a partial debt financing, are considered by Fehr (1999a and c).

We examine below these three proposals. First we consider the consequences of a transition to a fully funded system in an aging population, a case not yet investigated in a general equilibrium setting. Second, simulations of a switch to a flat basic pension system are performed where different financing schemes are modeled. And, finally, a hybrid or partially funded system is considered, where different financing methods are explicitly considered and a strong reduction in public pension benefits occurs.

9.2 Full Transition

A full transition can be carried out either instantaneously or gradually. In the former case old claims on the pension system are eliminated. In the latter case different scenarios are possible. For instance, claims on pension benefits acquired before the year of reform are paid out as pension benefits after the reform. This so-called phase-out policy reform does not disadvantage the elderly as much as the immediate switch to the fully funded system. But each transition, at least if there are no compensation payments, disadvantages the initially middle-aged but improves utility for the younger and future cohorts. This is a well known result established by many CGE studies. The first CGE study for Germany simulating such a case was performed by Raffelhüschen (1993). While he considered only a two period life cycle, Hirte and Weber (1997b) examined the transition in a more sophisticated model. They implemented the main features of the German pension system and considered a life cycle of 75 years. In addition Fehr (1999a and b) discussed the intragenerational effects of the transition schemes. Since consumption taxes are regressive a financing of the transition by consumption taxes increases the losses and benefits of the lower income quintile (Fehr, 1999a, 205). Similar results have been obtained by Kotlikoff (1996 and 1998, 1999) for the U.S..

In a partial equilibrium study Börsch-Supan (1998c) examines a transition to a fully funded system, which is to be carried out over the next 40 years. All entitlements to pension benefits collected before the start of the reform are fully acknowledged. Pension benefits are computed according to the pension formula in force until part II of the Pension Act of 1992 becomes effective in 2001. The reform starts in 2008. The transition is not Pareto improving in his scenario. Referring to the so-called non-insurance benefits, i. e. that portion of pension benefits used for intragenerational redistribution, Börsch-Supan suggests that these benefits should also be granted and financed in a PAYGO way in the future. Hence, only about 70% to 75% of current pension benefits should be replaced by a fully funded system. Börsch-Supan claims that his computation proves that a fully funded system is possible because the transition is not too expensive. Further discussion on this point can be found in Burger (1998), Eitenmüller and Hain (1998), and DIW (1999).

Generally, modeling a fully privatized pension system is easy in the Auerbach-Kotlikoff framework. As long as there is no rationing of credit a fully funded system is equivalent to private savings and, thus, must not be modeled explicitly. Though this equivalence can break down if credit for individuals is rationed, as shown by Cifuentes and Valdés-Prieto (1997), we do not model credit rationing. The reason is that in the present study only the youngest cohort would be affected by credit rationing. But this is the case only if they are forced to contribute more than 5% of labor income to a private pension plan.

An immediate transition which does not satisfy claims to pension benefits already accumulated is not feasible in the German case because these claims are private property which is protected by the constitution ('Grundgesetz'). Nonetheless many studies have examined the effects of such an immediate switch in Germany (see Raffelhüschen, 1993, Hirte and Weber, 1997b, Fehr, 1999a). Since the findings show that the degree of intergenerational redistribution produced by the reform is higher than under any phase-out scheme, we consider the immediate switch not to be feasible. Instead we implement a slow transition to a fully funded system where all claims accumulated before the year of reform are satisfied. This constitutes the phase-out of the old PAYGO system and the phase-in of a fully funded or privatized scheme. Pension benefits decrease from cohort to cohort. The last cohort which pays contributions before the reform starts in 2001, the cohort 1980, is also the last generation to receive pension benefits. However, aggregate earning points of this cohort are very low, about 1/40 of the earning points of the individuals already retired in 2001. Therefore pension benefits amount only to 1/40 of those of the initial pensioners. Since the youngest cohort knows in advance that its benefits are going to be so low it increases its savings or invests in a private pension scheme. Thus the reform scheme considered below contains a transition period of about 40 years. This is exactly what Börsch-Supan (1998) suggested.

Each full or partial transition faces some problems not discussed in other studies. We consider new regulations for contributions to health and long term care insurance, the ceiling on labor income when retired, and the so-called non-insurance benefits.

The contributions to health and long term care insurance are shared equally between the pension system and the pensioner. The contribution base is the size of pension benefits actually paid to a retiree. However, in the case of a private pension plan contributions have to be fully paid by the retirees. In addition, it is assumed that contributions are independent of pension benefits received from the private insurance. This is necessary since individuals can replace private pension plans by investing in other assets. Hence they could evade contributions to health insurance provided these depend on private pensions. On the other hand all savings could be used as a contribution base. In this case, the tax base of contributions to health insurance would be considerably higher compared to the initial tax base which consists only of pension benefits. Moreover, during the transition individuals receive pension benefits and interest income. This complicates the situation. To cope with this issue the tax base of contributions to health insurance is set to a fixed proportion of average income. These contributions have to be paid by each pensioner independent of the source of his income. To be specific the tax base is set to 50% of the average wage income. If the size of public pensions exceeds this minimal tax base, contributions also exceed the minimal contribution payments. If pensions benefits are lower, individuals have to make additional contribution payments so that their aggregate contribution payments, which include the contributions paid by the public pension system, are equal to the minimal size of the contributions.

The second regulation needed is a change in the amount one is permitted to earn by working in the first five years after retiring. Such a restriction is useful to deter individuals from retiring too early. In a private pension plan, contributions and payments of benefits are not tied to the working life but to a duration stipulated by contract. Consequently restricting working after retiring is not reasonable in a privatized pension system. However, there is a long transition period where restrictions on working are needed. This is implemented as follows: during the forty years of the transition the restriction on earnings is relaxed by 1/40 of the initial ceiling per year, so that after forty years individuals are free to earn as much as they want. In this way, the ceiling is relaxed at the same pace as the replacement rate of public pension benefits decreases.

The third measure in the reform scheme is that earning points collected on account of education under the old pension scheme plus expenditure of the public pension system for rehabilitation, etc., are now financed by taxes and paid by the government. Hence individuals receive additional payments after the public pension system is completely abolished. These benefits are equivalent to the so-called non-insurance benefits which individuals receive under the public pension system.

In addition different ways of financing the transition are considered. In a first scenario the remaining public pensions are financed in a PAYGO manner by a rise in the consumption tax rate and a 15% surcharge on the wage tax liability (see also Fehr, 1999a). The second scenario is a mixed debt and tax financing system. The debt to public expenditure ratio, which is about 2.137 in 1996 is raised by 1.25% per year between 2001 and 2040. The final ratio is 3.938. This is equivalent to a rise in the debt to GDP ratio from 54.7% in 1996 to 80% in the final steady state. Without debt financing this ratio would only amount to 47.1% . The taxes used to finance additional interest rates and public pensions during the transition are consumption taxes together with a 15% surcharge on the wage tax. Finally, it is assumed that the Pension Act of 1992 is inoperative.

9.2.1 Social Insurance and Macroeconomic Effects

Figures 9.1, 9.2, 9.3 show the results of the simulation of the transition. In a first experiment pension outlays are financed by a linked rise in direct and indirect taxes. This is modeled as a 15% surcharge on the wage tax and a rise in the consumption tax rate. In the second scheme part of these outlays is financed by issuing debt. The results are compared with the benchmark path obtained if there is no policy change.

In both cases the rate of contribution and the implicit tax rate of the pension system fall to zero in 2001, as shown in panel (b) of Figure 9.1. Panel (a) of Figure 9.1 shows some deviations from the old age dependency ratio in the benchmark in the second half of the transition period due to postponing the retirement age. Since changing the retirement decision after the reform is launched in 2001 does not affect future pension benefits, the retirement decision depends only on net wages earned and pension benefits lost when working, and on labor income after retirement. As a consequence, the incentive to lengthen the working life grows with time because the size of pension benefits individuals lose when working as well as the tax burden on wages are lowered. Therefore in some years retirement is postponed and the old age dependency ratio decreases.

There arises, however, an opposite effect caused by relaxing the restric-

Figure 9.1: Fully funded: social insurance variables

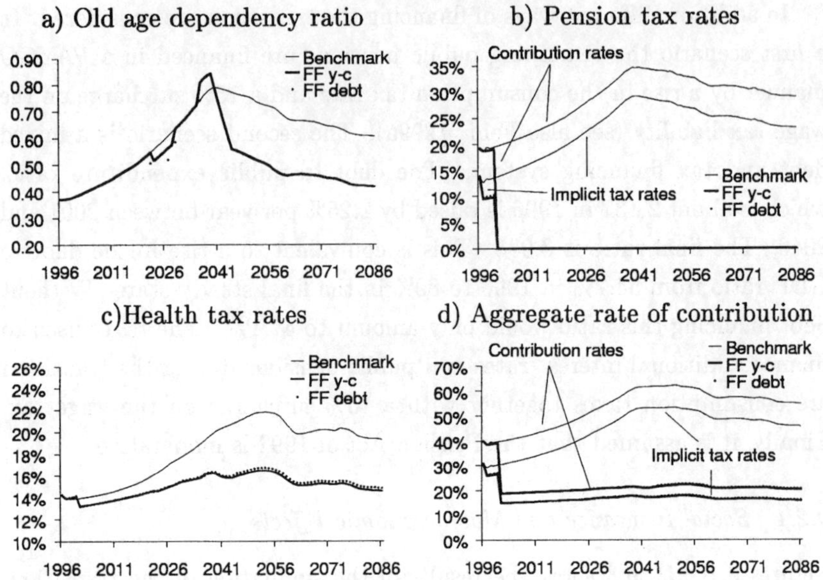

tion on working after retiring. Since the ceiling for working after retiring is gradually increased, retiring earlier is more attractive at the end of the phase-out path. Then small pension benefits can be obtained by retiring in addition to an almost equal income from working. This explains why the old age dependency ratio increases at the end of the phase-out period in all cases, as shown by Figure 9.1(a). Thereafter individuals are assumed to retire at 65, the year when they receive additional transfers to be based on former non-insurance benefits.

Labor supply is also affected. The cut in the implicit tax rate raises the effective wage and, thus, encourages labor supply. This is reflected in the increase in employment per capita shown in panel (c) of Figure 9.2. This effect is relatively large between the announcement and the year the reform is launched. Then the increase in the wage tax rate is far higher than the reduction in the implicit tax rate. But with time the later outweighs the former. Hence the effective wage increases before the reform, falls in the year of reform below the benchmark level, and increases thereafter. Since the extremely high change in the implicit tax rate affects the younger

Figure 9.2: Fully funded: employment and unemployment

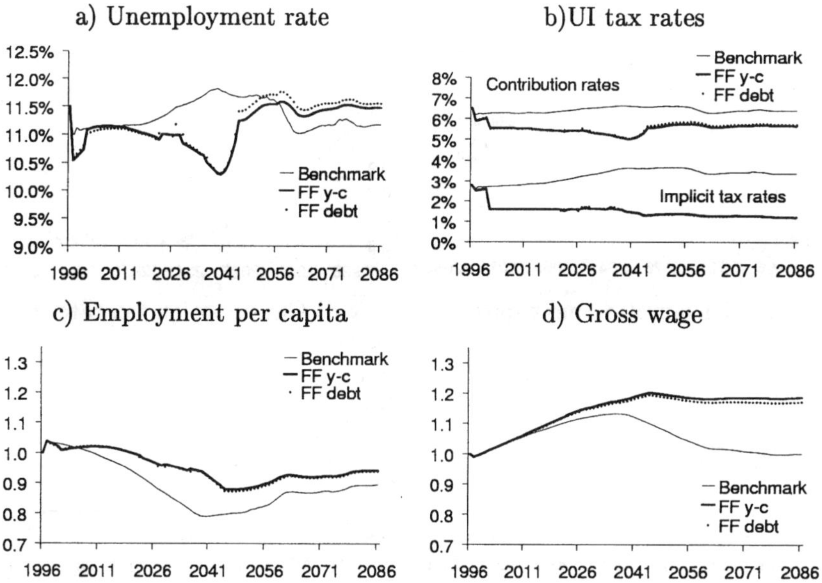

individuals, their labor supply is expanded during the pre-reform period and during the second part of the demographic transition period. In the year of reform it falls below the benchmark level and recovers thereafter with an increasing rate.

The elder working cohorts face only a small reduction in their marginal rate of implicit tax which is already very low. Hence the substitution effect is also low. As the average net wage starts to increase in the year of reform, the current pension value also increases because it is tied to the change in net wages. This raises the value of each personal earning point collected before the year of reform and, thus, the size of pension benefits which the elder working individuals receive after retiring. Hence these cohorts experience a positive income effect which allows them to consume more leisure and reduce their labor supply. Since this effect is relatively high compared to the impact of the implicit tax rate on aggregate labor supply, employment per capita is reduced before the reform is put into effect (see panel (c) of Figure 9.2). After 2001 the elder working cohorts entering retirement receive benefits which decrease from period to period. Hence

Figure 9.3: Fully funded: capital stock and consumption

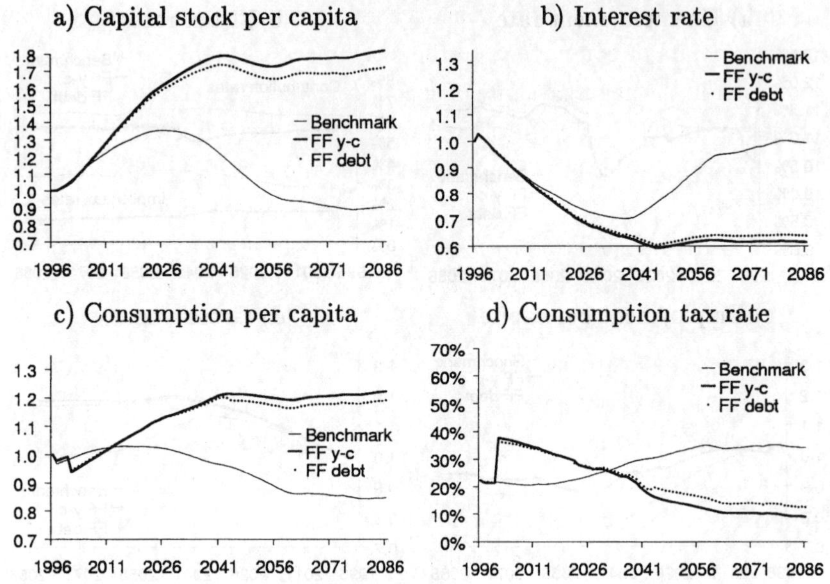

the positive income effect which occurs initially vanishes with time and is replaced by a negative income effect with the result that the elder cohorts start to expand their labor supply. Hence all working cohorts supply more labor and, finally, employment per capita increases above the benchmark level.

The same effects explain the dynamic behavior of the rate of unemployment shown in Figure 9.2(a). Since the labor supply of the younger cohorts is higher during the pre-reform period, their share in the effective labor force increases and the aggregate rate of unemployment diminishes. Since in 2001 the labor supply of the younger cohorts falls while the labor supply of the elder cohorts starts to rise again, the rate of unemployment returns to the benchmark level. But in course of time the younger cohorts expand their labor supply more than the elder cohorts so that the rate of unemployment decreases again.

The growth in employment and later in wages allows the rate of contribution to health insurance to decrease even though the elderly pay lower contributions. Panel (c) of Figure 9.1 shows that the rate of contribution to health insurance is only between two and four percentage points above its initial level in the 2040s. This is a reduction of approximately 6 percentage points in comparison to the benchmark case. Far stronger is the reduction in the aggregate rate of contribution and implicit tax in the year of reform. In 2001 the aggregate rate of contribution falls from 40% to 19% and the aggregate rate of implicit tax from about 30% to 15% (see panel (d) of Figure 9.2). Thereafter both are almost constant. Even in the 2040s and 2050s the aggregate rate of contribution does not exceed 21% and the aggregate rate of implicit tax stays below 18%. This is a reduction of the former by more than 40 points and of the latter by more then 38 points.

Figure 9.3 shows that there is a strong rise in the capital stock, an opposite fall in the interest rate, and an increase in consumption per capita which allows the consumption tax rate to fall from between 35% to 40% in 2001 to 10% in the long term. Nonetheless, the initial rise in the consumption tax is so high that it deters one from considering such a policy reform as feasible. But note that a similar level of the consumption tax rate will be reached under many other pension policies if taxation of consumption is used to balance the public budget. The only difference is that, for instance in the benchmark case or in the case of the Pension Act of 1992, such a high level of the consumption tax rate will not occur until the 2040s. Also the initial upward shift of the consumption tax rate allows labor taxes to be reduced by a similar amount.

Next a remark on capital accumulation. Individuals increase their savings with time compared to the benchmark case since they invest in private pension plans used as compensation for the abolition of the public pension system. In this way capital accumulation is enhanced. Considering the graphs of Figure 9.3 it appears that the relative increase in the capital stock per capita in the final steady state is lower by about 10 percentage points in the case of a transition financed partially by debt. Hence one can conclude that public debt issued to finance the transition crowds out private savings and thus reduces the capital stock per capita. Finally, since the surcharge on the wage tax is levied from 2001 for ever, consumption per capita as well as the capital stock per capita are lower in this case compared to a pure tax financing scheme.

Table 9.1: Fully funded system: decomposition of changes in utility

Year of	Mixed tax				Mixed tax plus debt			
birth	ΔU^a	ΔP^b	$-\Delta T^c$	ΔEB^d	ΔU	ΔP	$-\Delta T$	ΔEB
1921	0.03	-0.04	0.09	0	-0.01	-0.04	0.04	0
1936	-4.81	-0.54	-3.25	-0.11	-4.52	-0.54	-3.08	-0.08
1946	-3.24	0.51	-4.19	-0.31	-2.97	0.52	-4.06	0.62
1956	-1.18	3.33	-4.88	-0.41	-0.98	3.34	-4.80	0.55
1966	1.43	6.37	-5.73	-0.37	1.20	6.22	-5.84	1.31
1976	5.69	11.11	-7.05	-0.31	5.63	11.12	-7.12	2.61
1986	10.26	15.66	-8.82	-0.06	9.90	15.67	-9.06	5.16
1996	14.87	19.82	-8.75	0.95	14.28	19.79	-9.28	7.07
2006	18.46	24.21	-8.79	3.05	17.71	24.13	-9.69	8.95
2016	20.82	26.60	-8.51	6.71	19.87	26.45	-9.89	10.04
∞	18.61	20.05	-5.71	12.43	18.09	19.95	-7.22	7.74
$\sum$	0.75		-2.08	1.62	0.83		-1.95	1.58

All changes as percentage of all remaining lifetime resources.
[a]Change in utility.
[b]Change in net pension benefits.
[c]Change in net tax liabilities
[d]Change in efficiency.

9.2.2 Welfare Effects

For the reasons outlined above efficiency gains and welfare improvement should be higher in the case of a purely tax financed transition than when debt is permanently raised to partially finance the transition. The results shown in Table 9.1 support these expectations.

The figures shown in Table 9.1 show that strong efficiency gains accrue to all future cohorts. Overall efficiency gains amount to 1.62% of remaining wealth under the mixed tax scheme and 1.58% in the case of debt and mixed tax financing. The index of redistribution effects is -1.95% in the partial debt financing schemes and -2.08% if a mixed tax structure is used.

Altogether, both schemes lower the utility of the cohorts 1936 to 1956 and raise the utility of the cohorts born in 1966 or later. The reform schemes do not affect the initially eldest cohort whereas all other cohorts are disadvantaged by the rise in consumption taxes. The reduction in marginal wage taxes accounts for the gains of the same cohorts under all other reform schemes. Hence both reform schemes cause an intergenerational redistribution in favor of the future cohorts and at the expense of the initially middle-aged cohorts. However, issuing debt relatively lowers the intergenerational redistribution since the generations currently alive have a relatively lower consumption tax rate while a relatively high tax rate is levied on the consumption of future cohorts.

Let us summarize the findings. The transition to a fully funded system disadvantages the initially middle-aged cohorts but raises efficiency if consumption taxes are involved[3]. Thus the results confirm the outcomes of all other studies. Though further simulations suggest that it is possible to reduce the costs of the transition (for instance Hirte and Weber, 1997b, or some simulations not reported here) this reform seems not to be included in pension reform schemes likely to be enacted in Germany either now or in the near future. The main reason for this is that the high redistribution prevents this proposal being accepted by a majority of voters (see Hirte, 2000b). Therefore we turn to the investigation of the effects caused by a partially funded system.

9.3 Partially Privatization Strategies

9.3.1 The Flat Basic Pension Scheme

Miegel and Wahl (1985) propose a flat, basic pension scheme with a long phase-in period. In their proposal flat pension benefits are financed by a consumption tax but a wage tax is used to finance the transition. These flat pension benefits would be uniform for each type of pension and would be paid from the age of 63 onwards. They amount to 55% of the average wage income per capita, which is about 40% of the average net income. Since individuals would be not allowed to retire earlier, deductions from pension benefits are not included in the proposal. However there would be a supplement rate to pension benefits of 0.4% for each month retirement

[3] This is confirmed by further simulations of a pure consumption tax and a pure contribution financed transition. Then the pure consumption tax scheme produces the largest welfare improvement but the most adverse redistribution index. The opposite is true under the contribution financed transition.

is postponed. On account of the many objections[4] to financing only by a consumption tax they published a new proposal in Miegel and Wahl (1999). Here the flat pension scheme would be financed by a mix of a consumption and an income tax, where the consumption tax would account for 60% of the required revenue. The uniform pension benefits would be only 52.5% of wage income per capita. Only claims on pension benefits which are accumulated before the reform starts would be valid during the phase-in period. The net pension level would decrease to about 45% due to contributions to health and long term care insurance. Miegel and Wahl expect that this reform would not make any generation worse off in comparison with the current situation (Miegel and Wahl, 1999, p. 156).

However, many arguments against these proposals have been published, for instance, by Schmähl (1993) or Hof (1999, p. 2). Hof argues that a flat basic pension system is not favorable because it is not based on the principle of equivalence, and thus reduces incentives to work. Furthermore, the transition to a flat basic pension system has very strong redistribution effects (see also Schmähl, 1993). Fehr examines the effects of such a scheme in a framework with constant population but heterogeneous cohorts (Fehr, 1999a), and in the setting of the German demographic development (Fehr, 1999c). He compares this proposal with a scheme with the same mix of taxes but a reduction in pension benefits. He infers that the flat basic pension system should be adopted in the case of a fixed population (Fehr, 1999a). But if there is an aging trend a flat basic pension system reduces efficiency and increases redistribution at the expense of the initial elderly (Fehr, 1999c). Hence, the flat basic pension scheme is inferior to a scheme with lower benefits which are tied to contributions if one considers demographic factors.

In the flat pension scheme examined below individuals receive uniform benefits with a gross replacement rate of about 55%, the level proposed by Miegel and Wahl (1985). This is equivalent to a net replacement rate, i. e. the ratio of net pensions to average net income, of approximately 40%, though this ratio fluctuates with time. Pension outlays are financed by a

[4]For instance, the Advisory Board of the Ministry of Economics expects that the consumption tax rate ought to be raised by 15 to 20 percentage points. It considers this large increase not to be feasible (WISSENSCHAFTLICHER BEIRAT 1998, p. 15).

combination of a 15% surcharge on the wage tax liability and a rise in the consumption tax rate. But, deviating from the Miegel and Wahl proposal, the retirement age can be less than 63 because it is not very realistic to assume that individuals are willing to postpone retiring until that age. As long as there is a pension scheme for those disabled or not able to work, both can be considered as substitutes for normal old age pensions. For this reason we assume that individuals can retire earlier.

Following Fehr (1999), it is assumed that only the computation of personal earning points is altered in comparison to the current German regulations. These earning points are now independent of the relative income level. For each year of working an individual receives 0.77 earning points. Consequently pension benefits depend on the length of the working life but not on relative income. Furthermore the restriction on working after retiring is relaxed. The maximum income ceiling is raised proportionally to the reduction in the pension level. In addition the transition to the basic pension scheme takes time. Although personal earning points are reduced to 0.77 per year of working from 2001 on, earning points collected prior to this year are fully valued when computing pension benefits. This is required by the guarantee of property included in the German constitution[5].

In a second experiment the proposal is slightly modified. The supplement and deduction scheme of the Pension Act of 1992 is added to the flat pension scheme in order to encourage individuals to retire later.

Social Insurance and Macroeconomic Effects

We discuss first the case of the flat pension scheme without deductions, called 'FL tax' in the relevant figures. Panel (a) of Figure 9.4 shows that this leaves the average retirement age unchanged in comparison to the benchmark case. The reason is that the true wage is not affected enough to cause a postponement of retirement since the proposal does not include any deductions. Hence, future pension benefits are not raised enough if the retirement age increases to compensate for the loss in current pensions. Nevertheless there is a positive effect on the pension system. While benefits

[5] To be exact, only contributions of the employees but not those paid by the employer are acknowledged as property which are to be guaranteed.

Figure 9.4: Basic pensions: social insurance variables

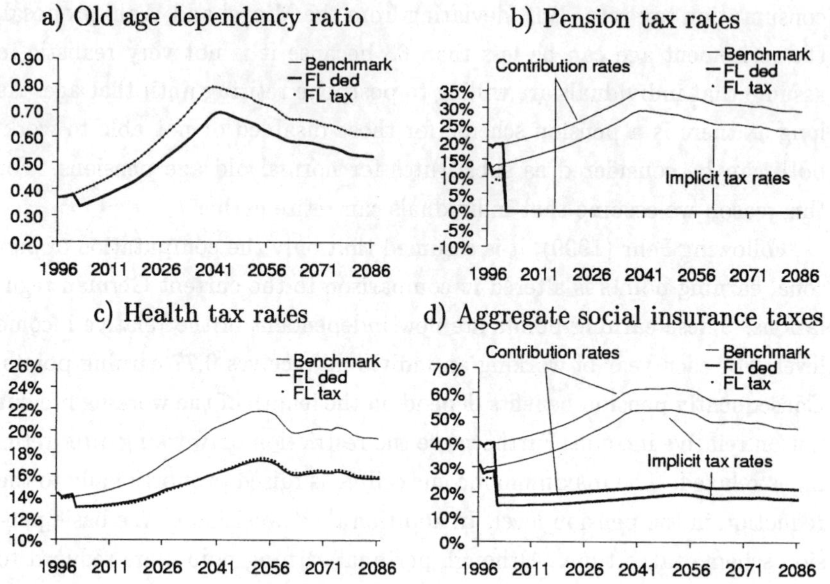

do not change initially, the reduction in personal earning points after 2000 slowly reduces pension benefits from cohort to cohort of retirees. After 45 years all pensioners receive only flat pension benefits.

Since the tax benefit linkage vanishes and the rate of contribution is replaced by wage and consumption taxes, both the rate of contribution to and the implicit tax rate of the pension system fall to zero in 2001. Since the older working cohorts know that in 2001 consumption taxes increase, intertemporal substitution and income effects occur. The income effect dominates since the period subject to a higher consumption tax rate is much longer than the remaining period of low tax rates. Consequently current consumption and leisure demand are reduced and labor supply increases. Furthermore, since the aggregate tax burden on labor is expected to fall heavily due to the switch to taxation of consumption, net wages are expected to increase considerably in the future. As the computation of the current pension value, which determines the money value of the earning points, is unaltered by the reform, higher net wages cause a rise in the current pension value and thus in pension benefits. Therefore the absolute

Figure 9.5: Basic pensions: employment

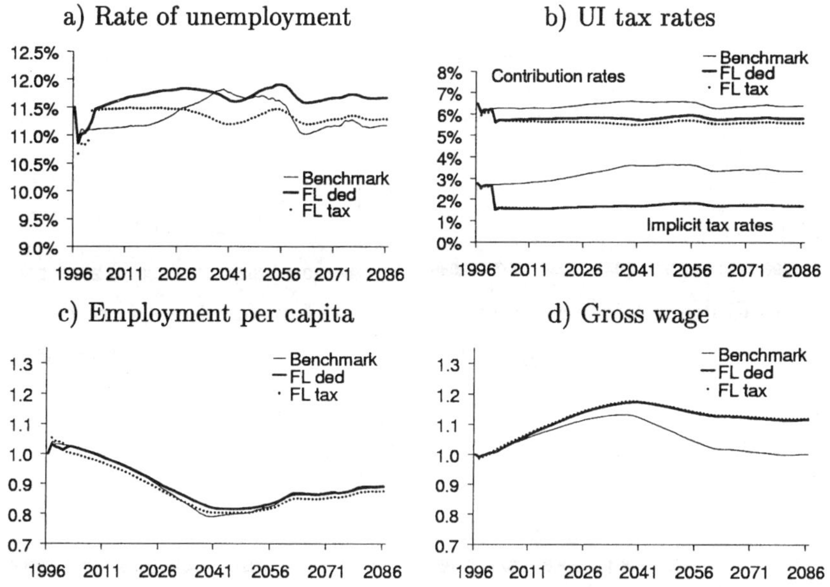

size of pensions increases though the flat pension scheme ensures that the net replacement rate will decline from about 65% in 1996 to about 55% in 2041. Hence, the tax benefit linkage increases immediately after the announcement of the reform.

This lowers the implicit tax rate of the pension system and thus encourages the individuals to supply more labor. This effect is higher for the younger individuals and raises overall employment per capita above the benchmark level. This in turn reduces the rate of unemployment. In 2001 all the cohorts reduce their labor supply since they suffer from the upward shift in the wage tax rate. Hence employment per capita falls and the rate of unemployment increases. The latter is due to the immediate reduction in the proportion of younger labor in the effective labor force in 2001.

In the case of deductions, i. e. the graphs called 'FL ded', there is an opposite effect on the labor supply of the elder working cohorts. Since they are going to retire two years later part of the negative income effect is eased by their longer working life. Therefore their labor supply increases more than without deductions in the pre-reform years. For the young

Figure 9.6: Basic pensions: per capita variables

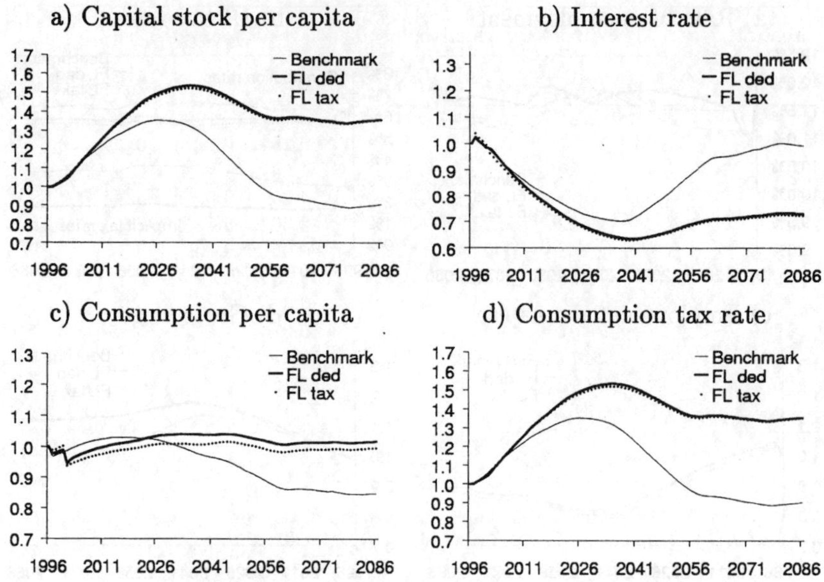

an opposite intertemporal income effect occurs before the year of reform. They supply less labor since they also expand their working life and, thus, earn income in future periods which allows more leisure to be consumed today. Hence, employment per capita decreases before the year of reform while the rate of unemployment is above the rate in the tax financing scheme. Both effects are shown in panels (a) and (c) of Figure 9.5. After 2001 individuals shift their retirement age into the future if confronted with lower pension benefits. This raises the proportion of elder labor in the effective working force and, thus, increases the rate of unemployment. The aging trend strengthens this effect so that the rate of unemployment in the case of deductions exceeds the rate of unemployment in the case without deductions by roughly 0.4 percentage points after 2040.

Finally, consider consumption and the capital stock per capita. The rise in the consumption tax rate lowers consumption per capita, but only for a time (see Figure 9.6(c)). As time goes by the efficiency gains which are caused by the partial switch to consumption taxation increase and allow the capital stock per capita and consumption per capita to increase.

Table 9.2: Basic pension system: decomposition of changes in utility

Year of	Tax financed/deductions				Tax financed			
birth	ΔU^a	ΔP^b	$-\Delta T^c$	ΔEB [d]	ΔU	ΔP	$-\Delta T$	ΔEB
1921	-0.03	-0.01	-0.01	0	0.28	0.02	0.30	0.01
1936	-3.57	0.89	-3.62	-0.17	-4.64	1.25	-4.60	-0.25
1946	-4.95	0.78	-4.81	-0.18	-4.26	3.59	-5.86	-1.09
1956	-1.98	5.22	-6.23	-0.35	-2.36	6.72	-7.21	-1.18
1966	0.91	8.71	-7.31	0.20	-0.05	9.46	-8.34	-0.58
1976	4.26	13.32	-9.30	1.12	2.86	13.77	-10.58	0.19
1986	7.81	18.12	-12.24	2.97	6.32	18.58	-13.88	1.87
1996	10.79	22.07	-14.48	4.39	9.67	22.55	-16.15	3.46
2006	14.05	26.11	-16.71	5.92	13.41	26.52	-18.23	5.45
2016	16.44	28.16	-18.24	7.06	16.16	28.47	-19.44	6.86
∞	14.72	21.89	-14.99	5.07	14.47	22.02	-15.75	4.62
$\sum$	-0.15	-1.82		0.58	-0.78	-1.59		-0.13

Changes as percentage of all remaining lifetime resources.
[a]Change in utility.
[b]Change in net pension benefits.
[c]Change in net tax liabilities.
[d]Change in efficiency.

Welfare Effects

On account of the rise in the absolute size of pensions no cohort loses pension benefits under either scheme. The increased pension benefits even compensate for the reduction in the length of the retirement period if deductions are introduced. This is shown in column 'ΔP' of Table 9.2. In addition, as the rate of contribution to the pension system falls to zero in 2001 all cohorts receive higher net pension benefits. But these gains grow inversely to age until 2041, the year in which the first cohort benefits from the vanishing rate of contribution over its whole working life retires. Since the reform transforms implicit into explicit taxes, net tax liabilities increase. Again, they are higher for younger cohorts which are subject to higher tax rates for a larger part of their remaining lifetime.

The sharp rise in the consumption tax rate and the wage tax rate in 2001 creates an excess burden which initially exceeds the efficiency gains caused by the lower implicit tax rate. However in the course of time

Table 9.3: Basic pensions: sensitivity analysis – macro effects

	Tax financed plus deductions				Tax financed plus deductions			
Year of birth	Base case	No UI[a]	No HI[b]	Low α[c]	Base case	No UI	No HI	Low α
	Old age dependency ratio				Unemployment rate: x			
1996	0.37	0.37	0.37	0.37	11.5	–	11.5	11.5
1997	0.37	0.37	0.37	0.37	10.9	–	10.8	10.8
2001	0.36	0.36	0.36	0.36	11.5	–	11.5	11.2
2041	0.69	0.69	0.69	0.69	11.6	–	11.3	11.5
∞	0.56	0.56	0.56	0.56	11.5	–	11.3	11.4
	Consumption tax rate: τ^c				Pension contr. rate: θ^P			
1996	22.2	21.7	17.3	22.2	19.2	19.2	19.2	19.2
1997	21.7	21.6	17.1	21.4	18.7	18.8	18.7	18.7
2001	36.9	35.3	30.5	36.9	0	0	0	0
2041	47.5	39.7	32.2	45.3	0	0	0	0
∞	39.2	31.8	24.6	35.9	0	0	0	0
	Implicit pension tax: τ^P				Aggregate contr. rate: θ^{SI}			
1996	13.9	14.7	13.2	14.0	39.9	34.2	25.7	40.0
1997	10.7	11.6	8.8	10.5	38.8	33.5	24.7	38.7
2001	0	0	0	0	18.6	13.8	5.4	18.6
2041	0	0	0	0	21.9	16.6	5.2	22.2
∞	0	0	0	0	21.2	16.0	5.2	21.6
	Aggregate implicit tax: τ^{SI}				Employment per capita			
1996	31.0	29.7	15.4	31.1	1.00	1.00	1.00	1.00
1997	27.2	26.3	10.8	27.1	1.01	1.06	1.03	1.03
2001	14.5	13.8	0.76	14.6	1.02	1.02	1.02	1.02
2041	17.9	16.6	0.72	18.2	0.82	0.82	0.82	0.83
∞	17.3	16.0	0.75	17.6	0.88	0.89	0.89	0.89
	Capital stock per capita				Consumption per capita			
1996	1.00	1.00	1.00	1.00	1.00	1.00	1.00	1.00
1997	1.00	1.00	1.00	1.00	0.98	0.98	0.98	0.98
2001	1.05	1.04	1.05	1.04	0.94	0.95	0.94	0.95
2041	1.51	1.55	1.57	1.53	1.04	1.09	1.08	1.05
∞	1.41	1.48	1.57	1.45	1.03	1.10	1.10	1.06

[a]No unemployment and no unemployment insurance.
[b]No health insurance.
[c]Slower increase in the strength of the preference for leisure.

the excess of the consumption tax rate over its benchmark level decreases and efficiency gains occur. Moreover efficiency gains caused by a reduced marginal rate of implicit tax increase until the 2050s. Therefore efficiency gains increase until generation 2006.

These effects determine changes in utility. The cohorts 1936 to 1956 in the case with deductions, and the cohorts 1936 to 1966 in the case without deductions, lose mainly due to higher consumption taxes. In contrast subsequent cohorts are better off. They benefit from efficiency gains and higher net pension benefits. However the high losses of the elder cohorts outweigh the gains of the younger cohorts when welfare is computed. Thus welfare is reduced by 0.78% of remaining wealth in the case without deductions and by 0.15% in the case with deductions. Changes in aggregate excess burden differ considerably from changes in welfare. Obviously the decomposition of welfare is not very successful. The index of redistribution is -1.59% in the case without deductions and otherwise -1.82%. The reform causes a strong redistribution to the younger cohorts from the cohorts 1936 to 1956 in the case of deductions and from cohorts 1936 to 1966 in the case without deductions. Redistribution is stronger in the case of deductions since the rise in the retirement age increases the losses of the middle-aged cohorts who did not retire in the base year.

Sensitivity Analysis

Table 9.3 shows the results of the sensitivity analysis of the tax financing scheme with deductions and Table 9.4 the results of the pure tax financing scheme. As most differences between the schemes arise from reasons outlined in the discussion of the Pension Act of 1992, we refer to the explanations provided on pages 132–137. The most noticeable differences between all the simulations where unemployment is considered and those *without unemployment* ('NO UI') are caused by the strong fall in the rate of unemployment which occurs immediately after the announcement of the reform in 1997. This lowers the short term aggregate rate of contribution, the rate of contribution to the pension system, and both implicit tax rates much more than in all cases which include unemployment. In addition the changes in the consumption tax rate are stronger in these cases.

Table 9.4: Basic pensions: sensitivity analysis – macro effects

	Tax financed				Tax financed			
Year	Base case	No UI[a]	No HI[b]	Low α[c]	Base case	No UI	No HI	Low α
	Old age dependency ratio				Unemployment rate: x			
1996	0.37	0.37	0.37	0.37	11.5	–	11.5	11.5
1997	0.37	0.37	0.37	0.37	10.7	–	10.7	10.6
2001	0.38	0.38	0.38	0.38	11.4	–	11.7	11.4
2041	0.79	0.79	0.79	0.79	11.2	–	11.0	11.2
∞	0.60	0.60	0.60	0.60	11.3	–	11.3	11.3
	Consumption tax rate: τ^c				Pension contr. rate: θ^P			
1996	22.2	21.7	17.3	22.2	19.2	19.2	19.2	19.2
1997	20.8	21.2	16.7	20.5	18.4	18.8	18.5	18.4
2001	39.1	36.2	32.0	39.3	0	0	0	0
2041	51.7	49.7	38.2	53.6	0	0	0	0
∞	41.2	44.7	29.5	42.3	0	0	0	0
	Implicit pension tax: τ^P				Aggregate contr. rate: θ^{SI}			
1996	13.9	14.7	13.2	14.0	39.9	34.2	25.7	40.0
1997	8.3	12.0	6.4	8.4	38.1	33.6	24.4	38.1
2001	0	0	0	0	18.6	13.8	5.5	18.7
2041	0	0	0	0	21.7	16.8	5.0	21.9
∞	0	0	0	0	21.2	16.8	5.2	21.4
	Aggregate implicit tax: τ^{SI}				Employment per capita			
1996	31.0	29.7	15.4	31.1	1.00	1.00	1.00	1.00
1997	24.6	26.7	8.4	24.7	1.05	1.04	1.05	1.05
2001	14.6	13.8	0.9	14.6	1.00	1.00	0.99	1.00
2041	17.9	16.8	0.7	18.1	0.80	0.81	0.81	0.80
∞	17.3	16.8	0.8	17.4	0.88	0.88	0.87	0.88
	Capital stock per capita				Consumption per capita			
1996	1.00	1.00	1.00	1.00	1.00	1.00	1.00	1.00
1997	1.00	1.00	1.00	1.00	0.99	0.98	0.98	0.99
2001	1.06	1.05	1.06	1.05	0.94	0.94	0.94	0.94
2041	1.49	1.50	1.52	1.48	1.01	1.05	1.05	1.00
∞	1.40	1.42	1.50	1.40	1.02	1.06	1.06	1.02

[a]No unemployment and no unemployment insurance.
[b]No health insurance.
[c]Slower increase in the strength of the preference for leisure.

Table 9.5: Basic pensions: sensitivity analysis – welfare effects

	Tax financed plus deductions				Tax financed			
Year of birth	Base case	No UI[a]	No HI[b]	Low α^c	Base case	No UI	No HI	Low α
ΔU								
1921	-0.03	-0.06	0.09	-0.08	0.28	0.28	0.40	-3.24
1936	-3.57	-3.34	-3.80	-3.34	-4.64	-4.44	-4.91	-4.61
1946	-4.95	-4.52	-5.29	-4.74	-4.26	-3.86	-4.29	-4.17
1966	0.91	1.04	0.48	1.04	-0.05	0.24	-0.23	-0.15
1976	4.26	4.24	3.56	4.24	2.86	2.99	2.38	2.48
1996	10.79	10.93	9.52	10.95	9.67	9.34	8.06	9.03
∞	14.72	15.78	12.83	14.84	14.47	14.90	12.01	13.67
Σ	-0.15	0.17	-0.37	0.04	-0.78	-0.44	-0.88	-0.88
ΔEB								
1921	0	0.01	0	-0.02	0.01	0.01	0.01	0
1936	-0.17	-0.15	-0.13	-0.13	-0.25	-0.23	-0.21	-0.22
1946	-0.18	-0.35	-0.32	0.24	-1.09	-1.08	-0.97	-1.11
1966	0.20	-0.10	-0.16	0.61	-0.58	-0.63	-0.77	-0.65
1976	1.12	-0.86	0.50	1.92	0.19	0	-0.29	0.03
1996	4.39	3.88	2.69	4.82	3.46	2.78	1.72	3.16
∞	5.07	5.36	3.05	5.29	4.62	4.63	2.38	4.23
Σ	0.58	0.44	0.23	0.93	-0.13	-0.21	-0.38	-0.20

Changes as percentage of all remaining lifetime resources.
[a]No unemployment insurance.
[b]No health insurance.
[c]Slower increase in the strength of the preference for leisure.

Finally, a short look at welfare effects reveals that here the 'No UI' case is not the worst case as it is in the benchmark case. The reason is that due to the strong fluctuations in unemployment, changes in efficiency and utility are stronger in the short and medium term when unemployment is included. In addition the strong immediate fall in the rate of unemployment turns into a strong rise in the rate of unemployment when the reform starts. This offsets the initial gains and lowers the utility of the initially living cohorts compared to the case without unemployment. The difference between the four modifications of the model amounts to about 0.54 percentage points in the scenario with deductions or 0.44 percentage points in the other case. The most striking result is that the sign of changes in welfare in the case of deductions is ambiguous. Depending on the modification society is either worse off or better off.

Let us summarize the findings. A flat, basic pension scheme, as for instance suggested by the "Grünen" or Miegel and Wahl, does not perform very well. It lowers welfare as well as efficiency, produces bad results for redistribution, and disadvantages the initially middle-aged cohorts. Despite the strong reductions in the rate of contribution and the replacement rate, the consumption tax rate reaches a level of more than 50% in the 2040s. Therefore the scheme without deductions is not very attractive. In addition, since individuals can substitute pensions for disability or inability to work for normal old age pensions, the retirement age does not change. The opposite is expected by Miegel and Wahl. To initiate a change in the retirement age additional policies are needed, for instance a reduction in pension benefits in the case of early retirement. Furthermore, the costs of the proposal for tax financing are strongly underestimated when considering only the pension system. This might be the reason for the appeal of this proposal. Another result is that a flat basic pension scheme can be implemented without reducing the nominal level of pension benefits. The strong reduction in the implicit tax rate enables a pension level of 55% of wage income to be achieved by either fixing the nominal pension level or increasing it at a rate slower than the growth rate of wages.

The results for the basic pension scheme confirm the main results of Fehr (1999c). Since Fehr considers different income groups he also calculates intragenerational redistribution. According to his simulations the lowest income quintile is relatively better off than the other income groups. But his model is different from the model used in the present study. For instance the implicit tax rate and the retirement decision are exogenous in his model. Therefore he can neither compute effects on the retirement decision nor the exact change in the implicit tax rate, nor the impact on the whole social insurance system.

If this reform scheme is completed by deductions from pension benefits in the case of early retirement, the same as stipulated in the Pension Act of 1992, there is indeed a strong response in the average retirement age. It increases from the age of 60 to 62. This disadvantages the initially middle-aged cohorts since they cannot adjust their optimal consumption plans sufficiently. In contrast younger cohorts benefit from this scheme. As a result reductions in welfare are not as large as in the case without deductions. Unfortunately, the better performance under this reform scheme occurs at the expense of stronger redistribution effects.

9.3.2 Lower Level of Pension Benefits – A Partially Funded System

The Advisory Board at the Ministry of Economics recommends a partially funded system where the contributions to the private and the PAYGO system add up to 24.5% in the beginning and at most 27% at the peak of the demographic transition (Wissenschaftlicher Beirat, 1999, p. 49). To implement such a system individuals would be forced to invest about 4% of their salary in a private pension scheme. This would increase the share of pensions received from the private pension plans to a final value of 50% of all pensions. This, so the expectation of the Advisory Board, would lower the burden of aging imposed on employees since these gain from the higher rate of return of the private pension scheme.

Some CGE analyses have been published which examine similar partially funded schemes. Broer (1999a) discusses a reduction in pension benefits in the Netherlands. Though this policy disadvantages the currently elderly and poor households it would be preferred by the majority of voters in comparison to a funded system if there is a minimum level of pension benefits. Fehr (1999a and b) presents simulation results in which pension benefits are reduced by 40%. In his study with a constant population this reform is inferior to a minimum pension scheme financed by tax, at least with respect to efficiency and redistribution effects (Fehr, 1999a). However, in his second study, where demographics are modeled, a reduced level of pension benefits becomes more favorable compared to a minimum benefit scheme (Fehr, 1999b). Note that there are other simulation studies which do not use the micro based CGE framework, for instance Boldrin et. al. (1999) who also support a combination of financing by tax and a reduction in pension benefits.

Since we have already presented the results of a reform scheme consisting of financing by tax and a reduction in pension benefits in the previous chapter, we only summarize here the findings of these simulations. The scheme considered in the previous chapter includes a full adjustment in pension benefits so that the rate of contribution can be smoothed. If the rate of contribution increases to 22% and is held at this level thereafter, this implies a gradual reduction in the net pension level from 70.1% of average net wage income in 1996 to 38.8% in 2041. To be exact, this reform scheme is equivalent to a partially funded system where the rate of contribution to the public pension system is fixed at 22% and individuals join a private pension scheme which complements public pensions. On account of the slow rate of reduction in pension benefits the extent of the private pension scheme grows from cohort to cohort up to the cohorts retiring in the 2040s. Beyond that the public pension level increases again which allows investments in private pension plans to be lowered.

There are positive welfare and efficiency gains of about 0.25% of all remaining wealth (see Table 8.2) which are caused by the large reduction in the implicit tax rate. The index of redistribution is -0.41%, which is not very high. This scheme causes an intergenerational redistribution from the currently middle-aged to the youngest and future cohorts. The reason is that the strong reduction in the implicit tax rate lowers the burden of the future cohorts more than they are disadvantaged by reduced pension benefits. On the other hand the initially middle-aged cohorts who experience a strong loss in pension benefits hardly benefit from the reduction in the implicit tax rate because their remaining working life is very short.

9.4 Conclusions

The findings of this chapter confirm that only a switch away from financing by contribution allows welfare and efficiency gains to be realized (see Homburg, 1990, and Fenge, 1995). It is not the switch to a fully privatized pension system but the switch in the tax base which produces the high welfare and efficiency gains reported above. In addition welfare and efficiency also depend on many specific regulations such as the change in the income ceiling for working after retiring or the size of health contributions to be paid by retirees when the link between health contributions and pension benefits is no longer applicable. While the latter also constitutes a change in taxation, the former is not linked to taxation. Hence modifying other instruments than taxes can also affect efficiency. This is not yet discussed in the literature.

The transition scheme to a fully funded pension system examined above causes an intergenerational redistribution from currently elder and middle-aged cohorts to the younger and future generations. As shown in the preceding chapter, this redistribution can be reduced by the use of debt to finance part of the pension outlays during the transition. But it does not appear to be possible to eliminate all adverse redistribution effects when aging occurs. This is confirmed by additional experiments in which it was not possible to find a Pareto improving transition to a fully funded system in the current setting.

Another reform scheme which is very popular among politicians and economists is a flat basic pension scheme. Regardless of its popularity almost nothing could be found in favor of this proposal. The consumption tax rate would reach a hardly acceptable level. And, worse, welfare and efficiency would deteriorate, and almost all currently living cohorts would lose. Hence it appears to be politically infeasible.

In contrast, providing nothing else is changed, a large reduction in pension benefits improves welfare and efficiency if it is implemented as outlined above. Then the implicit tax rate can be lowered and the losses of the initially middle-aged cohorts are relatively low. Furthermore, young cohorts already alive benefit from this reform. Nevertheless, intergenerational redistribution caused by this reform scheme is not too large. Hence, the German reform of 2001, which is similar to this reform scheme, is probably not a bad policy either with respect to welfare or efficiency, or with respect to redistribution.

Chapter 10

Evaluating Pension Policies: the Conclusions

The various results presented in the preceding chapters only state which policy causes which effects. A comparison of the different reform schemes which helps to choose the 'best' pension policy has not yet been provided. This is the first task of this chapter. The criteria used to select the best policy are the aggregate changes in welfare, efficiency, redistribution, and changes in the rate of contribution and the size of pensions as variables representing the effects on the pension system. It is however not certain that the proposals obtained by using these criteria are politically feasible, i. e. coincide with the preferences of the majority of the voters. For this reason we also examine the results of a voting process.

The second task to which this chapter is devoted is to summarize the main findings and evaluate the technical innovations presented in this study, and, finally, provide suggestions on future research.

10.1 Choice of a Reform Scheme

In the preceding chapters fifteen reform schemes have been examined. We review the results of these schemes except three scenarios. One proposal is not considered since it implies a rate of contribution higher than the rate resulting from the Pension Act of 1992. This is the introduction of supplements without raising the mandatory retirement age. Another scheme not considered is the scheme where the rate of contribution is fixed at its 1996 level. In this case pension benefits would decrease to an extremely low size. The third reform scheme not included in the comparison is the immediate switch to consumption taxation which we omit because of the

Table 10.1: Comparing the pension schemes

	$\sum \Delta U^a$	$\sum \Delta EB^b$	$\sum \Delta EE^c$	$\theta^{P\,d}$	b^P/BE^e
T40[f]	1.48	1.33	-0.89	0	69.3
T10	1.01	1.04	-0.69	22.2	68.8
H92	0.98	0.98	-0.53	29.6	71.0
FD	0.83	1.58	-1.95	0	2.7
FT	0.74	2.29	-2.35	0	2.7
R99	0.72	0.78	-0.56	27.3	68.5
A99	0.62	0.60	-0.54	27.0	63.5
A92	0.50	0.53	-0.44	30.0	70.3
CC	0.25	0.29	-0.41	22.0	38.7
B	—	—	—	34.7	70.3
KS	-0.02	0.22	-0.45	24.0	70.9
L92	-0.15	-0.58	-1.82	0	54.8
LT	-0.78	-0.13	-1.59	0	55.0

[a]Change in Welfare.
[b]Aggregate change in efficiency.
[c]Index of redistribution.
[d]Rate of contribution to the pension system.
[e]Gross replacement rate of pension benefits.
[f]T40 = phase-in of consumption tax financing; T10 = ten year rise in consumption tax rate and the subsidy rate; H92 = Pension Act of 1992 with higher deductions; FD = fully funded system with partial debt financing; FT = fully funded system with tax financing; R99 = reform of 1999; A99 = Pension Act of 1999; A92 = Pension Act of 1992; CC = constant rate of contribution fixed at 22%; B = benchmark case; KS = capital stock for the pension system; L92 = flat pensions plus deductions; LT = flat pensions financed by taxes.

extremely high rise in the consumption tax rate in 2001. This leaves twelve pension schemes which can be compared to the benchmark case.

10.1.1 Welfare, Efficiency, Redistribution, and the Pension System

Table 10.1 shows the ranking of the twelve reform schemes and the benchmark case with regard to changes in welfare. In addition changes in aggregate efficiency effects, the index of redistribution, the rate of contribution in 2041, and the gross replacement rate defined as the gross pension to average wage income ratio in 2041 of an individual who has paid contributions for 45 years are given in this table.

The first unexpected result is that the transitions to a fully funded system financed either by consumption tax and a 15% surcharge on the wage tax liability, 'FT', or by the same mix of financing by tax and issuing debt, 'FD', produce less welfare than three other reform schemes. The reason is that the initially elder cohorts experience high losses in both schemes. The highest welfare gains can be achieved by implementing a gradual transition to a complete financing by a consumption tax, 'T40'. But even the two schemes which include an extension of the reform of 1999, 'T10', or the Pension Act of 1992, 'H92', improve welfare more than the fully funded schemes.

However under the last scheme, 'H92', the rate of contribution fluctuates more under this scheme because the retirement age is changed more often. For instance in 2041 two cohorts enter retirement, which immediately raises the rate of contribution. Far better results for the pension system are achieved if the rise in the consumption tax rate is spread over ten years, 'T10'. The rate of contribution to the pension system increases only to 22% in this scenario, a level not much higher than in 1996, without considerably lowering the size of pension benefits.

The three policies adopted in Germany in the 90s, 'A92', 'A99', 'R99', are not much worse than the fully funded pension system financed by tax, 'FT'. This shows that enacting the Pension Act of 1992, 'A92', was rational from a welfare point of view, since it raises welfare by 0.5% of aggregate lifetime resources. Furthermore it causes a reduction in the rate of contribution by 4.7% in 2041 without reducing the size of pension benefits for the ideal retiree, a pensioner paying contributions for 45 years and earning average labor income in each year. This fictitious individual is the retiree who is at the center of the political debate on the size of pension benefits. That this policy actually lowers the relative pension level of the real pensioner due to deductions is another issue.

The Pension Act of 1999, 'A99', was also rational with respect to welfare. It raises welfare by 0.12 points compared to the Pension Act of 1992 and produces a larger reduction in the rate of contribution which becomes 27% in 2041. Nonetheless suspending the Pension Act of 1999 and replacing it by the pension reform of 1999 was also rational. This is expected to imply almost the same rate of contribution, 27.3% in 2041, as the Act of 1999 but to increase welfare by 0.72% of aggregate remaining lifetime resources. Moreover this improvement is not achieved at the expense of the retirees whose pension benefits amount to 68.5% of average wage income, compared to only 63.5% under the Pension Act of 1999. It is the switch to the more efficient consumption tax which causes the better performance. This is shown by the higher change in aggregate excess burden.

All these policies mentioned above are clearly better than the switch to a defined contribution system where the rate of contribution is fixed at 22% and pension benefits are adjusted to balance the budget, 'CC'. This proposal is equivalent to a transition to a partially funded system since pension benefits are enormously reduced so that individuals are forced to invest in a private pension plan. However, this reform has not been investigated together with the Pension Act of 1992 or the reform of 1999. Therefore, the outcome is very pessimistic with respect to the replacement rate and welfare effects. For this reason one cannot deduce from the proposal 'CC' whether the German pension reform of 2001 will do better or worse than the Pension Act of 1992 or the pension reform of 1999.

Accumulating a capital stock in the public pension system, the scheme 'KS', promises no welfare gains compared to the benchmark situation. But it leads to a lower rate of contribution in 2041 without reducing the relative size of pension benefits. The proposals for a flat pension scheme, 'L92' and 'LT', are at the bottom of the list. Though clearly easing the financial situation of the pension system they reduce welfare compared to all other cases and even to the benchmark situation. The welfare losses can be reduced by introducing a reduction in pension benefits in the case of early retirement[1]. The reason for these losses is the reduction in efficiency caused by abolishing the tax benefit linkage or the link between labor income and benefits.

Looking only at welfare and the pension system the recommendation for future policy is straightforward: switch to financing by consumption tax as far as possible! Moreover, it does no harm if the Pension Act of 1992

[1] We have also simulated a flat pension scheme financed by contributions. Since it creates higher welfare losses than a scheme financed by tax, we do not present these simulations in this study.

and the pension reform of 1999 are both implemented. Both are included in the proposal 'T10'. The second best policy option is a transition to a fully funded system. This solves the problems of the public pension system which result from the aging trend, and creates welfare gains not much lower than in the case of financing by consumption tax. On the other hand, a fully funded system reduces income from interest due to a reduction in the interest rate and thus lowers the income of the old in a similar way to a pure reduction in the pension benefits.

These are the two policies recommended when considering efficiency, welfare, and the effects on the pension system. In contrast the policy actually chosen is only for the short term but allows further reform schemes to be considered. It does not improve the sustainability of the pension system. Though the reform of 2001 improves the situation of the pension system compared to the pension reform of 1999, it also does not ensure the sustainability of the pension system in the middle of this century. Hence, one can expect further reforms in the future.

Next to redistribution effects. These are extremely high in the flat pension schemes, 'L92' and 'LT', and the fully funded systems, 'FD' and 'FT'. However the decomposition of welfare effects does not really work in the latter case. This is shown by the huge difference between efficiency and welfare effects, which are supposed to be the same. Therefore there is no point in considering fully funded schemes in this case. The flat, basic pension schemes produce the highest index of redistribution. This is another reason not to implement such a scheme.

The results show that there is something like a trade-off between efficiency and distribution, but only within the same type of pension scheme. Since a partial switch to financing by consumption tax , 'T10', does not cause much more redistribution than current policies, 'A92', 'A99', and 'R99', redistribution is not an argument against the partial switch to financing by consumption tax.

However, the likelihood of implementation of a proposal does not depend on the aggregate performance. It rather depends on the preferences of the majority – see the Pension Act of 1999. For this reason we turn now to the issue of the political feasibility of reform schemes.

10.1.2 The Feasibility of Pension Policies

The political feasibility of pension schemes can be examined by simulating referenda on the different pension schemes. To simplify matters we assume that the voters have the choice between two proposals at each referendum. In addition, it is assumed that each pension scheme opted for by the majority of voters is actually enacted and is unchanged for all the future, so that problems of time inconsistency are excluded.

The voters maximize utility and prefer that reform scheme which provides the higher utility. All decisions take place in 1996, which in every simulation is the year the reform is announced. Though it is possible to carry out the referenda in other years, this requires the algorithm to allow for unexpected shocks (see Hirte, 2000b). All individuals at least 18 years old in 1996 are entitled to vote. Therefore the utility of future cohorts is not considered. In other words, individuals are not interested in the utility of their children. This flaw in the model could easily be avoided by using the utility obtained when calculating efficiency effects.

Table 10.2 documents the outcome of the respective referenda. Each element (i, j) of the matrix reflects the decision between the policy i and j. If the proposal i is preferred by majority the element (i, j) is filled with an 'X'. Then the element (j, i) is empty, and vice versa.

Let us omit the benchmark case 'B' for the time being. Then all components of Table 10.2 which are above the diagonal are not empty. Hence there is a unique ranking of the reform schemes and there is no paradox of voting. Regardless of the sequence of the decisions the outcome is always the same. Each scheme shown in the first column of Table 10.2 always wins the referendum against each scheme printed in any row below and loses the referendum against each scheme written above. This changes if the benchmark case is also considered. Then there is a voting paradox between the four schemes 'T10', 'A99', 'T40' and the benchmark case 'B'.

What can be learned from this table? At first, the Pension Act of 1992, 'A92', was a rational choice not only from a welfare point of view but also for a government seeking the approval of the majority of the voters. Almost 63.4% of the population entitled to vote prefers this policy to doing nothing, i. e. the benchmark case 'B', in the computation carried

Table 10.2: Voting on pension policy

	H92	A92	R99	T10	A99	T40	B	CC	KS	FD	FT	L92	LT
H92[a]	■	X	X	X	X	X	X	X	X	X	X	X	X
A92		■	X	X	X	X	X	X	X	X	X	X	X
R99			■	X	X	X	X	X	X	X	X	X	X
T10				■	X	X		X	X	X	X	X	X
A99					■	X	X	X	X	X	X	X	X
T40						■	X	X	X	X	X	X	X
B				X			■	X	X	X	X	X	X
CC								■	X	X	X	X	X
KS									■	X	X	X	X
FD										■	X	X	X
FT											■	X	X
L92												■	X
LT													■

[a]H92 = Pension Act of 1992 with higher deductions; A92 = Pension Act of 1992; R99 = reform of 1999; T10 = ten year rise in the consumption tax rate and the subsidy rate; A99 = Pension Act of 1999; T40 = gradual transition to consumption tax financing; B = benchmark case; CC = constant rate of contribution fixed at 22%; KS = capital stock for the pension system; FD = fully funded system with partial debt financing; FT = fully funded system with tax financing; L92 = flat pensions plus deductions; LT = flat pensions financed by taxes.

out in this study. For the same reason it was equally rational for the new German government not to promise to suspend the Pension Act of 1992 if elected. Second, though the Pension Act of 1999, 'A99', would improve welfare, passing this Act was an inferior policy with respect to the 1998 election – though this is only shown above for a referendum carried out in 1996. Since the Pension Act of 1992 was already announced and the opposition party did not suggest another policy, the decision at this election was also a choice between the Pension Act of 1992 and that of 1999. In our calculation the former obtains a majority of 2/3 of all votes. Hence promising to suspend this act was rational for the opposition party. And in fact the change of government seems to have been at least partially influenced by the decision on the pension policy.

Even if the pension policy carried out by the new government in 1999 had been known at the election of 1998, the decision between the reform of 1999 and the Pension Act of 1999 would also have been in favor of the former, though with a smaller majority of 56%. It is also not astonishing that there was heavy protest against the reform of 1999 after its announcement in the spring of 1999. Although only 52% of the voters would prefer the Pension Act of 1992 to the reform of 1999 according to the simulation, 71% of the individuals opting for the Pension Act of 1992 and against the Pension Act of 1999 would prefer the Pension Act of 1999 to the reform of 1999. According to this result a large group of individuals voting for the change in government, i. e. for suspending the Pension Act of 1999, is going to blame the new government for cheating.

These are the findings with respect to past policy. The outcomes of the simulation are very pessimistic with respect to further policy reform. But remember that the referenda are supposed to have been carried out in 1996, hence other outcomes cannot be excluded when the policy is announced, for instance in 2000, and the voting takes place in that year. This, however, is not within the scope of this study[2]. Table 10.2 shows that there is no policy scheme other then the return to the Pension Act of 1992, 'A92', or an extension of this act, 'H92', which will obtain a majority once the reform of 1999, 'R99' is implemented.

However the reform of 1999 is preferred to two schemes only with a small majority. These are

(1) the extension the reform of 1999 by raising the consumption tax rate and the subsidies to the pension system for further eight years, 'T10', a policy only disapproved of by 52% of the voters in comparison to the reform of 1999, ' R99',
(2) the Pension Act of 1999, 'A99', with a majority of 56% against it.

Fortunately, the policy which extends the financing by consumption tax also performs very well with respect to welfare and the pension system. Though a majority of 70% would vote against a complete switch to financing by consumption tax, 'T40', this scheme seems not entirely infeasible. If the scheme 'T10' is implemented first, then only 52% of the voters opt against the full switch to financing by consumption tax. The other reform schemes appear to have only small prospects of being chosen as policies on pensions to deal with the problems of aging.

[2]In HIRTE (2000b) we examine the political feasibility of a partially or fully funded system. There the timing of the implementation is considered and referenda in different years are simulated. It is shown that the timing of pension policies is important.

Since mandatory and voluntary private pension plans are equivalent in the model used in this study, one cannot draw any conclusion about whether policy reform should include a mandatory partial privatization scheme. It is only possible to infer that a policy which reduces pension benefits raises the incentive to invest in a private pension plan. The results suggest that a commitment to implement a huge private pension plan will not be accepted by a majority. The low degree of approval of both the scheme with a constant contribution rate and the flat basic pension scheme supports this suggestion. Nonetheless, it is yet to be shown that this is true if a scheme of financing by consumption tax is combined with a lower extent of pension benefits. At least the reform of 1999 shows that an enlargement of private pension plans can be accepted in this case.

The consideration of welfare and political feasibility leads to almost the same conclusion about the best policy: choose a reform scheme which extends the financing of pension outlays by a tax on consumption. But one should neither strongly worsen the *relative* standard of living of the pensioners nor abolish the principle of equivalence, i. e. the link between income and the size of pension benefits a retiree receives.

However, the transition to a fully funded system, though a second best alternative to financing by a consumption tax when considering welfare, efficiency, and the sustainability of the pension system, appears not to be feasible because it lacks approval by the population. One can infer from these computations of the voting that the introduction of a demographic factor or an equivalent reduction in pension benefits and/or higher grants which are financed by consumption tax are very likely to be the major components of the next pension reforms. If this includes a reduction in pension benefits, a moderate expansion of private pension schemes, either mandatory or voluntary can also be expected.

10.2 Résumé

In the introduction we outlined the main tasks of this study. These are:

(1) to examine and evaluate the pension policies which seek to solve the pension crisis by performing a dynamic computable general equilibrium (CGE) analysis,

(2) demonstrate that a dynamic CGE analysis is an appropriate approach to evaluating different kind of pension policies,

(3) develop this approach further by extending the Auerbach-Kotlikoff model if useful for exploring pension policies.

Let us start with the last point, the *innovations and their implications.* The most prominent innovation of our study is the fully endogenized retirement decision. Since many studies have shown that the retirement decision is very responsive to changes in pension policies (e. g. for the German case Siddiqui, 1995, Riphahn and Schmidt, 1997), it appears absolutely necessary to consider explicitly the retirement decision. It is therefore surprising that this is not yet a common feature of dynamic CGE studies on pension policies (an exception is Hirte, 1999a). Modeling endogenous retirement decisions also reveals which other features should be included in the model. For instance, omitting unemployment changes the retirement decision in some simulations. Hence the implementation of unemployment appears complementary to an endogenous retirement decision.

The most striking result about this feature is that the retirement decision appears to be almost immune against some of the strongest changes in the pension system. For instance, a full switch to financing of pension outlays by a consumption tax, a constant rate of contribution, a partially and fully funded system, or the accumulation of a capital stock in the pension system affect the retirement decision at most in the short term. Nonetheless the retirement age is one of the key determinants of the extent of the problems aging imposes on the pension system. Hence a policy aiming at changing this age could be very effective. The computations presented above have shown that the introduction of deductions from pension benefits in the case of early retirement is a very effective device for influencing the retirement age.

A second new feature of the model is the way in which the continuous rise in longevity is modeled. Life expectancy increases by 0.1 years per period so that almost no discontinuities appear in the economic effects. This specification is the key to a closer replication of the expected demographic changes in the German population. It also allows the effects of aging to be decomposed into a life expectancy component and a fertility component. This shows that the latter is far more significant. Nonetheless the increase in life expectancy affects social insurance and also the values of macroeconomic variables.

Third, we have implemented the whole social insurance system including the public pension system, health and long term care insurance, and unemployment insurance. This shows that aging is a far larger problem than it appears when only the pension system is taken into account. Though this is common knowledge the amount and changes in welfare, efficiency effects, or macroeconomic variables are not marginal compared to a pure pension model and not yet examined. In some simulations the differences between a pure pension model and the full social insurance model amount to more than 50% of the computed changes in welfare. In one case the sign of welfare changes when the whole insurance system is not considered.

Fourth, to allow an unemployment insurance to be considered we have also modeled unemployment. Though this is done in a very simple way, it is sufficient for our purpose. As far as we know it is the first CGE model in which unemployment differs with age. This feature is especially important in the retirement decision. Since unemployment of the eldest working cohorts is relatively high, it strongly affects the retirement decision. As it turns out some policy schemes produce very different results for the average retirement age and, thus, for the pension system, depending on whether or not unemployment is considered. Furthermore the response of the average retirement age is at first glance counterintuitive in some simulations in the short term when considering unemployment. This might explain why the empirical studies of Siddiqui (1995, 1997a, b and c) find no evidence that the retirement age is influenced by unemployment (note the opposite results of Schmidt, 1995, or Riphahn and Schmidt, 1997).

And finally, it is the first study which implements an implicit tax rate in an *endogenous* way in a CGE model together with demographics for Germany. It is furthermore the first study where the implicit tax rate consists not only of an implicit tax of the pension system but also of an implicit tax of health, long term care, and unemployment insurance. The results make clear that implicit taxes have a large influence in an economy with endogenous demographics. Furthermore they show that efficiency effects generated by changes in the marginal rate of implicit tax are far larger in the model with social insurance than in a pure pension model.

Let us now summarize the *insights into pension policies for aging* one gains from the present study. The best policy for welfare, efficiency, and the rescue of the current pension system is a switch to financing by a consumption tax, even if it is only a partial switch. For this reason the policy of raising the subsidy rate and the consumption tax rate which has been enacted in Germany is a first step to a more efficient pension system. However, the efficiency gains, improvement in welfare, and alleviation of the financial problems of the pension system which occur due to a switch to financing by a consumption tax almost completely vanish if pension benefits are granted as flat pension benefits. This result speaks unambiguously in favor of the principle of equivalence, i. e. the link between income earned when working and pension benefits, and against a flat, basic pension scheme. The latter is clearly an inferior policy scheme.

A policy aiming at raising the retirement age is also not a bad choice when considering all the criteria. As it turned, out among the schemes considered only deductions from pension benefits in the case of early retirement appear to be effective in encouraging individuals to retire later. However, the size of deductions enacted in the Pension Act of 1992 is too low to ensure the sustainability of the pension system. A higher deduction rate is far better but provokes a stronger fluctuation in the average retirement age. As a consequence the rate of contribution to the pension system is much lower in many periods but might be even higher in some periods in comparison with the case of a lower deduction rate. This shows that the decision on the optimal level of the deduction rate is a difficult task.

Furthermore efficiency gains arising under a tax smoothing scheme are positive but small. Hence a fixed rate of contribution with a full adjustment of pension benefits, i. e. a partial privatization policy with a high share of private pension plans, is also inferior to a switch to financing by a consumption tax.

Moreover, the political feasibilityf all these policies, i. e. whether they are likely to be supported by the majority of voters, has been considered.

The results show that it seems to be rational from that point of view that the Pension Act of 1992 has been enacted, the Pension Act of 1999 has been suspended by the new government, and that the reform of 1999 has been implemented. The results also suggest that a policy reform will be oriented towards these three reform schemes and a partial financing by consumption tax. Hence this explains why neither a switch to a fully funded system nor an introduction of a flat basic pension scheme are considered in Germany – a vast majority of the voters is likely to vote against both schemes. Furthermore, a strong change of the pension system will also not obtain a majority. This is true for a switch to a fully funded pension system, a large partially funded system if it is accompanied by a smooth contribution rate, the accumulation of a capital stock within the current pension system, as well as a flat basic pension scheme.

Another result obtained is that public savings via the public pension system fully crowd out private savings. A last finding is that efficiency gains depend not only on the tax base used to finance pensions (Fenge, 1995) but also on restrictions on working after retiring.

Finally, we turn to the usefulness of a *dynamic CGE study for evaluating pension policies*. This approach provides manifold results about different criteria. For instance, as in other studies, changes in macroeconomic variables and the pension system are computed. But it is the strength of this method that changes in individual behavior can be considered. Then for each representative individual preferences - measured in income equivalents of utility - for different reform schemes can be compared. This shows the gains or losses of each cohort in terms of utility when implementing specific pension policies. This might completely differ from changes in income effects as computed in a generational accounting approach[3]. The reasons are that income effects are computed by considering changes in individual behavior which is not the case in a generational accounting study,

[3]FEHR and KOTLIKOFF (1996) show that a generational accounting and a CGE analysis can produce very similar changes in 'utility'. However, this is not shown for the general case, because they compute the generational accounts by using the income effects which they compute using the CGE model. Hence, changes in individual behavior are taken into account in the generational accounts. This, however, is not the case in a generational accounting study (see Börstinghaus and Hirte (2001).

and that efficiency effects are taken into account in the CGE approach. Therefore one can even compute the excess burden imposed on different cohorts. Finally, aggregate measures such as welfare, aggregate efficiency or an index for the extent of redistribution can be calculated. Hence, much more information is obtained than by other methods. This makes policy advice more differentiated. Furthermore, it is possible to simulate voting on pension policies and, thus, help to judge the rationality of economic policy and to assess the feasibility of specific pension policies.

Since a CGE analysis is based on a theoretical model it should be understood as an enlargement of a specific theoretical approach. It allows the solution of models which cannot be solved analytically. This is also the strength of the method. It can use a purely theoretical approach and implement nearly all the relevant institutional arrangements of a real economy. Moreover it can apply theoretical arguments to interpret the results. This can be reinforced by sensitivity analysis which examines whether specific modifications of the model or significant changes in the parameters alter the signs or values of the computed results. These sensitivity analyses are also required to examine the reliability of the results, since the model can only be solved for specific values of the parameters. The sensitivity analyses presented in this study show that most results appear to be robust with respect to the changes applied in the sensitivity analysis. There is only one case where the sign changed as a result of changing the settings.

On the other hand, a weakness of this method is that it provides results which are true only within the chosen model. This applies to all theoretical and econometric studies. But compared to the latter the results of a CGE analysis are not derived from real data by econometric methods. Hence the significance of the results, in an econometric sense, cannot be investigated. However, a similar problem arises in almost all studies which forecast the future of the pension system, such as the report of the Prognos-Institute (Eckerle and Oczipka, 1998) on the future of the pension system or other studies examining the effects of policy changes, for instance studies on generational accounting.

Of course, the complexity of the model introduced and employed in the present study implies that some features which are also significant have not been considered. Some of them, for instance heterogeneous individuals, have been included in other models, which are on the other hand less sophisticated with respect to some features included in our model (e. g. Altig et. al., 1997, or Fehr, 1999a or c). It is a task for further research to model different income groups together with the endogenous retirement decision, unemployment and health insurance. This is easier to do in a small open economy where factor prices are fixed than in a closed economy. Another flaw of the life cycle model is the strong rise of consumption near the end of life. It might be useful to tie consumption or leisure to investments in health. This is partially done in a recent paper of Broer (1999b). Finally, economic growth should be implemented. This can be done in an ad hoc manner with exogenous growth (see Chauveau and Loufir, 1997). Otherwise endogenous growth ought to be modeled. Although this opens a wide field of possibilities, it is a severe problem that the equilibrium solution one finds in the simulation is fully determined by the initial guess. Hence the results of simulations of endogenous growth models are far less reliable than those of other CGE studies.

Of course, there are some further issues of aging or social insurance which would also be useful to be examined with a dynamic CGE analysis. One is migration, which can be expected to increase due to the enlargement of the EC. Others are further fiscal reforms, such as tax reforms or fiscal consolidation. All these policies affect social insurance. Examining these issues with 'simple' approaches which do not consider incentives and behavior responses might be useful to produce first results in a quick way. However, efficiency effects matter even for redistribution, so that this quick methods can be misleading. In contrast, dynamic CGE studies can provide further insights into the significance and direction of changes in behavior and provide many more insights into the effects of economic policy than these approaches.

Appendix: The Marginal Tax Benefit Linkage

The present value of pension benefits in period s is

$$PV_s^i = \sum_{\nu=M}^{J} R_k^{n,\nu} \left(1 - \overline{\tau}_k^{b,\nu} - 0.5\tau^H\right) b_k^{P,\nu},$$

where average tax rates are applied to pension benefits.

Differentiating with respect to current labor supply of individual aged i in period s yields

$$\frac{\partial PV_s^i}{\partial l_s^i} = \sum_{\nu=M}^{J} R_k^{n,\nu} \left(1 - \overline{\tau}_k^{b,\nu} - 0.5\tau^H\right) \frac{\partial b_k^{P,\nu}}{\partial l_s^i}$$
$$- \sum_{\nu=M}^{J} R_k^{n,\nu} b_k^{P,\nu} \frac{\partial \overline{\tau}_k^{b,\nu}}{\partial b_k^{P,\nu}} \frac{\partial b_k^{P,\nu}}{\partial l_s^i}$$
$$+ \sum_{\nu=M}^{J} \left(1 - \overline{\tau}_k^{b,\nu} - 0.5\tau^H\right) b_k^{P,\nu} \frac{\partial R_k^{n,\nu}}{\partial l_s^i}$$

which is

$$\text{(a)} \quad \frac{\partial PV_s^i}{\partial l_s^i} = \sum_{\nu=M}^{J} R_k^{n,\nu} \left[\left(1 - \overline{\tau}_k^{b,\nu} - 0.5\tau^H\right) - b_k^{P,\nu} \frac{\partial \overline{\tau}_k^{b,\nu}}{\partial b_k^{p,\nu}}\right] \frac{\partial b_k^{P,\nu}}{\partial l_s^i} \Omega_{s,i}$$

where

$$\Omega_{s,i} = \prod_{s=v+1}^{t} \left(\frac{1 + r_s^m}{1 + r_s^{n,i}}\right),$$

reflects the effect of the marginal change in l_s^i on the net interest rate. $\Omega_{s,i}$ is the correction factor which is equivalent to the correction factor derived by Auerbach and Kotlikoff (1987, p. 44) when solving for the optimal consumption/leisure demand. Since

$$R_k^{m,\nu} = R_k^{n,\nu} \Omega_{s,i}$$

(a) turns into

$$\text{(b)} \qquad \frac{\partial PV_s^i}{\partial l_s^i} = \sum_{\nu=M}^{J} R_k^{m,\nu} \left[\left(1 - \overline{\tau}_k^{b,\nu} - 0.5\tau^H\right) - b_k^{P,\nu} \frac{\partial \overline{\tau}_k^{b,\nu}}{\partial b_k^{P,\nu}} \right] \frac{\partial b_k^{P,\nu}}{\partial l_s^i}$$

Since

$$\overline{\tau}_k^{b,\nu} = \frac{T_k^{b,\nu}}{b_k^{P,\nu}},$$

where $T_k^{b,\nu}$ is tax liability of individual ν, one obtains

$$\frac{\partial \overline{\tau}_k^{b,\nu}}{\partial b_k^{P,\nu}} b_k^{P,\nu} = \frac{\partial T_k^{b,\nu}}{\partial b_k^{P,\nu}} - \frac{T_k^{b,\nu}}{b_k^{P,\nu}} = \tau_k^{b,\nu} - \overline{\tau}_k^{b,\nu}.$$

Insertion into (b) gives

$$\frac{\partial PV_s^i}{\partial l_s^i} = \sum_{\nu=M}^{J} R_k^{m,\nu} \left(1 - \tau_k^{b,\nu} - 0.5\tau^H\right) \frac{\partial b_k^{P,\nu}}{\partial l_s^i}.$$

Inserting the derivation of equation (2.31) with respect to labor supply gives

$$\frac{\partial PV_s^i}{\partial l_s^i} = w_s^i \frac{1}{BE_s} \sum_{\nu=M}^{J} R_k^{m,\nu} a_k^R \left(1 - \tau_k^{b,\nu} - 0.5\tau^H\right) \frac{\partial b_k^{P,\nu}}{\partial l_s^i}.$$

Division by w_i leads to the marginal benefit rate $\phi_s^{P,i}$ in equation (2.36).

The marginal tax benefit linkage of unemployment insurance is the change in unemployment benefits and the change in future pension benefits which is caused by contributions of unemployment insurance to the pension system per unit of wage income. Contributions of unemployment insurance amount to about 80% of the net wage income. This net income is computed by using the wage income in the preceding period net of the average marginal tax rates. Let us approximate this by using the individual net wage. Using equation (2.38) on page 47 and (2.36) on page 44 yields

$$\begin{aligned} \phi_s^{X,i} &\approx \frac{\partial b_s^{X,i}}{\partial w_s^i l_s^i} + 0.8 \frac{\partial b_s^{X,i}}{\partial w_s^i l_s^i} \\ &= x_{s+1}^{i+1} \left(\frac{\pi_{s+1}^X}{1 + r_{s+1}^m} \frac{w_s^{n,i}}{w_s^i} + 0.8\, \phi_s^{P,i} \right). \end{aligned}$$

References

AARON, H.J. (1966), The Social Insurance paradox, *Canadian Journal of Economics and Political Science* 32, 371-374.

AARON, H.J. and W.G. GALE (1996), *Economic Effects of Fundamental Tax Reform*, Washington D.C.: Brookings Institutions.

AKERLOF, G.A. (1982), Contracts as Partial Gift Exchange, *Quarterly Journal of Economics* 97, 543-69.

ALTIG, D., A.J. AUERBACH, L.J. KOTLIKOFF, K.A. SMETTERS, and J. WALLISER (1997), Simulating U.S. Tax Reform, NBER Working Paper no. 6248, Cambridge, MA..

ANBA(1997): Amtliche Nachrichten der Bundesanstalt für Arbeit, Nürnberg, 1997.

ATKINSON, A.B. (1987), Income Maintenance and Social Insurance, in: A.J. Auerbach and M.S. Feldstein, eds., *Handbook of Public Economics*, Vol. 2, Amsterdam: North-Holland, 779-908.

AUERBACH, A.J. (1996), Tax Reform, Capital Allocation, Efficiency, and Growth, in: H.J. Aaron and W.G. Gale, eds., *Economic Effects of Fundamental Tax Reform*, Washington, D.C.: Brookings Institution Press, 29-73.

AUERBACH, A.J. and L.J. KOTLIKOFF (1983a), An Examination of Empirical Tests of Social Security and Savings, in: E. Helpman, A. Razin, and E. Sadka, eds., *Social Policy Evaluation: An Economic Perspective*, New York: Academic Press, 161-179.

AUERBACH, A.J. and L.J. KOTLIKOFF (1983b), National Savings, Economic Welfare, and the Structure of Taxation, in: M. Feldstein, ed., *Behavioral Simulation Methods in Tax Policy Analysis*, Chicago: University of Chicago Press, 459-498.

AUERBACH, A.J. and L.J. KOTLIKOFF (1984), Social Security and the Economics of Demographic Transition, in: H. Aaron and G. Burtless, eds., *Retirement and Economic Behavior*, Washington, D.C.: The Brookings Institution.

AUERBACH, A.J. and L.J. KOTLIKOFF (1985), Simulating Alternative Social Security Responses to Demographic Transition: *National Tax Journal* 38, 153-168.

AUERBACH, A.J. and L.J. KOTLIKOFF (1987a), *Dynamic Fiscal Policy*, Cambridge: Cambridge University Press.

AUERBACH, A.J. and L.J. KOTLIKOFF (1987b), Evaluating Fiscal Policy with a Dynamic Simulation Model, *American Economic Review* 77, 49-55.

AUERBACH, A.J. and L.J. KOTLIKOFF (1992), Tax Aspects of Policy toward Aging Populations, in: J.B. Shoven and J. Whalley, eds., *Canada-U.S. Tax Comparisons*, Chicago: University of Chicago Press, 255-273.

AUERBACH, A.J., L.J. KOTLIKOFF and J. SKINNER (1983), The Efficiency Gains from Dynamic Tax Reform, *International Economic Review* 24, 81-100.

BA:Bundesministerium für Arbeit und Sozialordnung (1997), *Statistisches Taschenbuch 1997. Arbeits- und Sozialstatistik*, Bonn.

BALLARD, C. and L. GOULDER (1985), Consumption Taxes, Foresight, and Welfare: A Computational General Equilibrium Analysis, in: J. Piggott and J. Whalley, eds., *New Developments in Applied General Equilibrium Analysis*, Cambridge: Cambridge University Press, 253-282.

BALLARD, C., D. FULLERTON, J.B. SHOVEN and J. WHALLEY (1985), *A General Equilibrium Model for Tax Policy Evaluation*, Chicago: University of Chicago Press

BARRO, R.J. (1974), Are Government Bonds Net Wealth?, *Journal of Political Economy* 82, 1095-1117.

BARRO, R.J. (1979), On the Determination of Public Debt, *Journal of Political Economy* 87, 940-971.

BARRO, R.J. (1984), The Behavior of United Stated Deficits, NBER Working Paper 1309, Cambridge, MA.

BECKER, G.S. and R.J. BARRO (1988) A formulation of the economic theory of fertility, *Quarterly Journal of Economics* 103, 1–26.

BELAN, P., P. MICHEL, and P. Pestieau (1996), Pareto Improving Social Security Reform with Endogenous Growth, CORE Discussion Paper no. 9657, Universite Catholique de Louvain.

BELLMAN, L. and U. BLIEN (1996), Die Lohnkurve in den neunziger Jahren. Der Zusammenhang zwischen regionalen Durschnittslöhnen und regionaler Arbeitslosigkeit in einer Mehrebenenanalyse mit dem IAB-Betriebspanel, *Mitteilungen der Arbeitsmarkt- und Berufsforschung* 29, 467-470.

BERTHOLD, N. and E. THODE (1996), Auslagerung versicherungsfremder Leistungen - Ausweg oder Sackgasse, *Wirtschaftsdienst*1996/VII, 350-358.

BESENDORFER, D., C. BORGMANN and B. RAFFELHÜSCHEN (1998), Ein Plädoyer für intergenerative Ausgewogenheit. Rentenreformvorschläge auf dem Prüfstand, *ifo-studien* 44, 209-231.

BETTENDORF, L. (1994), *A Dynamic Applied Generation Equilibrium Model for a Small Open Economy*, K.U.Leuven, Leuven.

BIS:Bank for International Settlements (1998), *The Macroeconomic and Financial Implications of Ageing Populations: A Report by the Group of Ten*, Basel.

BLANCHARD, O. (1985), Debt, Deficits and Finite Horizons, *Journal of Political Economy* 93, 223-247.

BLANCHARD, O and S. FISCHER (1989), *Lectures on Macroeconomics*, Cambridge, MA: MIT-Press.

BLANCHARD, O. and N. KIYOTAKI (1987), Monopolistic Competition and the Effects of Aggregate Demand, *American Economic Review* 77, 647-666.

BLANCHFLOWER, D.G. and A.J. OSWALD (1994), *The Wage Curve*, Cambridge, MA.: MIT-Press.

BLANCHFLOWER, D.G. and A.J. OSWALD (1996), Effizienzentlohnung und die deutsche Lohnkurve, *Mitteilungen der Arbeitsmarkt- und Berufsforschung* 29,460-466.

BLIEN, U. (1996a), Die Lohnkurve: Eine Einführung zu den Workshop Beiträgen, *Mitteilungen der Arbeitsmarkt- und Berufsforschung*29, 455-459.

BLIEN, U. (1996b), Die Lohnkurve in den achtziger Jahren. Eine Mehrebenenanalyse mit der IAB-Beschäftigtenstichprobe, *Mitteilungen der Arbeitsmarkt- und Berufsforschung* 29, 471-478.

BMF:Bundesministerium der Finanzen (1997), *Unsere Steuern von A-Z*, Bonn.

BOADWAY, R., M. MARCHAND and P. PESTIEAU (1991), Pay-as-you-go social security in a changing environment, *Journal of Population Economics* 4, 257-280.

BOLDRIN, M., J.J. DOLADO, J.F. JIMENO, and F. PERACCHI (1999), The Future of Pensions in Europe, *Economic Policy* 29, 289-320.

BÖRSCH-SUPAN, A., (1991), The Implication of an Aging Population: Problems and Policy Options in the U.S. and Germany, *Economic Policy* 12, 103-139.

BÖRSCH-SUPAN, A., (1992), Population Aging, Social Security Design, and Early Retirement, *Journal of Institutional and Theoretical Economics* 148, 533-557.

BÖRSCH-SUPAN, A., (1998a), Germany: A Social Security System on the Verge to Collapse, in: H. Siebert, ed., *Redesigning Social Security*, Tübingen: Mohr Siebeck, 129-159.

BÖRSCH-SUPAN, A., (1998b), Incentive Effects of Social Security on Labor Force Participation: Evidence in Germany and Across Europe, *Journal of Public Economics*, forthcoming.

BÖRSCH-SUPAN, A., (1998c), Zur deutschen Diskussion eines Übergangs vom Umlage- zum Kapitaldeckungsverfahren in der gesetzlichen Rentenversicherung, *Finanzarchiv* 55, 401-428.

BÖRSCH-SUPAN, A. and R. SCHNABEL (1998), Social Security and Declining Labor Force Participation in Germany, *American Economic Review, Papers and Proceedings* 88, 173-178.

BÖRSTINGHAUS, V. and G. HIRTE (2001), Generational Accounting versus Computable General Equilibrium Analysis of Fiscal Reforms, Diskussionsbeiträge der Kath. Universität Eichstätt, Wirtschaftswissenschaftliche Fakultät Ingolstadt.

BOVENBERG, A.L., D.P. BROER and E.W.M.T. WESTERHOUT (1993), Public Pensions and Declining Fertility in a Small Open Economy: An Intertemporal Equilibrium Approach, in: B.L. Wolfe, ed., *On the Role of Budgetary Policy During Demographic Changes* (Supplement to Public Finance, Vol. 48), 43-59.

BREYER, F. (1989), On the Intergenerational Pareto Efficiency of Pay-as-you-go Financed Pension Systems, *Journal of Institutional and Theoretical Economics* 145, 643-658.

BREYER, F. (1990), *Ökonomische Theorie der Alterssicherung*, München: Vahlen.

BREYER, F. (1994), The Political Economy of Intergenerational Redistribution, *European Journal of Political Economy* 10, 61-84.

BREYER, F. (1998), The Economics of Minimum Pensions, in: H. Siebert, ed., *Redesigning Social Security*, Tübingen: Mohr Siebeck.

BREYER, F., M. KIFMANN, and K. STOLTE (1997), Rentenzugangsalter und Beitragssatz zur Rentenversicherung, *Finanzarchiv* 54, 187-202.

BREYER, F., and M. STRAUB (1993), Welfare Effects of Unfunded Pension Systems When Labor Supply is Endogenous, *Journal of Public Economics* 50, 77-91.

BREYER, F. and D.E. WILDASIN (1993), Steady-State Welfare Effects of Social Security in a Large Open Economy, in: B. Felderer, ed., *Public Pension Economics*, (Journal of Economics, Supplementum 7), Wien, New York: Springer, 43-49.

BROER, D.P. (1999a), Growth and Welfare Distribution in an Ageing Society: An Applied General Equilibrium Analysis for the Netherlands, OCFEB Research Memorandum 9908, Erasmus University Rotterdam.

BROER, D.P. (1999b), Social Security in an Ageing Society, An Applied General Equilibrium Analysis, mimeo, Erasmus University Rotterdam.

BROER, D.P., E.W.M.T. WESTERHOUT and A.L. BOVENBERG (1994), Taxation, Pensions and Saving in a Small Open Economy, *Scandinavian Journal of Economics* 96, 403-424.

BROER, D.P. and J. LASSILA, eds. (1997), *Pension Policies and Public Debt in Dynamic CGE Models*, Heidelberg: Physica-Verlag.

BROER, D.P. and E.W.M.T. WESTERHOUT (1997), Pension Policies and Lifetime Uncertainty in an Applied General Equilibrium Model, in: D.P. Broer and J. Lassila (eds.), *Pension Policies and Public Debt in Dynamic CGE Models*, Heidelberg: Physica-Verlag, 110-138.

BRUNNER, J.K. (1994), Redistribution and the Efficiency of the Pay-as-you-go Pension System, *Journal of Theoretical and Institutional Economics 150, 511-523.*

BRUNNER, J.K. (1996), Transition from a Pay-as-you-go to a Fully Funded Pension System: The Case of Differing Individuals and Intragenerational Fairness, *Journal of Public Economics* 60, 131-146.

BUEB, E., M. SCHREYER and M. OPIELKA (1984), Das alternative Rentenmodell für alle!, in: E. Bueb and M. Opielka, eds., *Sozialstaatskrise und Umbaupläne: Materialien zur sozialpolitischen Diskussion der Grünen* (Die Zukunft des Sozialstaats, 1), Stuttgart, 236.

BURGER, A. (1998), Reform der Rentenversicherung: Chancen und Risiken des Kapitaldeckungsverfahrens, *Deutsche Rentenversicherung*, 655-672.

BURTLESS, G. and R. A. MOFFITT (1984), The Effect of Social Security Benefits on the Labor Supply of the Aged, in: H. Aaron and G. Burtless, eds., *Retirement and Economic Behavior*, Washington, D.C.: Brookings Institute.

BURTLESS, G. and R. A. MOFFITT (1985), The Joint Choice of Retirement Age and Postretirement Hours of Work, *Journal of Labor Economics* 4, 209-236.

BUSLEI, H. and F. KRAUS (1996), Wohlfahrtseffekte eines graduellen Übergangs auf ein niedrigeres Rentenniveau, in: V. Steiner and K.F. Zimmermann, eds., *Soziale Sicherung und Arbeitsmarkt: Empirische Analyse und Reformansätze*, Baden-Baden: Nomos, 57-92.

CHAUVEAU, T. and R. LOUFIR (1997), The Future of Public Pensions in the Seven Major Economies, in: D.P. Broer and J. Lassila, eds., *Pension Policies and Public Debt in Dynamic CGE Models*, Heidelberg: Physica-Verlag, 20-73.

CIFUENTES, R. and S. VALDÉS-PRIETO (1997), Transition in the Presence of Credit Constraints, in: S. Valdés-Prieto, ed., *The Economics of Pensions*, Cambridge: Cambridge University Press, 160-189.

CORNEO, G. and M. MARQUARDT (1999), The Social Security System, Growth and Unemployment, Discussion Paper No. A-570, University of Bonn.

CUTLER, D.M., J.M. POTERBA, L.M. SHEINER, and L.H. SUMMERS (1990), An Aging Society: Opportunity or Challenge?, *Brookings Papers on Economic Activity* 1990:1, 1-56.

Deutsches Institut für Altersvorsorge(1998), *Renditen der gesetzlichen Rentenversicherung im Vergleich zu alternativen Anlageformen*, Köln.

Deutsches Institut für Altersvorsorge(1999a), *Reformvorschläge zur gesetzlichen Alterssicherung in Deutschland. Ein systematischer Überblick*, Köln.

Deutsches Institut für Altersvorsorge(1999b), *Gesetzliche Alterssicherung: Reformerfahrungen im Ausland. Ein systematischer Vergleich aus sechs Ländern*, Köln.

DIAMOND, P.A. (1965), National Dept in a Neoclassical Growth Model, *American Economic Review* 55, 1126-1150.

DIAMOND, P.A. (1997a), Insulation of Pensions from Political Risk, in: S. Valdés-Prieto, ed., *The Economics of Pensions*, Cambridge: Cambridge University Press, 33-57.

DIAMOND, P.A. (1997b), Macroeconomic Aspects of Social Security Reform, *Brooking Papers on Economic Activity*, 1-66.

DIAMOND, P.A., D.C. LINDEMAN, and H. YOUNG, eds., (1996) *Social Security: What Role for the Future?*, (National Academy of Social Insurance) Harrisonburg, Virginia: Donelly and Sons.

DIW– Deutsches Institut für Wirtschaftsforschung (1998), Kapitaldeckung: Kein Wundermittel für die Altersvorsorge, *Wochenbericht* 46, 833-840.

ECKERLE, K. and T. OCZIPKA (1998), *Prognos-Gutachten 1998: Auswirkungen veränderter ökonomischer und rechtlicher Rahmenbedingungen auf die gesetzliche Rentenversicherung in Deutschland*, DRV Schriften, vol. 9, Frankfurt a. M..

EITENMÜLLER, S. (1996), Die Rentabilität der gesetzlichen Rentenversicherung - Kapitalmarktanaloge Renditeberechnung für die nahe und ferne Zukunft, *Deutsche Rentenversicherung* 12, 784-798.

EITENMÜLLER, S. and W. HAIN (1998), Potentielle Effizienzvorteile kontra Übergangskosten: Modellrechnungen zu den Belastungswirkungen bei einem Wechsel des Finanzierungsverfahrens in der gesetzlichen Rentenversicherung, *Deutsche Rentenversicherung*, 634-654.

ELMENDORF, D. (1996), The Effects of Interest Rate Changes on Household Savings and Consumptions: A Survey, mimeo, Federal Reserve Board.

ELMENDORF, D.W. and N.G. MANKIW (1999), Government Debt, forthcoming in: J.B. Taylor and M.Woodford, eds., *Handbook of Macroeconomics*, Amsterdam: North-Holland.

ENDERS, W. and H.E. LAPAN (1982), Social Security Taxation and Intergenerational Risk Sharing, *International Economic Review* 2, 647-658.

ENGEN, E.M., J. GRAVELLE and K. SMETTERS (1997), Dynamic Tax Models: Why They Do the Things They Do, *National Tax Journal* 50, 657-682.

ESSEN, U. van (1994), *Alterssicherung und direkte Besteuerung*, Frankfurt: Peter Land Verlag.

EVANS, J.L. and M.C. AMEY (1996), Seigniorage and Tax Smoothing: Testing the Extended Tax-Smoothing Model, *Journal of Macroeconomics* 18, 111-125.

FEHR, H. (1996), Welfare Effects of Investment Incentive Policies: A Quantitative Assessment, *Finanzarchiv* 53, 515-544.

FEHR, H. (1997), Belastungswirkungen aktueller Reformvorschläge zur Einkommmensbesteuerung und zur Alterssicherung, *Vierteljahreshefte zur Wirtschaftsforschung* 66, 363-381.

FEHR, H. (1998), From Destination- to Origin-Based Consumption Taxation: A Dynamic CGE Analysis, forthcoming *International Tax and Public Finance.*

FEHR, H. (1999a), *Welfare Effects of Dynamic Tax Policies*, Tübingen: Mohr Siebeck.

FEHR, H. (1999b), Privatization of Public Pensions in Germany: Who Gains and How Much?, *Jahrbücher für Nationalökonomie und Statistik* (*Journal of Economics and Statistics*) 218, 674-694.

FEHR, H. (1999c), Pension Reform during the Demographic Transition, *Scandinavian Journal of Economics*, forthcoming.

FEHR, H. and L.J. KOTLIKOFF (1996), Generational Accounting in General Equilibrium, *Finanzarchiv* 53, 1-27.

FEHR, H. and A. RUOCCO (1997), Equity and Efficiency Aspects of Italian Debt Reduction, *Tübinger Diskussionsbeiträge* no. 104, University of Tübingen.

FEHR, H. and W. WIEGARD (1996), Numerische Gleichgewichtsmodelle: Grundstruktur, Anwendungen und Erkenntnisgehalt, in: *Ökonomie und Gesellschaft, Jahrbuch 13*: Experiments in Economics, Frankfurt, 296-339.

FEHR, H. and W. WIEGARD (1998a), Effizienzorientierte Steuerreformen – läßt sich die Verteilungsfrage vernachlässigen?, in G. Krause-Junk, ed., *Steuersysteme der Zukunft*, Schriften des Vereins für Socialpolitik, vol. 256, Berlin: Duncker & Humblot, 199-245.

FEHR, H. and W. WIEGARD (1998b), German Income Tax Reforms: Separating Efficiency from Redistribution, forthcoming in: A. Fossati and J. Hutton, eds., *Policy Simulation in the European Union*, London: Routledge, 235-263.

FEHR, H. and W. WIEGARD (1998c), Effizienz- und Verteilungswirkungen einer zinsbereinigten Einommen- und Gewinnsteuer, Tübinger Diskussionsbeiträge no. 124, University of Tübingen.

FEHR, H. and W. WIEGARD (1999), Lohnt sich eine konsumorientierte Neugestaltung des Steuersystems?, in: C. Smekal, R. Sendlhofer and H. Winner, eds., *Einkommen versus Konsum – Ansatzpunkte zur Steuerreformdiskussion*, Heidelberg, 65-84.

FELDERER, B, ed., (1990) *Bevölkerung und Wirtschaft* (Schriftenreihe des Vereins für Socialpolitik, vol. 202), Berlin: Duncker & Humblot.

FELDERER, B., ed., (1993), *Public Pension Economics*, (Journal of Economics, Supplementum 7), Wien, New York: Springer.

FELDSTEIN, M.S. (1974), Social Security, Induced Retirement, and Aggregate Capital Formation, *Journal of Political Economy* 23, 905-926.

FELDSTEIN, M.S. (1977), Social Security and Private Savings: International Evidence on the Extended Life-cycle Model, in: M.S. Feldstein and R. Inman, eds., *the Economics of Public Services*, London: MacMillan, 174-205.

FELDSTEIN, M.S. (1982), Social Security and Private Saving: Reply, *Journal of Political Economy* 90, 630-642.

FELDSTEIN, M.S. (1995), Would Privatizing Social Security Raise Economic Welfare, NBER Working Paper no. 5281, Cambridge, MA.

FELDSTEIN, M.S. (1996), The Missing Pies in Policy Analysis: Social Security Reform, *American Economic Review* 86, 1-14.

FELDSTEIN, M.S. (1998), *Privatizing Social Security*, Chicago: Chicago University Press.

FELDSTEIN, M.S. and A. SAMWICK (1998), The Transition Path in Privatizing Social Security, in: M.S. Feldstein, ed., *Privatizing Social Security*, Chicago: Chicago University Press.

FENGE, R. (1995), Pareto-efficiency of the Pay-as-you-go Pension System with Intragenerational Fairness, *Finanzarchiv* 53, 515-544.

FENGE, R. (1997), *Effizienz der Alterssicherung*, Heidelberg: Physica.

FENGE, R. and R. SCHWAGER (1995), Pareto Improving Transition from a Pay-as-you-go to a Fully Funded Pension System in a Model with Differing Earning Abilities, *Zeitschfrift für Wirtschafts- und Sozialwissenschaften* 115, 367-376.

FONTAINE, J.A. (1997), Are there (good) Macroeconomic Reasons for Limiting External Investments by Pension Funds? The Chilean Experience, in: S. Valdés-Prieto, ed., *The Economics of Pensions*, Cambridge: Cambridge University Press, 251-274.

FLAIG, G. (1988), Einkommen, Zinssatz und Inflation – Ein Beitrag zur Erklärung von Konsumwachstumsschwankungen, in: G. Bombach, B. Gahlen, A.E. Ott, eds., *Geldtheore und Geldpolitik*, Tübingen: Mohr Siebeck, 291-314.

Frankfurter Institut, ed., (1997), *Rentenkrise – und wie wir sie meistern können*, Bad Homburg.

FRANZ, W. (1996), *Arbeitsmarktökonomik*, 3rd edition, Berlin, New York: Springer-Verlag.

FREDERIKSEN, N.K. (1997), Macroeconomic and Efficiency Effects of the Flat Tax, mimeo, Economic Policy Research Unit, Copenhagen Business School.

FULLERTON, D. and D.L. ROGERS (1993), *Who Bears Lifetime Tax Burden?*, Washington, D.C.: Brookings Institutions.

GALI, J. (1996), Unemployment in Dynamic General Equilibrium Economies, *European Economic Review* 40, 839–845.

GARDNER, G.W. and K.P. KIMBROUGH (1992), Tax Smoothing and Tariff Behavior in the United States, *Journal of Macroeconomics* 14, 711-729.

GENOSKO, J. (1985), *Arbeitsangebot und Alterssicherung*, Regensburg: Transfer-Verlag.

GENOSKO, J. (1993), Hinkt der Generationenvertrag. *Diskussionsbeiträge* der Wirtschaftswissenschaftlichen Fakultät Ingolstadt no. 36.

GIERSCH, H. ed., (1997) *Reforming the Welfare State*, Berlin: Duncker & Humblot.

GHEZ, G.R. and G.S. BECKER (1975), *The Allocation of Time and Goods over the Life Cycle*, New York.

GLISMAN, H.H. and E.J. HORN (1997), Hat das umlagefinanzierte Rentensystem noch eine Chance?, in: Wie sicher ist unsere Zukunft? Entwicklungsperspektiven der sozialen Sicherung, Beihefte zur *Konjunkturpolitik* 46, 49-74.

GORDON, R.H. and H.R. VARIAN (1988), Intergenerational Risk Sharing, *Journal of Public Economics* 24, 450-459.

GOSH, A. R. (1995), Intertemporal Tax-Smoothing and the Government Budget Surplus: Canada and the United States, *Journal of Money, Credit and Banking* 27, 1033–1045.

GRUBER, J. and D. WISE, eds., (1998), *Social Security and Retirement Around the World*, Chicago: University of Chicago Press.

GUSTAFSSON, B.A. and N.A. KLEVMARKEN, eds. (1989), *The Political Economy of Social Security*, Amsterdam: North-Holland, 83-95.

HAGEMANN, R.P. and G. NICOLETTI (1989), Population Ageing: Economic Effects and some Policy Implications for Financing Public Pensions, *OECD Economic Studies* 12, 51-96.

HARRISON, G.W., S.E.H. JENSEN, L.H. PEDERSEN, and T.F. RUTHERFORD, eds., (1999), *Using Dynamic General Equilibrium Models for Policy Analysis*, Amsterdam: North-Holland.

HANSEN, H.J. (1996), Der Einfluß der Zinsen auf den privaten Verbrauch in Deutschland, Diskussionspapier 3/96, Volkswirtschaftliche Forschungsgruppe der Deutschen Bundesbank.

HANSEN, L.P. and J.P. SINGLETON (1982), Generalized Instrumental Variables Estimation of Nonlinear Rational Expectations Models, *Econometrica* 50, 1269-1286.

HIRSCH, B.T., J.T. ADDISON and J. GENOSKO (1989), *Eine ökonomische Analyse der Gewerkschaften*, Regensburg: Transfer-Verlag.

HIRTE, G. (1996), *Effizienzwirkungen von Finanzausgleichsregelungen. Eine Empirische Allgemeine Gleichgewichtsanalyse für die Bundesrepublik Deutschland* (Finanzwissenschaftliche Schriften vol. 76), Frankurt a. M.: Peter Lang Verlag.

HIRTE, G (1998), Anhebung des Rentenzugangsalters - muß es Verlierer geben?, Diskussionsbeiträge der Katholischen Universität Eichstätt, Wirtschaftswissenschaftliche Fakultät Ingolstadt, no. 99.

HIRTE, G (1999a), Renditen in der Gesetzlichen Rentenversicherung und ihr Aussagegehalt, *Applied Economics Quarterly* (*K*onjunkturpolitik) 45, 1-23.

HIRTE, G. (1999b), Raising the Retirement Age - Why Should Anybody Lose?, *Jahrbücher für Nationalökonomie und Statistik* (*Journal of Economics and Statistics*) 219, 393-408.

HIRTE, G. (1999c), Welfare and Macroeconomic Effects of the German Pension Act of 1992 and 1999, Diskussionsbeiträge der Kath. Universität Eichstätt, Wirtschaftswissenschaftliche Fakultät Ingolstadt, 109.

HIRTE, G. (2000a), Pension Policies in Germany - Economic Effects and Feasibility, Diskussionsbeiträge der Katholischen Universität Eichstätt, Wirtschaftswissenschaftliche Fakultät Ingolstadt, no. 133.

HIRTE, G. (2000b), Privatising Old Age Insurance – Economic Effects and Political Feasibility, Diskussionsbeiträge der Katholischen Universität Eichstätt, Wirtschaftswissenschaftliche Fakultät Ingolstadt, no. 138.

HIRTE, G. (2000c), Struktur der impliziten Steuersätze der Gesetzlichen Rentenversicherung, *ifo*-studien 46 , 315-334.

HIRTE, G. and R. WEBER (1997a), Pareto-Improving Transition from PAYG to a Fully Funded System – a Critical Reexamination, Diskussionsbeiträge der Katholischen Universität Eichstätt, Wirtschaftswissenschaftliche Fakultät Ingolstadt, no. 93.

HIRTE, G. and R. WEBER (1997b), Pareto-improving Transition from a PAYG to a Fully Funded System - is it Politically Feasible?, *Finanzarchiv* 54, 303-330.

HOF, B. (1999), *Rentenreformkonzepte in der Diskussion*, Institut der deutschen Wirtschaft: Beitäge zur Wirtschaft- und Sozialpolitik 251, Köln: Deutscher Instituts-Verlag.

HOLZMANN, R. (1993), Economic Aspects of Pension Reform in OECD Countries, in: B.L. Wolfe, ed., *On the Role of Budgetary Policy During Demographic Changes* (Supplement to Public Finance, vol. 48), 269-292.

HOLZMANN, R. (1997), On Economic Benefits and Fiscal Requirements of Moving from Unfunded to Funded Pensions, *European Economy Reports and Studies.*

HOMBURG, S. (1990a), The Efficiency of Unfunded Pension Schemes, *Journal of Institutional and Theoretical Economics* (JITE) 146, 640-647.

HOMBURG, S. (1990b), Interest and Growth in an Economy with Land, *Canadian Journal of Economics* 24, 450-459.

HOMBURG, S. (1992), *Efficient Economic Growth*, Berlin: Springer.

HOMBURG, S. (1997), Old-age Pension Systems: A Theoretical Evaluation, in: H. Giersch, ed., *Reforming the Welfare State*, Berlin: Springer, 233-246.

HOMBURG, S. and W. RICHTER (1990), Eine effizientorientierte Reform der GRV, in: B. Felderer, ed., *Bevölkerung und Wirtschaft*, Schriften des Vereins für Socialpolitik, Bd. 202, Berlin: Duncker & Humblot, 233-246.

HUANG, C.H. and K. S. LIN (1993), Deficits, Government Expenditures and Tax Smoothing in the United States: 1929–1988, *Journal of Monetary Economics* 131, 317–339.

Huber, B. (1990), *Staatsverschuldung und Allokationseffizienz: Eine theoretische Analyse,* Baden-Baden: Nomos Verlagsgesellschaft.

HURD, M. D. (1990), Research on the Elderly: Economic Status, Retirement and Consumption and Saving, *Journal of Economic Literature* 28, 565-627.

HUTTON, J. and T. KENC (1996), Replacing the UK Income Tax with a Progressive Consumption Tax, in: A. Fossati, ed, *Economic Modelling under the Applied General Equilibrium Approach*, Aldershot: Ashgate, Avebury, 215-246.

HUTTON, J. and A. RUOCCO (1999), Tax Progression and Employment in a General Equilibrium Model of Europe, mimeo, University of York, U.K.

HU, S.C. (1979), Social Security, the Supply of Labor, and Capital Accumulation, *American Economic Review* 69, 274-283.

ifo Institut für Wirtschaftsforschung (1997), *Entlastungspotential eines Teilkapitalstocks unter alternativer Bevölkerungsannahmen*, Studie im Auftrag der Entquete-Kommission Demographischer Wandel, München.

İMROHOROĞLU, S. (1998), A Quantitative Analysis of Capital Income Taxation, *International Economic Review* 39, 307-328.

İMROHOROĞLU, A., S. İMROHOROĞLU and D.H. JOINES (1995), A Life Cycle Analysis of Social Security, *Economic Theory* 6, 83-114.

İMROHOROĞLU, A., S. İMROHOROĞLU and D.H. JOINES (1998), The Effect of Tax-Favored Retirement Accounts on Capital Accumulation, *American Economic Review* 88, 749-768.

Institut der Deutschen Wirtschaft(1996, 1997, 1998), Zahlen zur wirtschaftlichen Entwicklung der Bundesrepublik Deutschland, Köln, 1996, 1997, 1998.

Institut für Wirtschaft und Gesellschaft(1997), *Mängel des bestehenden Systems der gesetzlichen Alterssicherung*, Bonn.

Interministerielle Arbeitsgruppe(1996), Bevölkerungsprognose, Variante A, Bonn.

JÄGER, N. (1990), *Die Umstellung der Gesetzlichen Rentenversicherung auf ein partiell kapitalgedecktes Finanzierungsverfahren. Eine Simulationsstudie*, Frankfurt a.M.: Peter Lang.

JENSEN, S.E.H. (1997), Debt Reduction, Wage Formation and Intergenrational Welfare, in: D.P. Broer and J. Lassila, eds., *Pension Policies and Public Debt in Dynamic CGE Models*, Heidelberg: Physica-Verlag, 167-189.

JENSEN, S.E.H. and S.B. NIELSEN (1993), Aging, Intergenerational Distribution and Public Pension Systems, in: in: B.L. Wolfe, ed., *On the Role of Budgetary Policy During Demographic Changes* (Supplement to Public Finance, Vol. 48), 29-42.

JENSEN, S.E.H., S.B. NIELSEN, L.H. PEDERSEN, P.B. SØRENSEN (1994), Labour Tax Reform, Employment and Intergenerational Distribution, *Scandinavian Journal of Economics* 96, 381-404.

JENSEN, S.E.H., S.B. NIELSEN, L.H. PEDERSEN, P.B. SØRENSEN (1996), Tax policy, housing and the labour market: An intertemporal simulation approach, *Economic Modelling* 13, 355-382.

JORGENSEN, D.W. (1984), Econometric Methods for Applied General Equilibrium Analysis, in: H.E. Scarf and J.B. Shoven, eds., *Applied General Equilibrium Analysis*, Cambridge: Cambridge University Press, 139-203.

KEHOE, T.J. and D.K. LEVINE (1990), Indeterminancy in Applied Intertemporal General Equilibrium Models, in: L. Bergman, D.W. Jorgenson and E. Zahlai (eds.), *General Equilibrium Modelling and Economic Policy Analysis*, Cambridge, 111-148.

KENC, T. and W. PERRAUDIN (1997), Pension Systems in Europe, in: D.P. Broer and J. Lassila (eds.), *Pension Policies and Public Debt in Dynamic CGE Models*, Heidelberg: Physica-Verlag, 74-109.

KEUSCHNIGG, C. (1991), How to Compute Perfect Foresight Equilibria, Diskussionsbeiträge des SFB 178, Serie II-Nr 150, Universität Konstanz.

KEUSCHNIGG, C. (1992), Intergenerationally Neutral Taxation, *Public Finance* 47, 446-461.

KEUSCHNIGG, C. (1994), Dynamic Tax Incidence and Intergenerationally Neutral Reform, *European Economic Review* 38, 343-366.

KIMBROUGH, K.P. (1986), Foreign Aid and Optimal Fiscal Policy, *Canadian Journal of Economics* 19, 35-61.

KING, M.B. and D. FULLERTON (1984), *Capital Income Taxation*, Chicago and London: Chicago University Press.

KINGSTON, G. H. and A. P. LAYTON (1986), The Tax Smoothing Hypothesis: Some Australian Empirical Results, *Australian Economic Papers* 25, 247–251.

KNAPPE, E. and U. RACHOLD (1999), Demographischer Wandel und Gesetzliche Krankenversicherung, in: E. Knappe and A. Winkler, eds., *Sozialstaat im Umbruch: Herausforderungen and die deutsche Sozialpolitik*, Frankfurt a. M., New York: Campus, 91-118.

KOTLIKOFF, L.J. (1988), Intergenerational Transfers and Savings, *Journal of Economic Perspectives* 2, 41-58.

KOTLIKOFF, L.J. (1993), From Deficit Delusion to the Fiscal Balance Rule – Looking for a Sensible Way to Measure Fiscal Policy, *Journal of Economics*, 7th Supplement, 17-41.

KOTLIKOFF, L.J. (1996a), Privatization of Social Security: How it Works and Why it Matters, in: J.M. Poterba, ed., *Tax Policy and the Economy* 10, 1-32.

KOTLIKOFF, L.J. (1996b), Replacing the U.S. Federal Tax System with a Retail Sales Tax – Macroeconomic and Distributional Impacts, Unpublished Report to Americans for Fair Taxation.

KOTLIKOFF, L.J: (1996c), Privatizing Social Security at Home and Abroad, *American Economic Review, Papers and Proceedings*.

KOTLIKOFF, L.J. (1998), Simulation the Privatization of Social Security in General Equilibrium, in: M.S. Feldstein, ed., *Privatizing Social Security*, Chicago: University of Chicago Press, 265-306.

KOTLIKOFF, L.J. (1999), The A-K OLG Model – Its Past, Present, and Future, forthcoming in: G.W. Harrison, S.E.H. Jensen, L.H. Pedersan, and T.F. Rutherford, eds, *Using Dynamic General Equilibrium Models for Policy Analysis*, Amsterdam: North-Holland.

KOTLIKOFF, L.J., K. SMETTERS and J. WALLISER (1998a), Social Security: Privatization and Progressivity, *American Economic Review, Papers and Proceedings* 88, 137-141.

KOTLIKOFF, L.J., K. SMETTERS and J. WALLISER (1998a), The Economic Impact of Privatizing Social Security, in: H. Siebert, ed., *Redesigning Social Security*, Tübingen: Mohr Siebeck, 327-348.

KOTLIKOFF, L.J., K. SMETTERS and J. WALLISER (1998c), Privatizing U.S. Social Security – A Simulation Study, forthcoming in: K. Schmidt-Hebbel (ed.), *Pension Systems: From Crisis to Reform*, Washington.

LAITNER, J. (1990), Tax Changes and Phase Diagrams for an Overlapping Generations Model, *Journal of Political Economy* 98, 193-220.

LAPAN, H.E. and W. ENDERS (1990), Endogenous Fertility, Ricardian Equivalence, and Debt Management Policy, *Journal of Public Economics* 42, 227-248.

LASSILA, J., H. PALM and T. VALKONEN (1997), Pension Policies and International Capital Mobility, in: D.P. Broer and J. Lassila, eds., *Pension Policies and Public Debt in Dynamic CGE Models*, Heidelberg: Physica-Verlag, 110-138.

LAU, L.J. (1984), "Comments", in: H.E. Scarf and J.B. Shoven (eds.), *Applied General Equilibrium Analysis*, Cambridge: Cambridge University Press, 127-137.

LAWRANCE, E. (1991), Poverty and the Rate of Time Preference: Evidence from Panel Data, *Journal of Political Economy* 88, 54-77.

LAYARD, R., S. NICKELL, and R. JACKMAN (1991), *Unemployment. Macroeconomic Performance and the Labour Market*, Oxford: Oxford University Press.

LAZEAR, E.P. (1986), Retirement from the Labor Force, in: O. Ashenfelter and R. Layard (eds.), *Handbook of Labor Economics*, Bd.I, Amsterdam: North-Holland, 305-355.

LEIMER, D.R. and S.D. LESNOY (1982), Social Security and Private Saving: New Time-Series Evidence, *Journal of Political Economy* 90, 606-29.

LINDBECK, A. and D.J. SNOWER (1988), Cooperation, Harassment, and Involuntary Unemployment: An Insider-Outsider Approach, *American Economic Review* 78, 167-188.

LORD, W. and P. RANGAZAS (1991), Savings and Wealth in Models with Altruistic Bequest, *American Economic Review* 81, 289-296.

LUCAS, R.E. and N.L. STOCKEY (1983), Optimal Fiscal and Monetary Policy in an Economy without Capital, *Journal of Monetary Economics* 12, 55-93.

MANSUR, A. and J. WHALLEY (1984), Numerical Specification of Applied General Equilibrium Models: Estimation, Calibration, and Data, in: H.E. Scarf and J.B. Shoven, eds., *Applied General Equilibrium Analysis*, Cambridge: Cambridge University Press, 69-127.

MARCHAND, M. and P. PESTIEAU (1991), Public Pensions: Choices for the Future, *European Economic Review* 35, 441-453.

MEIJDAM, L. and H.A.A. VERBON (1997), Aging and Public Pensions in an Overlapping Generations Model, *Oxford Economic Papers* 49, 29-42.

MERTON, R.S. (1983), On the Role of Social Security as a Means for Efficient risk Sharing in an Economy where Human Capital is not Tradable, in: Z. Bodie and J.B. Shoven, eds, *Financial Aspects of the United States Pension System*, Chicago: Chicago University Press, 325-358.

MIEGEL, M. and S. WAHL (1985), *Gesetzliche Grundsicherung. Private Vorsorge – Der Weg aus der Rentenkrise*, Bonn.

MIEGEL, M. and S. WAHL (1999), *Solidarische Grundsicherung. Private Vorsorge – Der Weg aus der Rentenkrise*, München.

MILES, D. and A. IBEN (1998), The Reform of Pension Systems: Winners and Losers across Generations, CEPR Discussion Paper no. 1943.

MILES, D, and A. TIMMERMANN (1999), Risk Sharing and Transition Costs in the Reform of Pension Systems in Europe, *Economic Policy* 29, 253-286.

MITCHELL, O. and S. ZELDES (1996), Social Security Privatization: a Structure for Analysis, *American Economic Review* 86, 363-367.

MODIGLIANI, F. (1988), The Role of Intergenerational Transfers and Life Cycle Savings in the Accumulation of Wealth, *Journal of Economic Perspectives* 2, 15-40.

MODIGLIANI, F. and A. STERLING (1983), Determinants of Private Saving with special Refrence to the Role of Social Security, in: F. Modigliani and R. Hemming, eds., *The Determinants of National Saving and Wealth*, New York: St. Martins Press, 24-55.

MÖLLER, J. (1996), Die Lohnkurve im Rahmen eines allgemeinen regionalen Anpassungsmodells, *Mitteilungen der Arbeitsmarkt- und Berufsforschung* 29, 479-483.

NEUMANN, M.J.M: (1997), Vom Umlageverfahren zum Kapitaldeckungsverfahren: Optionen zur Reform der Alterssicherung, in: Frankfurter Institut, ed., *Rentenkrise – und wie wir sie meistern können*, Bad Homburg, 87-128.

NEUMANN, M.J.M: (1998), Ein Einstieg in die Kapitaldeckung der gesetzlichen Renten ist das Gebot der Stunde, *Wirtschaftsdienst*, 259-264.

OECD(1998), *The Tax/Benefit Position of Employees 1995-1996*, Paris.

PECHMAN, J.A., H.J. AARON and M.K. TAUSSIG (1968), *Social Security: Perspectives for Reform*, Washington D.C.: Brookings Institution.

PEREIRA, A.M. and J.B. SHOVEN (1988), Survey of Dynamic Computational General Equilibrium Models for Tax Policy Evaluation, *Journal of Policy Modeling* 10, 401-436.

PEREIRA, A.M. (1988a), DAGEM: A Dynamic Applied General Equilibrium Model for Tax Policy Evaluation (Complete Documentation), University of California, San Diego *Working Paper* 8-17.

PEREIRA, A.M. (1988b), *Corporate Tax Integration in the United States: A Dynamic General Equilibrium Analysis*, University of California, San Diego Working Paper 8-18.

PERRONI, C. (1995), Assessing the Dynamic Efficiency Gains of Tax Reforms when Human Capital is Endogenous, *International Economic Review* 36, 907-925.

PETERS, W. (1989), *Theorie der Renten- und Invalidittsversicherung*, Berlin: Springer-Verlag.

PETERS, W. (1990), Reform oder Privatisierung der Alterssicherung – Spielraum der Umlagefinanzierung oder Chances des Kapitaldeckungsverfahrens, in. H.-J. Ramser, ed., *Theore und Politik der Sozialversicherung*, Tübingen: Mohr Siebeck, 103-132.

PISSARIDES, C.A. (1979), Job Matchings with State Employment Agencies and Random Search, *Economic Journal* 89, 818-833.

RAFFELHÜSCHEN, B. (1989), *Anreizwirkungen des Systems der sozialen Alterssicherung – Eine dynamische Simulationsanalyse*, Frankfurt a. M.: Peter Lang Verlag.

RAFFELHÜSCHEN, B. (1993), Funding Social Security: Through Pareto Optimal Conversion Policies, in: B. Felderer, ed., *Public Pension Economics*, (Journal of Economics, Supplementum 7), Wien, New York: Springer, 105-131.

RAFFELHÜSCHEN, B. (1997), Sanfte Umstellung, *Finanzen*12, 21-22.

RAFFELHÜSCHEN, B. and W. KITTERER (1990), Übergangsprobleme eines Systemwechsels in der sozialen Alterssicherung – Eine dynamische Simualtionsanalyse, in: B. Felderer, ed., *Bevölkerung und Wirtschaft* (Schriftenreihe des Vereins für Socialpolitik, vol. 202), Berlin: Duncker & Humblot, 405-424

RAFFELHÜSCHEN, B. and A.E.RISA (1995), Reforming Social Security in a Small Open Economy, *European Journal of Political Economy* 11, 469-485.

RANGAZAS, P. C. (1996), Fiscal Policy and Endogenous Growth in a Bequest-Constrained Economy, *Oxford Economic Papers* 48, 52-74.

RAZIN, A. and L.E.O. SVENSSON (1983), The Current Account and the Optimal Government Debt, *Journal of International Money and Finance* 2, 215-24.

REISEN, H. and J. WILLIAMSON (1997), Pension Funds, Capital Controls, and Macroeconomic Stability, in: S. Valdés-Prieto, ed., *The Economics of Pensions*, Cambridge: Cambridge University Press, 227-250.

RICHTER, W. (1993), Intergenerational Risk Sharing and Social Security in an Economy with Land, in: Felderer, B., ed., (1993), *Public Pension Economics*, (Journal of Economics, Supplementum 7), Wien, New York: Springer, 91-103.

RIMBAUX, E. (1996), Marginal Effective Tax Rates in Retrospect: 1970-1995, *Public Finance* 51, 92-137.

RIPHAHN, R. and P. SCHMIDT (1997), Determinanten des Rentenzugangs: Eine Analyse altersspezifischer Verrentungsraten. *Jahrbuch für Wirtschaftswissenschaften* (Review of Economics) 48, 113-147.

SAMUELSON, P.A. (1958) An Exact Consumption-Loan Model of Interest With or Without the Social Contrivance of Money, *Journal of Political Economy* 66, 467-482.

SAMUELSON, P.A. (1975), Optimum Social Security in a Life-Cycle-Growth Model, *International Economic Review* 16, 539-544.

SANDMO, A. (1985), The Effects of Taxation on Savings and Risks, in: A.J. Auerbach and M.S. Feldstein (eds.), *Handbook of Public Economics*, Vol. I., Amsterdam: North-Holland, 265-311.

SCHIEBER, S.J. and J.B. SHOVEN, eds., (1997), Public Policy Toward Pensions, Cambridge, MA: MIT-Press.

SCHMIDT, P. (1995), *Die Wahl des Rentenalters – Theoretische und empirische Analyse des Rentenzugangsverhaltens in West- und Ostdeutschland.* Frankfurt a.M.: Peter Lang.

SCHMÄHL, W. (1990), Reformen der Rentenversicherung: Gründe, Strategien und Wirkungen – Das Beispiel der "Rentenreform 1992", in: B. Gahlen, H. Hesse, H.J. Ramser, eds.: *Theorie und Politik der Sozialversicherung*, Tübingen: Mohr Siebeck, 203-255.

SCHMÄHL, W. (1993), Übergang zu Staatsbürger-Grundrenten – Ein Beitrag zur Deregulierung in der Alterssicherung?, in: W. Schmähl, ed., *Mindestsicherung im Alter. Erfahrungen, Herausforderungen, Strategien*, Frankfurt a. M., New York: Campus, 265-333.

SCHMÄHL, W. (1994), Perspektiven der Alterssicherung in Deutschland, *Wirtschaftsdienst* 8, 390-395.

SCHNABEL, R. (1998), Rate of Return of the German Pay-As-You-Go Pension System, *Finanzarchiv* , 55, 374-399.

SCHNEIDER, D. (1990), Capital Income Taxation in the Federal Republic of Germany – An Assessment from an Efficiency Perspective, in: H. Siebert (ed.), *Reforming Capital Income Taxation*, Tübingen: Mohr Siebeck, 259-273.

SCHNEIDER, J. (1987), *Marktfehler und Arbeitslosigkeit*, Regensburg: Transfer.

SEATER, J.J. (1993), Ricardian Equivalence, *Journal of Economic Literature* 31, 142-190.

SHAPIRO, C. and J.E. STIGLITZ (1984), Equilibrium Unemployment as a Worker Discipline Device, *American Economic Review*, 74, 433-444.

SIDDIQUI, S. (1995a), Labour Supply Disincentive Effects of Old Age Public Pensions: A Case Study for West Germany combining Panel Data and Aggregate Information, University of Konstanz, Diskussionpapier 28-1995.

SIDDIQUI, S. (1997a), Early Retirement in West Germany: A Sequential Model of Discrete Choice, *Zeitschrift für Wirtschafts- und Sozialwissenschaften* 117, 1997, 391-415.

SIDDIQUI, S. (1997b), The Pension Incentive to Retire: Empirical Evidence for West Germany, *Journal of Population Economics* 10, 463-86.

SIDDIQUI, S. (1997c), *Der Übergang in den Ruhestand. Eine theoretische und empirische Untersuchung für die Bundesrepublik Deutschland*, (Applied Econometrics, vol. 1), Münster: Lit.

SINN, H.W. (1999), Why a Funded System is Needed and Why It is Not Needed, Paper presented at the 55th IIPF Congress in Moscow.

SMITH, A. (1982), Intergenerational Transfers as Social Insurance, *Journal of Public Economics* 19, 97-106

SMITH, E. O. (1994), *The German Economy*, London, New York: Rutledge.

SØRENSEN, P.B. (1997), Public Finance Solutions to the European Unemployment Problem?, *Economic Policy* 25, 223-264.

SPREMAN, K. (1984), Intergenerational Contracts and Their Decomposition, *Journal of Economics* 44, 237-253.

Statistisches Bundesamt(1994), *Achte koordinierte Bevölkerungsvorausberechnung, Variante 2*, Wiesbaden.

Statistisches Bundesamt(1996), Fachserie 1, Reihe 4.1.1: *Erwerbstätigkeit und Bevölkerung*, Wiesbaden.

Statistisches Bundesamt(1997), *Statistical Yearbook 1997 of the federal Republic of Germany*, Wiesbaden.

Statistisches Bundesamt(1998), *Statistical Yearbook 1998 of the federal Republic of Germany*, Wiesbaden.

STRAZICICH, M. C. (1996), Are State and Provincial Governments Tax Smoothing?. Evidence from Panel Data, *Southern Economic Journal* 62, 979–988.

SUMMERS, L.H. (1988), Relative Wages, Efficiency Wages, and Keynesian Unemployment, *American Economic Review* 78, 383-388.

SWAROOP, V., (1989), Uniform Labor-income Taxation and Economic Efficiency, *Journal of Public Economics* 38, 117-136.

SWAROOP, V. (1995), Changes in Public Expenditure, Optimal Debt and Tax Policy, and Intertemporal Adjustments, *Public Finance* 50, 136–152.

TREHAN, B.; C. E. WALSH (1990), Seigniorage and Tax Smoothing in the United States, 1914-1986, *Journal of Monetary Economics* 25, 97–112.

TURNOVSKY, S. J. and W. A. BROCK (1980), Time Consistency and Optimal Government Policies in Perfect Foresight Equilibrium, *Journal of Public Economics* 13, 183–212.

VALDÉS-PRIETO, S., ed., (1997), *The Economics of Pensions*, Cambridge: Cambridge University Press.

VAN DER PLOEG, F. (1993), Monetary Discipline and the Real Value of Government Debt: The Case for an Independent Eurofed, in: H.A.A. Verbon and F.A.A.M. van Winden, eds., *The Political Economy of Government Debt*, Amsterdam: North-Holland, 157-177.

van Winden, eds., *The Political Economy of Government Debt*, Amsterdam: North-Holland, 157-177.

VDR(1999), Statistik, www.vdr.de.

Verbon, H.A. (1989), Conversion Policies for Public Pension Plans in a Small Open Economy, in: B.A. Gustafsson and N.A. Klevmarken, eds., *The Political Economy of Social Security*, Amsterdam: North-Holland, 83-95.

Wigger, B. (2000), Pareto-verbessernde intergenerationelle Transfers , Paper presented at the Jahrestagung des Vereins für Socialpolitik, September, 2000 in Berlin.

Wildasin, D.E. (1990), Non-neutrality of Debt with Endogenous Fertility, *Oxford Economic Papers* 42, 414–428.

Wissenschaftlicher Beirat(1998), *Grundlegende Reform der gesetzlichen Rentenversicherung*, Gutachten des Wissenschaftlichen Beirats beim Bundesministerium für Wirtschaft, Bonn.

World Bank(1995), *Averting the Old Age Crisis: Policies to Protect the Old and Promote Growth*, Washington, D.C.

Wrede, M. (1999), Pareto Efficient Pay-as-you-go Pension Systems with Multi-Period Lives, *Jahrbücher für Nationalökonomie und Statistik*(Journal of Economics and Statistics) 219, 494-503.

Yaari, M.E. (1965), Uncertain Lifetime, Life Insurance and the Theory of Consumer, *Review of Economic Studies* 32, 137-150.

Zhang, J. (1995), Social Security and Endogenous Growth, *Journal of Public Economics* 58, 185-213.

Authors Index

Subject Index

Beiträge zur Finanzwissenschaft

Edited by Hans-Werner Sinn and Wolfgang Wiegard

Volume 1
Eckhard Janeba
International Tax Competition
1997. IX, 130 pages. Cloth.

Volume 2
Helge Berger
Konjunkturpolitik im Wirtschaftswunder
Handlungsspielräume und Verhaltensmuster von Bundesbank und Regierung in den 1950er Jahren
1997. IX, 310 pages. Cloth.

Volume 3
Martin Werding
Zur Rekonstruktion des Generationenvertrags
Ökonomische Zusammenhänge zwischen Kindererziehung, sozialer Alterssicherung und Familienlastenausgleich
1998. XIV, 535 pages. Cloth.

Volume 4
Wilhelm Althammer
Internationale Aspekte der Umweltpolitik
1998. XIV, 272 pages. Cloth.

Volume 5
Hans Fehr
Welfare Effects of Dynamic Tax Reforms
1999. XIX, 268 pages. Cloth.

Volume 6
Andreas Scheuerle
Politisch erzeugte Konjunkturzyklen
1999. XXVII, 389 pages. Cloth.

Volume 7
Martin Kolmar
Optimale Ansiedlung sozialpolitischer Entscheidungskompetenzen in der Europäischen Union
1999. XV, 262 pages. Cloth.

Volume 8
Ulrich Scholten
Die Förderung von Wohneigentum
1999. X, 325 pages. Cloth.

Volume 9
Ronnie Schöb
Steuerreform und Gewinnbeteiliung
Neue Wege aus der Beschäftigungskrise
2000. VIII, 226 pages. Cloth.

Volume 10
Lars P. Feld
Steuerwettbewerb und seine Auswirkungen auf Allokation und Distribution
Ein Überblick und eine empirische Analyse für die Schweiz.
2000. XIV, 465 pages. Cloth.

Volume 11
Clemens Fuest
Steuerpolitik und Arbeitslosigkeit
2000. IX, 205 pages. Cloth.

Volume 12
Holger Feist
Arbeit statt Sozialhilfe
2000. IX, 241 pages. Cloth.

Volume 13
Matthias Wrede
Fiskalische Externalitäten im föderativen Staat
2001. XII, 252 pages. Cloth.

Volume 14
Georg Hirte
Pension Policies
2001. XXII, 288 pages. Paper.